THE BRAIN OVER BINGE RECOVERY GUIDE

A SIMPLE AND PERSONALIZED PLAN FOR ENDING BULIMIA AND BINGE EATING DISORDER

KATHRYN HANSEN

Camellia Publishing, LLC
Printed in the United States of America

First Printing, 2016

ISBN: 978-0-9844817-4-3
Library of Congress Control Number: 2015919056

Legal Disclaimer
This book is designed to provide helpful information on the topics discussed. It is not intended to replace the services of trained health professionals or be a substitute for medical advice. This book is not meant to be used to diagnose or treat any medical condition.

You are advised to consult with your health care professional with regard to matters relating to your health and, in particular, matters that may require diagnosis or medical attention. This book is sold with the understanding that the publisher is not engaged to render any type of psychological, medical, legal, or any other kind of professional advice.

The author and publisher disclaim any liability arising directly or indirectly from the use of this book. Any recommendations described within should be tried only under the guidance of a licensed health care practitioner. The author and publisher assume no responsibility for any outcome of the use of this book in self-treatment or under the care of a licensed practitioner.

This book is for the women and men who read my recovery story in Brain over Binge *and asked for more information and guidance, and for anyone who wants to be free of binge eating.*

Contents

Foreword
by Amy Johnson, Ph.D.

THE IDEAS IN THIS book changed my life.

In 2011, I was eight years into an overwhelming binge eating habit. At its worst, I was bingeing several times a day, terrified of—and feeling powerless over—my own thoughts about food.

As horrible as that was, my urges did subside for short periods of time. I had virtually no urges during my two pregnancies, and from time to time throughout those eight years, I was blessed with a few binge-free weeks here and there.

But even while I was enjoying a much-needed reprieve from my habit, I never felt completely free of it.

I believed what I had heard from conventional psychology—that I might learn to cope with my "disorder" and it might come to wreak *less* havoc on my life, but it would always be there to some degree; that it could lay dormant but then strike at any moment. I believed this habit was something I had to get to the bottom of, either through years of inner psychological work or by a massive effort to avoid triggers and white-knuckle my way through urges. Those looked like my only options.

I tried avoiding triggers and white-knuckling through urges, but that never helped for long. My attempts most often ended in an emotionally draining round of rebound binges. It looked like my only hope was the years-of-deep-inner-work route, and that hadn't been helping much either.

Then I read a book called *Brain over Binge* and everything changed.

In *Brain over Binge*, Kathryn Hansen shares the story of her own binge eating habit. The similarities between Kathryn's story and my experience blew me away. I knew *in theory* that others experienced the same cycle of overwhelming urges, giving in to those urges, shame and regret, (sometimes) restriction and compensatory behaviors, and then more urges, but I hadn't actually heard their stories firsthand, in detail.

Reading Kathryn's memoir made it clear that not only was I not alone, but what was happening to me was not about me at all. What I was experiencing was my brain caught up in an impersonal, very predictable cycle. It was my *healthy* brain doing what it had been innocently taught to do. I was no different than any other person who didn't fully understand her brain. I was doing the best I could, given what I (mis)understood about what was happening. *Brain over Binge* cleared up that misunderstanding and made way for permanent change. A binge eating habit is not a fundamental part of who anyone truly is. It is a relatively superficial, very impersonal, brain-wiring issue. It is created by thoughts (urges) that we can come to see in a new way, a way that renders them relatively powerless.

The simple truths in *Brain over Binge* and *The Brain over Binge Recovery Guide* perfectly converge with the broader spiritual principles I have studied and taught for years. All humans are innately habit-free and healthy by nature. We intuitively know how to eat by our natural hunger; we simply get confused by and caught up in a lot of emotional thinking (including urges), and we lose sight of our true nature. All human experience (urges, cravings, shame, etc.) is temporary. It passes through us, but it is not us. In the chapters I contributed to this book, I discuss these spiritual principles as they relate to ending binge eating.

I have been completely binge-free, with absolutely no fear of the habit resurfacing, since I read Kathryn's book nearly five years ago. Upon my own recovery, I started talking with anyone who would listen about *Brain over Binge* and the remarkable, rapid change I had experienced. The more I shared, the more people started showing up in my in-box, looking for support in ending their binge eating habit.

In early 2013, I taught a class based on the spiritual principles I had been studying and the brain-based principles I learned from *Brain over Binge*. The response was incredible. I was blown away by how many people struggle with binge eating and the similarities we all share. Most of all, I was blown away by the success of *Brain over Binge* in helping people end this habit (I've seen success rates well above what is often reported within traditional psychology and other treatment methods). I was so encouraged by what I was seeing that I devoted a portion of my coaching practice to working with binge eaters, and I've now written my own book—*The Little Book of Big Change: The No-Willpower Approach to Breaking Any Habit*—which is inspired by the recoveries I've witnessed in myself and many others.

Brain over Binge has changed countless lives for the better, and I'm honored to play a very small role in *The Brain over Binge Recovery Guide*. In this book, Kathryn goes into even more detail about the insights that set her, myself, and so many other *Brain over Binge* readers free. She points us toward the freedom that is far closer than it appears.

You're in the right place. Open your heart and your mind to a new way of viewing your habit. Allow the understanding and practices shared in this book to help you end your habit for good.

Amy Johnson, Ph.D.
November 25, 2015
Canton, MI

Preface

MY HUSBAND GREG AND I used to love to hike in the mountains near our previous home in Phoenix, Arizona. One day in early 2006, almost a year after I'd stopped binge eating, we were hiking and discussing our future plans. I felt like I had chosen the wrong degree in college, partially due to bulimia spoiling my four years at the university; and I was still unsure of my career direction. Even though I was only 24, my career indecision was causing me some anxiety, and to make matters a little more complicated, I was newly pregnant with our first child. So I wasn't even sure what pursuing a career would look like at that point.

At the time of this particular hike, I had already written some notes and a couple rudimentary chapters for the book I'd promised myself I'd write if I ever recovered from bulimia—the book that I eventually published in 2011 as *Brain over Binge*. All I knew in 2006 was that writing the book was something I wanted to do one day in some capacity, but I wasn't sure when or how it would materialize. I was and still can be perfectionistic about a lot of things, so my natural tendency was to push off writing until I could get it "right"—until I felt like I could say what I wanted to say in an optimal way that could help everyone who would read it.

As we continued walking up the mountain, with me mulling over career possibilities, Greg told me something that stayed with me until I completed *Brain over Binge*. He said, "If you put off writing your book, you'll soon be too far removed from your problem and your recovery to write anything authentic." He said I might forget exactly what it was like to binge, what it was like to feel that shame and lack of control, and exactly how I was able to put it all behind me. He warned me that looking too far back on my eating disorder might cause me to lose something or that my story might become distorted by future experiences.

He advised me to not worry about my future career at that time—to just keep working at my current job as a special education teacher's assistant, which I enjoyed, and to write my book in my spare time. After thinking it over for the next few months and making peace with the fact that my book would not be perfect and my story could not possibly help everyone, that is exactly what I decided to do. I began slowly documenting my eating disorder and recovery experience with the hope of helping just one person overcome bulimia or binge eating disorder. When my first child was born toward the end of 2006, being a mom took the place of my job in special education, and I continued to write in my harder-to-come-by spare time.

By 2009, I was actually finished saying all I wanted to say in the completed manuscript, but again, doubts surfaced. *Brain over Binge* contained a controversial message: that binge eating is not a coping mechanism for difficult emotions or life's problems, but instead a habit of the brain that can be extinguished without therapy. It was a message I felt was desperately needed in the eating disorder community, but being the one to deliver it felt a bit intimidating, to say the least. I wondered if my story and what I'd learned was enough, and I thought that people trying to recover might need more advice based on their own unique situations. I decided to put the project on the shelf for several months and again considered pursuing another career, all the while feeling a strong pull to quickly get my book to anyone who might be helped by it.

Out of this inner conflict, the idea for the book you are now holding was born in late 2009. Instead of altering *Brain over Binge* to include more direct advice to binge eaters in various situations, I decided that I would write another book down the road—a self-help version of *Brain over Binge* that would provide guidance to the reader instead of just sharing my own story and insights. With that new commitment to write a second book in mind, I got back to work editing and publishing the first one.

Now, five years removed from publishing *Brain over Binge* and over nine years removed from our hike in Phoenix, I see that Greg was spot-on when he advised me to get to work on my book right away. I see how much I needed to begin writing shortly after recovery. *Brain over Binge* was raw and genuine; it was my experience, fresh in my mind (for a brief version of my story, see Appendix B). It shared intimate details about my struggle and explained how my recovery didn't result in me becoming an ideal version of myself who had everything sorted out; instead, I remained an imperfect person who simply did not binge anymore. It's been truly amazing to hear from readers who recovered after reading my first book. I had hoped that my book would help just one person, and I've been over-whelmed to receive so many emails from people who say the book led them to complete recovery.

Most touchingly, people tell me that they see themselves in my story—they see their own thoughts, frustrations, emotions, and imperfections in those I shared; and from that, they are able to find hope, to feel like they are not alone, and to see a way out. If I were to begin writing *Brain over Binge* today, ten years after recovery, it's unlikely that I'd be able to capture so vividly what binge eating was like and everything that went along with it. Although I can no longer write as authentically about my days of bulimia, what I can do is share what I've learned since publishing *Brain over Binge*, which I hope will help move others toward complete cessation of binge eating.

I've gained much more insight into why some people are able to recover quickly and why others take more time; about what helps people achieve lasting recovery and what can hold people back. I've learned more about the brain science behind binge eating. From the first time I heard from a reader struggling to use concepts I talked about in *Brain over Binge* and asking for additional advice, my commitment to eventually write a second book was renewed. I was right that some binge eaters would need more than what I offered in *Brain over Binge*. Over the last five years, I've tried to offer extra guidance through my website and blog (www.brainover binge.com) and through *The Brain over Binge Workbook*—a brief, digital book I created in 2014 to help people better understand and overcome their binge eating. *The Brain over Binge Recovery Guide* is in many ways a compilation and expansion of those resources, but with greater depth and much more information added.

Although this book does retain the basic concepts and approach to recovery found in *Brain over Binge*, the focus here is on educating and empowering binge eaters to develop their own insights and implement the ideas in this book to best fit their own unique recovery. I've realized that people don't need more advice on how to copy my approach to recovery—or the approach of anyone who has recovered, for that matter. The reason my recovery was powerful was because it resonated so deeply as my own. After many failed attempts at recovery, I read information in Jack Trimpey's *Rational Recovery: The New Cure for Substance Addiction* that finally made sense to me; and following that, I had a significant mental shift, which allowed me to naturally start viewing my binge urges differently and overcome them.

Not everyone experiences a sudden change of perspective or success in over-coming their behaviors right away, and there is no need for self-criticism if your recovery does not look like someone else's. The concepts in this book may be very new to some readers, and it may take some time for the ideas to permeate and then gradually begin to lead to change. So trust your own intuition along the way and take only what feels like your own unique truth. Don't make things more complicated than they need to be and keep your focus on what you believe will help you recover in a way that feels authentic to you, and you'll be able to carve out your own individual path to a lifetime of recovery.

Important Considerations
and Disclaimers

THIS BOOK IS FOR anyone who wants to stop binge eating, whether or not you meet criteria for bulimia or binge eating disorder. It offers a self-directed approach to recovery, which is one alternative to eating disorder therapy and treatment programs. This book is not a substitute for medical or nutritional advice; and the author, contributors, and publisher are not responsible for adverse effects resulting directly or indirectly from the use of this book. Eating disorders have serious health consequences, and you are advised to seek medical help for any concerning symptoms.

Even if you don't have any identifiable symptoms, I strongly encourage you to undergo a medical evaluation to determine if you are in good enough health to attempt self-recovery. If you are found to be underweight or to have electrolyte imbalances or other health problems, you will need to be medically monitored to ensure proper healing. You will need to restore calorie intake and body weight to normal levels to be successful in recovery, and this process needs to be done *slowly* and with the supervision of a doctor or nutritionist.

A sudden increase in your calorie intake after a period of starvation can lead to a complication called "refeeding syndrome"—a serious metabolic condition involving dangerous electrolyte and fluid shifts.[1] Refeeding syndrome is prevent-able with medical monitoring and vitamin supplements, notably thiamine and B vitamins.[2] Remaining in a food-deprived state affects brain functioning in a way that can render you less capable of making sound decisions and prevent you from achieving recovery.

Any other mental or physiological disorder that affects judgment and cognitive decision making also warrants immediate professional help. Some examples are: drug or alcohol abuse, incapacitating anxiety or depression, and severe personality disorders. This book is for readers who, despite their eating disorder, can still function in a cognizant way in other parts of their lives. It is for the reader who feels like the eating disorder is interfering with who they truly are or who they can be; this book is for people who *want* to recover.

This doesn't mean you have to be unwaveringly certain of your desire to recover at all times; but at some level, you have to want better for yourself. This book is not for someone who can't see any reason to stop binge eating and purging; it is not for someone who wants to continue to deteriorate because of serious self-hatred or trauma; it is not for someone with suicidal thoughts or tendencies. People who don't want to find a way out or have no desire to live need more intensive monitoring and real-time help.

Young adults comprise another special group for consideration. Due to incomplete development of the parts of the brain responsible for self-control, the ability to make conscious choices is limited in those around 20 years old and younger.[3] Young people are still capable of making the changes they need to make to pursue recovery, but they may require more direction, support, and close monitoring for any signs of health problems. If you are a parent of a teenager or younger child experiencing an eating disorder and you want to help guide her or him through self-recovery, I strongly encourage you to find a doctor, therapist, or nutritionist who is willing to monitor your child and work with you to find the support they need in using the approach in this book.

Although this book offers a perspective that differs from traditional therapeutic approaches, that doesn't mean it's incompatible with other avenues to recovery. Different ideas work for different people in different ways, but the measure of any approach to recovery is its effectiveness to you personally. I will encourage you throughout the book to use the ideas in the best way you see fit and to use your own insights to move forward in a way that works for you. You may recover quickly, or you may see change in a more gradual way, and both are okay.

Meet the Contributors

SINCE WRITING MY FIRST book, I've been fortunate to get to know some great people who are doing amazing work helping others recover from bulimia and binge eating disorder, and I'm thankful that several have contributed their unique ideas to this book. All of the experts I've asked to contribute to this book have been where you are—in the grip of binge eating, looking for hope—and they all found their way to a full recovery.

The main contributor is Amy Johnson, Ph.D., a psychologist, master certified coach, and author of *The Little Book of Big Change: The No-Willpower Approach to Breaking Any Habit* and *Being Human: Essays on Thoughtmares, Bouncing Back, and Your True Nature*. Amy lived with bulimia/binge eating disorder for nearly eight years, and she recovered using concepts and ideas from *Brain over Binge*. Now part of her coaching practice is devoted to sharing those concepts with others. She works with clients worldwide, using innovative coaching tools and spiritual principles to help people not only overcome binge eating, but also change other harmful habitual patterns and experience peace of mind.

The second contributor is recovery mentor Katherine Thomson, Ph.D., whose expertise is primarily in helping people transition to eating a normal diet. Katherine is a medical sociologist who struggled with bulimia for six years and with lingering food obsessions after that. She is passionate about helping people feel good about how they are eating, feel positive about their body, and feel free of food struggles.

You will also hear from Cookie Rosenblum, M.A., another master certified coach and the author of *Clearing Your Path to Permanent Weight Loss: The Truth About Why You've Failed in the Past, and What You Must Know to Succeed Now*. Cookie has a deep understanding of binge eating because she has been through it herself, and through her coaching practice, she helps women not only to put aside binge eating, but also to return to a healthy weight in a way that doesn't involve dieting.

Additionally, you'll hear briefly from two integrative nutritionists—Stacey Cohen and Pauline Hanuise—who overcame binge eating and now offer holistic health and lifestyle coaching for those trying to recover. Pauline is also the creator of the successful online recovery program, Make Peace with Food.

Interspersed through the chapters of this book, you'll also read quotes from women and men* who read my first book and now have advice and insights to add

---

*The names of these men and women have been changed to protect their privacy.

to this one. I am so thankful to everyone who has offered expert advice and personal testimony, because it gives this book a greater chance of helping many more people than just my words could.

Introduction

RECOVERY FROM BINGE EATING does not have to be complicated. This book will help you do what you need to do to recover, and nothing else. Just like my first book, *Brain over Binge*, this book will not make you whole, happy, emotionally satisfied, or at peace with yourself and your body; but putting aside binge eating can certainly bring you closer to achieving those goals. Binge eating is an emotionally, physically, and mentally draining condition that produces shame, anxiety, depression, social withdrawal, and low self-esteem—just stopping the behavior can immediately give you a sense of freedom and a newfound ability to pursue whatever it is that matters to you.

This book will lay out a simple and clear framework that you can use to guide your own authentic recovery. No one will use the framework in exactly the same way, but it will direct your focus, choices, and actions in recovery so you can put aside binge eating in the most efficient way possible. Do not be misled by the length of this book. As I will explain, you will use only the parts that you need, and it contains ample blank space for your own writing and reflecting. Before explaining the recovery framework, it's necessary to briefly define a few terms used throughout the book:

> **Binge eating episode:** Eating, in a discrete period of time (such as a two-hour period), an amount of food that is definitely larger than most people would eat during a similar period of time and under similar circumstances. Binge eating episodes are accompanied by a sense of lack of control over what or how much is being eaten.[4] Although there is some subjectivity in what each person considers a binge eating episode (addressed in Chapter 4), binge eating is not the simple overeating that most people do from time to time, like having an extra serving of an especially delicious meal, having some dessert after you are already full, or eating more than usual on a holiday. Binge eating is a much more unsettling and abnormal behavior, which is why it's primarily done in secret.

> **Bulimia:** An eating disorder characterized by recurrent episodes of binge eating, followed by recurrent inappropriate compensatory behaviors in order to prevent weight gain (purging).[5] About 80 percent of bulimics are female;[6] approximately 1–4 percent of all females will suffer from bulimia in their lifetime.[7] According to the most recent version of the *Diagnostic and Statistical Manual of Mental Disorders* (DSM-5), to be formally diagnosed with bulimia, one has to binge/purge one time per week for at least three months;[8] but when the

term *bulimia* is used in this book, it refers to the binge/purge cycle regardless of how frequently it occurs.

Compensatory behaviors (purging): Unhealthy behaviors used in an attempt to prevent weight gain from binge eating. These behaviors primarily include self-induced vomiting, laxatives, diuretics, excessive exercise, and fasting or restrictive dieting. It is important to note that purging is not effective for weight loss: Laxatives and diuretics cause only the loss of water, not weight; with self-induced vomiting, the body still absorbs approximately 50–75 percent of the binge calories;[9] and all forms of purging can cause the body to become more efficient at storing calories as fat.

Binge eating disorder (BED): A type of eating disorder characterized by recurring episodes of binge eating, without the regular use of compensatory behaviors (purging). The binge eating episodes are accompanied with marked distress. BED is the most common eating disorder in the United States, with an estimated 3.5 percent of women and 2 percent of men being formally diagnosable with BED.[10] Just like bulimia, to be diagnosed with BED, the DSM-5 states that one has to binge one time per week for three months;[11] however, for the purposes of this book, when "people with binge eating disorder" are addressed, it refers to anyone who is troubled by binge eating.

Urge to binge: Any thought, feeling, or sensation that encourages binge eating. Urges to binge are compelling, intrusive, and irrational; and as will be discussed, it's the urges that are responsible for driving people to binge.

"Dismissing" urges to binge: The practice of viewing urges as meaningless, powerless, and harmless, and allowing them to come and go without acting on them. Both *Brain over Binge* and *The Brain over Binge Workbook* used the term *"resisting"* urges to binge. But since the time of their publication, Amy Johnson (the main contributor to this book) insightfully began replacing the word *resist* with *dismiss* while working with her clients, because, she says, *resisting* implies fighting against a process, and fighting binge urges is the opposite of what a binge eater wants to do. It's a simple but meaningful change in terminology that more accurately captures what needs to be done when urges arise.

Restrictive dieting: The term *restrictive dieting* primarily refers to calorie restriction—purposefully eating less than what the body requires to function in an attempt to lose weight. Restrictive dieting can also include any self-imposed rigid food rules, such as elimination of specific food groups, in order to lose weight. Trying to eat well to nourish the body and become healthier is not restrictive dieting.

Traditional therapy: There are numerous treatment options for bulimia and BED, but the most common overarching theory that guides therapy is that binge eating is a coping mechanism for underlying problems, difficult emotions, and/or daily stressors. Popular forms of therapy, then, focus on developing healthier coping skills and addressing emotional issues, problems, and stressors—in an attempt to eliminate the *need* to binge. Of course, every therapist is different, but when *traditional therapy* is used in this book, it refers to treatments that are guided by this mainstream theory.

With the meaning of common terms in this book understood, the recovery framework can now be introduced, consisting of just two goals. The purpose of the two-goal recovery framework is to keep recovery focused on what matters while still empowering you to tailor it to your particular situation. On the surface, the two goals look much too simple, and you may find yourself thinking that if doing the following two things were easy, you'd have already accomplished both by now. For the time being, please suspend any judgment and keep an open mind, remembering that there is an entire book ahead that will explain the reasons for this framework and will guide you through it.

Recovery Framework

1. Dismiss Urges to Binge
2. Eat Adequately

These two goals are all you need because: (1) if you can dismiss the urges to binge, you won't binge; and (2) if you can eat adequately while dismissing those urges, the urges will go away and you can return to a normal life. If you put these two goals into action every day, you will no longer be bulimic, you will no longer have binge eating disorder. You don't *need* to accomplish anything else, as far as recovery goes; but the benefit of this framework is that you *can* incorporate anything—authentic to you—that helps you dismiss urges and/or eat adequately. Likewise, you can prune any goal or activity in recovery that doesn't lead to improvement or realization of either of these two goals. That doesn't mean that other goals have no value for your life, but my job in this book is to simply make *recovery* accessible to you.

That brings me to important advice about how to use this book: *Stop reading when you feel like you have the information and insights you need to dismiss urges and eat adequately.* Many people find themselves in information overload when it comes to recovery; but more is not always better. You don't want to spend too much time thinking about your problem without putting ideas into action, or too much time reading about every possible scenario you might encounter or every problem that might come up. Women and men with eating disorders are smart and capable individuals, and a goal throughout this book will be to reignite trust in yourself.

This book has been designed in a logical sequence so that the overarching ideas that apply to most people who binge are presented first—both within the overall structure of the book and within each section—followed by discussions of concepts that apply only to some binge eaters or possible problems that might come up as you apply ideas. I suggest that you first gather the ideas that make the most sense to you and try them for yourself. Then if, later, if you feel like you need more information, come back and read more. It can take a while for new ideas to begin affecting your life and actions, so give yourself some time to absorb, practice, and incorporate what you read into your life before moving on. You will likely not need everything written here; so empower yourself to take only what helps you, and then get on with your life as soon as possible.

The book is organized as follows: The first part of this book—What You Need to Know Before Recovery—will help you understand why you binge and why a simple and targeted approach to recovery (the recovery framework presented here) is warranted, based on new science.

The second part of this book—Recovery—comprises the bulk of the book because it's where you will put into practice the two-goal recovery framework to end binge eating. The first section covers Recovery Goal 1: Dismiss Urges to Binge, and the reason that this is the first goal of recovery is because it's the only one many of you may need. If you already have general knowledge of how to eat in an adequate way, you won't need any more advice on this topic—more advice might just cause you to overthink your eating habits and complicate your recovery. Only if you are struggling with eating normally should you move on to the second section, Recovery Goal 2: Eat Adequately. This section will help you with a wide range of eating issues, like giving up dieting, dealing with weight problems, and learning about hunger and fullness. The intent of Recovery Goal 2 is to help you nourish your body properly, in a way that works for you.

One form of problematic eating in particular—restrictive dieting—deserves special discussion. If you aren't eating enough, it can make dismissing urges nearly impossible. If this is the case for you, you need to move directly to Recovery Goal 2 after learning the concepts from Recovery Goal 1. This is the exception to the suggestion above to give yourself ample time to work with new ideas. If you are depriving yourself of food, no amount of time is going to help your urges to binge go away. It's still important to have the knowledge of how to dismiss urges in place, so don't skip Recovery Goal 1, but as soon as possible, start gradually regulating your eating habits with the help of Recovery Goal 2 (and the support of a medical or nutritional professional if necessary).

In Part III of the book, Amy Johnson will help you extend your application of the concepts in this book to other aspects of your life. Even if you find that you don't need some of the chapters prior to this discussion, take the time to read Amy's words in Chapter 34, for you don't want to miss the opportunity to use what you've learned to end other habits or unproductive mental processes.

Finally, the book ends with two appendices that offer supplementary information, including a collection of helpful resources for readers interested in learning more or seeking additional help, and an abridged version of my own story.

Throughout the book, you will find writing prompts meant to help you discover and develop your own ideas on what works and doesn't work in your unique recovery. Use these prompts any way you wish—completing them as you go or simply keeping the questions in mind as you go about your day to spark your own insights. You don't have to actually put pen to paper or type up your answers on your computer/device for the prompts to be effective; but writing out your thoughts *will* help you better absorb what you learn along the way and give you a tool to refer back to as needed. You may find yourself spending ample time on the prompts in one chapter only to skim through those in the next, and that's perfectly fine. Remember, this is your own unique recovery story; this book is just meant to guide you with information and support.

However you use it, I hope you will come away from this book trusting yourself again and knowing that you are capable of living a life free of binge eating.

PART I

WHAT YOU NEED TO KNOW
BEFORE RECOVERY

[1]

Why You Binge

I think we overcomplicate things in our minds, like attach so many excuses as to why we binge. I could have made an entire shopping list of reasons why I binged. But your first book made that little light in my head go off, and I thought, "Ah, maybe it's not so complicated after all."

~Margaret

MOST BINGE EATERS ASK themselves one question after a binge: *Why?*

Countless books and articles have been written in an attempt to answer this question. Answers have been given by therapists, nutritionists, doctors, and by men and woman who are struggling with the problem or who have recovered. It's natural to want to look for answers, and it's not hard to find theoretical reasons for bulimia and binge eating disorder. When we talk about the *why* of binge eating, it's important to first make a distinction between two types of *why* questions and their answers:

1. Why did you develop bulimia/binge eating disorder?
2. Why, in the moments leading up to a binge, do you proceed to binge?

The first question is in the past tense, asking how you got where you are today. According to traditional therapy and mainstream thought, the answers to this first type of question are varied and also typically very complex and multifaceted. Low self-esteem, cultural pressure to be thin, lack of control over one's life, troubled personal relationships, genetic factors, childhood abuse, brain chemical imbalances, psychological problems, and personality traits, among other factors, have all been blamed.[12] There is no doubt that *something* put you at risk for developing bulimia or binge eating disorder; however, risk factors remain poorly understood.[13] In fact, to date, the evidence for psychological, biological, developmental, and sociocultural effects on the development of eating disorders is inconclusive, despite a large body of research examining possible risk factors.[14]

For every problem you think contributed to the development of your disorder, you could find countless people in the world with the same problem who do not binge.

In clinical research, there has been a move toward studying the underlying brain mechanisms of eating disorders and a marked increase in neuroscience data related to bulimia and BED.[15] Since patient response to current therapeutic interventions is inadequate—even poor—researchers theorize that a better understanding of the underlying neuroscience of eating disorders could improve treatment strategies.[16] The field of eating disorders lags behind other psychiatric conditions when it comes to understanding the brain's role,[17] but as we learn more, urgently needed treatment innovations will likely be in the form of brain-directed treatments, not talking therapies.

Although neuroscience still has a long way to go in pinning down exactly why eating disorders occur, this chapter and the next will discuss some simple—and, I believe, more practical—brain-based answers as to why you developed bulimia or binge eating disorder in the first place. While reading the explanations, know that even a brain-based answer for why you developed bulimia or BED has only limited value for your personal recovery, because when you are feeling driven toward a binge, it actually doesn't matter why your particular problem came about. What *does* matter is the answer to the second question above—the question in the present tense about why you actually binge. You need to know the more immediate reason why you do what you do in that moment when you are feeling compelled to binge. You need to know why you take that first compulsive bite.

By far, the most common reason given by traditional therapy and mainstream thought, as discussed in the Introduction, is that you binge to "cope." Supposedly, before you take the first bite, there is a need for relief from a problem or difficult emotion. This theory is so pervasive that even the well-known health website WebMD, which provides information stemming from more than 100 board-certified physicians and health experts nationwide,[18] says: "people who binge use food as a way to cope with unwanted emotions or stress."[19] I will discuss at length why the coping answer is flawed and often leads to increased reliance on binge eating. Everyone in this world has a need to cope, everyone has problems and emotions that they would like relief from; the need to cope does not drive binge eating in the present. There is only one reason why you binge.

THE CAUSE OF BINGE EATING

What makes you binge in the present is your desire to binge—the *urges*. No one would binge without binge urges, no matter what was going on in their life, no matter what emotions they were feeling, no matter what problems they were facing, no matter how well or how poorly they were coping with issues in their life.

No one binges without that compelling, intrusive, irrational desire to do so. That desire caused you to binge the first time, and every time after that.

Knowing that it's the urges that drive you to eat large amounts of food time after time simplifies recovery. You don't need to try to identify every risk factor or solve every problem that might (or might not) have theoretically led to the development of your bulimia or BED; you only have to learn to deal with the urges. Right now, you are dealing with the urges in the only way you know how, the only way that effectively (but temporarily) gets rid of them: by binge eating. Your binge eating isn't a symbolic way of coping with life's difficulties or negative feelings, it's your current way to cope with a very specific problem—the urges to binge.

Your urges to binge encompass all of the thoughts, feelings, physical sensations, and cravings that make you feel compelled to binge (and all the neurological and physiological processes underlying that experience). The urges can vary in how they feel from person to person and from moment to moment. Urges can feel like overpowering desire, like compulsion, like urgency, like a nagging itch, or even like a gentle push. Urges often include seemingly logical thoughts of why it makes sense to binge in that moment, as well as promises of what the binge will do for you, along with strong cravings or other physical symptoms.

When you are having an urge to binge, it can feel as if a large amount of food is like water in the desert and getting all you can is vital to your survival. In this way, urges can feel stressful and painfully demanding. Your urges may be predictable or unpredictable; they may always present themselves in a similar way, or the urges may surprise you. Regardless of when, where, how, and why the urges present themselves, no one binges without them. If you can learn to dismiss the urges, you'll no longer have anything driving you to binge, and nothing—no life event, no stressor, no emotion, no risk factor that might have led to the development of your problem—can sway you otherwise.

Knowing that urges to binge cause binge eating in the present transforms the way we will discuss the first question: Why did you develop bulimia/binge eating disorder? You developed bulimia or BED because you developed urges to binge. So the question now becomes: Why did you develop urges to binge? Bulimia and binge eating disorder cannot exist without them. Learning why you have them, from a brain-based perspective, can feel freeing—because you will realize you are not personally flawed or diseased—and can allow you to more easily dismiss them when the time comes.

WHY YOU HAVE URGES

Usually, urges to binge develop in your life for two very simple reasons:

1. **Survival instincts (dieting):** Binge eating is an adaptive response to dieting. Calorie restriction puts your body and brain in a survival-oriented state, causing you to crave and seek out large amounts of food, especially highly palatable food (high in sugar, fat, and carbohydrates). This is a normal reaction—a symptom of a healthy brain.[20]

2. **Habit (conditioning):** Once you binge eat many times, your body and brain become conditioned to expect and demand the binges, so your brain automatically sends out strong urges, as if binge eating is necessary for your survival. Habit formation is a vital brain function, not a sign of disease.[21]

The majority of bulimics can easily see that their binge urges developed after a period of dieting. The dieting may start as just an attempt to lose a few pounds, to go along with the crowd, to imitate a parent or friend who is dieting, or even to become healthier. The dangers are unknown to the new dieter, and the diet may seem to have positive benefits at first. But soon the dieting ignites increased food cravings and strong hunger, which eventually culminate in the first binge. This drive to eat more during and after a period of food restriction is not a sign of a lack of willpower; it's your brain trying to protect you. Research on both animals and humans has shown that calorie deprivation leads to increased food consumption and binge eating.[22] Even if calorie restriction isn't involved, giving yourself rigid food rules and trying to ban certain food sets up a mind-set of deprivation and a desire to rebel against the "rules," which often leads to out-of-control eating.[23]

> *I had no idea at the time that a diet would turn into a serious eating disorder. It started gradually and then accelerated. I started bingeing every few days, then every night. Then I started bingeing to the point where I felt I had to throw up. That started happening more often. I was afraid to tell anyone. I didn't know this was how it happened to other people, I felt like I was the only one who had ever experienced this shameful secret.*
>
> *~Janice*

The reason why some people binge eat after a period of restrictive dieting while others diet without ever binge eating is likely due to several factors, including brain and genetic differences.[24] But regardless of why your particular brain followed this common pattern, once that first binge occurs, you are immediately primed to do it again. This is because the first binge is usually pleasurable (temporarily), bringing immediate relief from restrictive dieting and activating the natural reward pathways in the brain with palatable foods.[25] The brain easily learns to repeat behaviors that are rewarding and reinforcing, and habit formation then occurs, so that the urges will surface even in the absence of food deprivation. Indeed, studies have shown that dieting alone does not maintain binge eating over time;[26] binge urges eventually become conditioned, habitual responses to environmental, sensory, or food cues.[27] A person's daily routine, surroundings, and experiences become associated with binge eating, and whenever the person is exposed to the cues, it can trigger automatic, powerful cravings, even if they are not restricting calories.

The binge eating habit doesn't actually require restrictive dieting as its catalyst; urges to binge can develop even if you've never purposefully deprived your body of necessary calories or set rigid food rules. Several studies have shown that the majority of those with BED started binge eating prior to any weight concerns or any attempt to diet.[28] When binge eating comes first, the onset of the problem is usually at a much earlier age.[29] Some research has linked these cases to irregular eating patterns, haphazard meal planning, and even the mere presence of highly palatable foods.[30] In some people, prolonged exposure to rewarding stimuli like palatable foods can lead to physical dependence, similar to the process observed in drug addiction.[31] Brain changes occur within the natural reward pathways, so that the person eventually transitions from overeating to binge eating, just like someone can transition from recreational drug use to drug abuse.[32]

Take a few minutes to think about how your binge urges first appeared in your life, considering both survival instincts and habit, and answer the questions below. As you reflect on your own history, it's possible you may recall significant stressful events tied in with the development of the urges. Know that there will be further discussion of this in Chapter 8; but for now, focus specifically on the urges in terms of survival instincts and habit—not dwelling on the circumstances in your life when the urges commenced. Stress (or at least an elevated level of perceived stress) *is* a factor that can tip the balance toward binge eating[33] and other bad habits, but that does not change how you will approach your binge eating problem as it is today. This doesn't discount whatever stressful life event may have preceded the onset of your urges; it only means that the urges were and still are the *direct* cause of your binge eating, and to recover, you'll still need to learn to dismiss them.

How did your urges to binge develop? Did you diet prior to the development of your urges to binge?

_____

_____

_____

_____

_____

_____

_____

_____

How do you think survival instincts and/or habit operated in the initiation and maintenance of your bulimia/BED?

_____

_____

_____

_____

_____

_____

_____

[2]

What Brain Processes Are Behind Urges to Binge?

It felt like an impossible task to fix everything in my life in order to stop binge eating. And rightly so! Knowing about the brain and how there wasn't anything wrong with me, rather that what was happening was a natural and expected consequence of dieting, made the problem a lot "smaller" and therefore more manageable. I finally felt like it was something I could overcome rather than a big mess I had to live with for the rest of my life.

~Lynn

MANY BINGE EATERS HAVE become accustomed to the idea that their desire to binge signals a deep psychological problem or emotional void in their life. Dismissing urges that are believed to be meaningful in their life can prove very difficult. Moving forward with a simpler two-goal recovery framework requires a shift toward a brain-based perspective that allows binge eaters to begin to see their urges differently. This chapter provides a fuller understanding of how binge urges work in the brain, going a little deeper into the science of urges than *Brain over Binge* did. Do not feel like you have to memorize the information that follows in order to recover; read it only to gain new insight and know that anything that may seem complex will be streamlined for ease of use in recovery.

In *Brain over Binge*, I warned that I am not a neuroscientist; the brain information included in that book and this one is meant to be useful, not highly technical. Even if I were a neuroscientist and tried to bring you a completely accurate picture of the brain of a binge eater, I could not, because neuroscience is not there yet. Nevertheless, there are some overarching themes and information emerging from current research that give us a glimpse into the brain processes behind binge urges. The goal is not to give you every detail of that research, but to help you understand your binge urges as a function of a temporary brain-wiring problem—one that you are capable of correcting.

Keep in mind here that I'm explaining the urges only in terms of the brain—because that's where our experience of the urges to binge ultimately comes from. Realize, however, that the brain is intimately connected to physiology. Brain systems interact with the various and complex bodily processes that influence eating behavior, especially with hormones that signal hunger and fullness and help maintain blood sugar levels.[34] Some of these hormones are indeed produced in the brain, such as the feeding stimulant neuropeptide Y and the feeding inhibitor peptide YY, both produced in the hypothalamus; but other hormones evoked in feeding behavior are produced throughout the body—in the adrenal and pituitary glands (epinephrine, cortisol), in fat cells (leptin), in the pancreas (glucagon, insulin), in the stomach (ghrelin), and in the gastrointestinal tract (cholecystokinin), just to name a few sites.

The cascade of physiological processes that signal your brain to create the urges, as well as the cascade of physiological processes that happen as a result of having those urges and acting on them, cannot yet be precisely pinned down or fully explained—nor does it need to be for recovery to occur. I personally believe that hormones and physiological processes that help shape patterns of eating are more relevant when it comes to minor forms of overeating, problematic cravings, food "addiction," and difficulty with weight loss, so we will talk a little more about this topic in the discussion of Recovery Goal 2 in Part II. When addressing *binge eating*, however, it's the brain-based habit, driven by urges, that is primary. Even though hormones are certainly involved, all of those signals are processed and integrated in the brain anyway, so it's the overarching experience of the binge urges that needs to be addressed.

WHERE DO BINGE URGES COME FROM NEUROLOGICALLY?

You now know that the urges to binge you experience today are the result of survival instincts (due to restrictive dieting) and/or habit (due to repeated binge eating). Both our survival functions and our habitual responses stem from a more primitive part of the brain that is responsible for maintaining our basic biological functions and driving us to act in ways that *it senses* will maximize our chance of survival. Note here that sometimes what the primitive brain *senses* will maximize our chance of survival is actually detrimental to us in the modern world. The primitive brain doesn't consider our long-term goals or the consequences of the behaviors it drives us toward; instead, it just responds to the environment or to how we have behaved in the past and then generates strong impulses, thoughts, cravings, desires, and urges that compel us to maintain habits.

Although the brain does not have neat boundaries, what's being referred to as the "primitive brain" is buried deep within and below the cerebral cortex—the wrinkled outer layer of the brain. The primitive brain, also known as the "animal brain," is nearly identical to the brains of animals. The primitive brain is pre-rational—it existed before rational thought—both developmentally in each person (meaning the primitive brain's development is complete early in life, before the rational brain centers are fully developed) and in the evolution/creation of our species (meaning the primitive brain existed on earth before rational brain networks existed). The vast majority of the activities in the primitive brain take place beyond our conscious awareness.

The primitive brain is composed of two basic parts:

1. **The brainstem:** The area at the base of the skull that connects the brain to the spinal cord and controls our basic life-sustaining functions, like breathing, heart rate, and blood pressure. This is the "simplest" part of the brain and closely resembles the brain of a reptile.

2. **The limbic system:** This is the most important part of the primitive brain for understanding binge urges because it has been directly implicated in binge eating.[35] The limbic system sits on top of the brainstem, buried under the cortex, and is involved in many of our emotions and motivations, particularly those related to survival.

The limbic system is often called the "pleasure center"; it links together a number of brain structures that control and regulate our ability to desire pleasure, to feel pleasure, and also the motivation to seek out pleasure. To this end, the limbic system contains the *reward circuit* or *reward system*, which is important in ensuring that pleasurable behaviors are repeated. The limbic system is involved in learning and the formation of memories—both integral to habit formation. The limbic system also contains the hypothalamus, which is a vital component of the primitive brain that plays a major role in regulating feeding hormones.[36]

The limbic system has three basic objectives: (1) to survive; (2) to seek pleasure; and (3) to avoid pain, both emotional and physical. In this way, the limbic system is vital to keeping us alive and safe by helping us avoid danger; but, as we will see, if poorly understood, it can work against us in bulimia and BED. The limbic system—charged with our survival and comfort—reacts as if binges are as necessary for survival as oxygen, as if the discomfort of binge urges must be avoided like a real, painful threat to your well-being.

REWARD SYSTEM GONE AWRY

A *reward* is anything we experience as pleasurable. A reward also typically serves as a *reinforcer*—a reward that, when presented after a behavior, causes the probability of that behavior to increase. There are countless examples of using rewards to reinforce behaviors, like giving a kid a sticker for being good or granting a dog a treat for learning a trick; but rewards and reinforcement are also vital tools of survival. The reward system is a powerful, primitive component within the limbic system that uses these tools to ensure that we repeat life-sustaining behaviors and any other behaviors that the system *senses* are beneficial to us.

The reward system is activated by healthy, life-promoting activities, like eating and sex and good habits that bring pleasure, but also by destructive habits that have become connected to reward and reinforced over time, especially habits that involve pleasurable substances like drugs[37] and large amounts of binge foods. Data from animal models suggest that binge eating, like substance abuse, may result from maladaptive processes within the natural reward system.[38] Indeed, there is evidence that changes in reward-related brain areas do occur in response to the binge eating of highly palatable foods,[39] and there have been some observed differences in the primitive brains of binge eaters and non–binge eaters.

For example, BED patients have been found to have a hyper-responsive reward network, meaning their reward system is more activated around food,[40] which could be a factor in explaining increased food consumption. In a study of bulimic patients, the act of tasting something sweet revealed a decreased reward system response, leading some to theorize that they may eat more to achieve the same reward system response as non–binge eaters.[41] More studies are needed, and so far, it's unclear whether the observed differences are only the results of repeated binge eating or if some are neurological risk factors for developing the problem.[42]

For a useful understanding of the urges, it doesn't matter exactly how the reward system goes awry; it only matters that it does. Regardless of how your binge eating starts or what neurological factors may have put you at risk, the binge urges result from a reward system that incorrectly drives you to large amounts of food, as if binge eating is vital to your survival. As we will see, it is possible to teach your primitive brain that binge eating actually *isn't* necessary or rewarding, and you'll do that by dismissing urges.

For the purposes of learning to dismiss urges, it's important to know that there is a divide within the reward system: The neural pathways and neurotransmitter systems involved in the desire and motivation for pleasure ("wanting") are actually different from the neural pathways and neurotransmitter systems involved in the actual experience of pleasure ("liking").[43] This explains why you have such strong urges that make you feel like binge eating is exactly what you desire; but then when you do it, aside from very brief pleasure, it's not as good as your urges promised and leads to more pain. How much you desire a reward is not always proportional to the pleasure experienced;[44] in other words, you "want" to binge more than you "like" to binge. It's the urges that make you want to binge, so we will focus on "wanting" first.

DOPAMINE DRIVES "PRIMAL WANTING"

The key neurotransmitter that stimulates the reward system is dopamine. Dopamine makes us "want" to perform survival-based behavior and habits. As Stanford University psychologist and expert in the science of self-control Kelly McGonigal, Ph.D., puts it: "When dopamine hijacks your attention, the mind becomes fixated on obtaining or repeating whatever triggered it."[45] The effect of dopamine makes it an apparent force behind binge urges.

While dopamine is certainly not the only factor involved, understanding how dopamine works is helpful in preparing to dismiss binge urges. In the past, the scientific consensus was that dopamine release actually *created* pleasurable feelings—the high or euphoria that one feels performing a pleasurable activity or taking in a rewarding substance. However, an increasing number of studies[46] now show that dopamine is not responsible for the direct experience of pleasure itself; it is instead responsible for *motivating us to seek pleasure.*[47]

When the brain recognizes an opportunity for reward, it releases dopamine in the limbic system; in fact, anything we think will make us feel good triggers dopamine release. The increase in dopamine marks the "object of desire as critical to your survival."[48] This reward system is not our enemy—we need it to keep us interested and engaged in life.[49] When this reward system is activated at normal levels, it motivates us toward natural and necessary behaviors—with eating obviously being one of the primitive brain's top priorities. It makes sense that we have a system that attracts us to food and motivates us to work to obtain it. But this system can become *over*stimulated with "unnatural rewards," like drugs of abuse or large amounts of highly palatable food.[50]

Dopamine increases in *anticipation* of a food reward[51] and is also elevated during food consumption, which keeps us wanting more and working to get more while we are eating. Highly palatable (high-sugar or high-fat) food doesn't flood the limbic system with as much dopamine as drugs do, but it causes a greater dopamine release than normal eating does; the sweeter the food, the more dopamine is released.[52] Furthermore, dopamine levels in the limbic system of binge eaters show a greater spike than in non–binge eaters at just the sight and smell of food.[53] This doesn't necessarily mean that binge eaters "like" the food more, just that their brains trigger them to "want" it more.

When I say "want" here, I am talking about a more primal form of wanting, different from the desires of our more rational, cognitive brain centers that make us human. Examples of cognitive, rational wanting would be: wanting to get a college degree, wanting to get married, wanting to meet certain goals, wanting to recover from bulimia or BED. In the scientific literature, the "primal wanting"— which stems from the limbic system as opposed to the higher brain centers—is called "incentive salience."[54] Incentive salience (which I'll continue to call "primal wanting" for ease of use and understanding) does not require "elaborate cognitive expectations,"[55] but instead focuses on immediate rewards.

In addictions and other bad habits, the fact that there are distinct neural pathways that drive primal wanting, as opposed to cognitive/rational wanting, often creates a situation where the two unique types of wanting conflict.[56] There is a primal wanting from the limbic system strongly driving the person toward a "reward" that their higher, rational brain doesn't *truly* want. This explains why binge eaters feel like the urges get in the way of their goals, their true desires, and the person they know they can be; and they are baffled by why they continue to *want* to binge. Understanding that the binge urges are just an expression of irrational, primal wanting gives you a clearer picture of why you have this inner dissonance. The promise of reward can be so powerful that you keep pursuing it even when it makes you miserable.

The promise of reward itself doesn't usually feel good either—anticipation of satisfying the primal wanting usually comes with a great deal of anxiety. This is because dopamine triggers our brain's stress response, making us feel like the object of our desire is a life-or-death situation.[57] We usually attribute this anticipatory anxiety to not yet having what we want (a binge), but it's our urges—mediated by dopamine—causing both the wanting *and* the anxiety of wanting. Giving in takes away the anxiety of the desire, and that's often a major driving force behind why we act on urges. Often the only reason we binge is to make that anxiety of not binge eating go away.

Once dopamine has driven us to the reward, its job is done and we are stuck with the consequences. That brain process that made binge eating seem so attractive and critical is gone in the blink of an eye after a binge, and that's when you wonder *why* you would possibly do this. It's as if something tricks you over and over, and for some reason, you can't learn your lesson. It's no wonder people search for deeper meaning in the urges to binge; otherwise, without an understanding of the primitive brain, it seems to make no sense on the surface. When I was bulimic, I remember thinking that at some point, I would feel like enough was enough. But it never felt that way. The desire kept coming up, just as strong as before.

In that way, I felt that it was like an addiction, and now there is evidence to support binge eating being an addictive process similar to substance abuse.[58] It has been shown that sugary foods persistently increase dopamine in a way that is similar to addictive drugs,[59] and it's been proposed that over time, continued stimulation of the dopamine pathways by binge eating results in some alterations of those pathways.[60] Research suggests that bulimics can eventually show tolerance similar to drug users, such that larger doses of the drug are required (in this case, larger amounts of food) to achieve the same effect.[61]

We aren't going to go too far down the path of comparing binge eating to addictions, because this implies a lack of control or a lack of choice, and this book is about giving you control back and putting the choice of whether or not to binge in your hands. If you want to say that you are "addicted" to binge eating, then that's perfectly valid, but that doesn't change how you will approach the problem. Addictions can be overcome; and as we'll discuss further in the next chapter, the brain processes that drive destructive habits and substance addictions are changeable.

An important concept that will be repeated throughout this book is that dopamine spikes and other brain processes that are temporarily faulty in bulimia or BED only *prime* your brain to binge, but those brain process do not move voluntary muscles—they don't pick up the food, chew it, swallow it. So the next time you start to feel all of that "wanting" and the anxiety that comes along with the urge, know that it's just dopamine doing its appointed task and it's only a temporary state you will learn to pass through.

Opioids Create "Primal Liking"

Once we give in to our dopamine-driven urges, our primitive brains reward us for eating by releasing pleasurable chemicals that have an impact on how much we "like" the food and the behavior itself, ensuring that the behavior is reinforced. The liking of food is more opioid-dependent than dopamine-dependent;[62] endogenous opioids within the reward system have been linked to the hedonic—or pleasurable—properties of food and help make binge eating reinforcing.[63] The brain rewards the consumption of palatable (fatty, sugary) foods by releasing these endogenous opioids, which help control pain and give you a sleepy, relaxing comfort. Research suggests that binge eating can lead to alterations within the endogenous opioid system.[64]

When the urges arise, you'll automatically be reminded of all of the ways that you "like" to binge. But just like "wanting" a behavior with your higher brain is different from primal wanting, it's important to recognize that "primal liking" is different from true pleasure. You may "like" some of the temporary feelings of a binge but, when considering it with your reasoning abilities, *not* like the behavior in your life. Furthermore, you may fully realize that even the temporary taste pleasure and fleeting good feelings aren't as good as the urges promise. Maybe when you first started binge eating, it felt really good because it was releasing you from food deprivation; but now it's probable that whatever you "like" about binge eating pales in comparison to what your rational brain *doesn't* like about binge eating.

The tricky part is that over time, the primal liking can translate into an illusion of true liking—through the conditioning process, you may have inadvertently connected binge eating to temporary relief from your emotions and problems, or you may have purposefully made that connection in therapy or through other self-help methods. The habit may have gotten so wrapped up in your life that the "primal liking" became more meaningful than it should have been. When you think you like and want to binge for rational reasons or true pleasure, it makes this reward system glitch more difficult to correct.

How to Use This Information

Understanding the reward system and how it drives us toward pleasurable behaviors and habits is meant to help you recognize the urges to binge as automatic functions of the primitive brain. It is vital for you to understand, however, that just because eating disorders have a basis in the brain, it doesn't mean you have a flawed or broken brain. Humans develop urges and cravings for all sorts of negative behaviors, and we could find evidence of any destructive habit in the brain with the proper technology. Feeling driven toward things that aren't good for us is nothing new, and the fact that we can now explain this drive in terms of the brain doesn't take away our personal responsibility.

> *A lot of women still get emotional about the binge eating; but once you realize what's happening in your brain, the science of it, the chemistry, the biology, the way we were created—it has nothing to do with emotion. Instead of becoming emotional, you can start thinking, "Wow, look at my brain, it's operating from survival; it's an amazing part of my body, but I don't need that response anymore—I have to reset it." It's not emotional, and it's not anything wrong with you. It's just your brain doing what it thinks it's supposed to be doing.*
> ~Cookie Rosenblum

In fact, as you will see, understanding this primitive brain function actually strengthens our capacity to use self-control. Without an understanding, you will feel overrun by the urges, but with this background information, you can start choosing your own path and stop letting your primal brain processes drive you to destructive actions. For now, you need to accept only that, yes, you do have some abnormalities in your primitive brain, specifically in your reward system involving dopamine and opioid functions—most of which were created by a history of caloric restriction and by binge eating itself.[65] These abnormalities are ultimately responsible for *urging* you to binge, but not for carrying out the action.

Every vice or detrimental activity human beings engage in involves neurons firing in a way that's not ideal, but that doesn't mean you aren't in control when those neurons are doing their thing. Start cultivating an attitude of acceptance toward your temporary reward system glitch. You don't have to fear it, or blame yourself or others or events for it, or think it signals something more than neurons firing in a pre-programmed way. Everyone is susceptible to something detrimental, and this just happens to be the challenge your brain is presenting.

We all "want" things we know we shouldn't have; and everyone has times when they feel they "like" to behave in ways that aren't going to bring them true pleasure. This is part of the human condition. Regardless of the exact neurotransmitters implicated, it's important to know that the processes of primal wanting and liking aren't in line with who we truly are, that when your reward center is flooded with dopamine and binge eating seems so appealing, those primal brain processes aren't deep and meaningful to *you*.

CAN DOPAMINE AND OPIOID SIGNALS JUST BE FIXED?

I've spent time here explaining how dopamine drives the primal wanting (the urges) and how opioids facilitate the temporary pleasure of binge eating. Wouldn't it follow, then, that we could just modify those specific neurotransmitters through pharmacological means and then the urges would cease? Due to the amazing complexity of the human brain, it's not that straightforward. It is impossible for a medication to tweak one neurotransmitter without affecting other brain mechanisms and without side effects.

There is also no way to change opioids and dopamine as they relate to one behavior and not others. We fundamentally need the activities of these neurotransmitters to live a normal and healthy life. Furthermore, changing dopamine or opioid signaling (or any other brain chemical, for that matter) is no guarantee that the brain wouldn't adapt in order to keep your habit alive. As already stated, the above discussion is simplified and there are certainly other neurotransmitters and brain functions involved, and so far, no pharmacological intervention is able to fully eradicate binge eating.[66]

That being said, in 2015, the U.S. Food and Drug Administration approved the first drug to specifically treat BED,[67] which does affect dopamine. The drug—Vyvanse®—is a nervous system stimulant that acts like an amphetamine and increases dopamine in the brain. Two twelve-week studies showed that Vyvanse reduced binge days per week significantly more than a placebo;[68] however, there are yet to be any long-term outcome studies, and the drug has a high potential for abuse and a risk of dangerous side effects. It is not currently known exactly how Vyvanse reduces binge eating episodes, but here are two of the theories.

One theory is that Vyvanse (and other nervous system stimulants) are natural appetite suppressants; and it's assumed that reducing a binge eater's hunger levels overall might naturally reduce the appeal of a binge. Another theory is that the increase in dopamine actually increases a person's capacity for self-control, which seems counterintuitive to what we've been discussing. It is true that a spike in dopamine motivates us to seek instant gratification (pleasure); but it also has a biological connection to our motivation to achieve[69]—and to that end, it can raise alertness and the ability to concentrate, as well as reduce impulsiveness, which, hypothetically, can help a person *not* be swept away by binge urges.[70] This is just one small example of the brain's complexity and why it's currently impossible to target only binge-specific pathways with a pill.

The way to directly affect the parts of the brain that are temporarily abnormal in bulimia or BED—the ones we can pinpoint and the countless ones we cannot— is to stop binge eating. As discussed in the next chapter, dismissing binge urges and eating adequately will give you the brain changes you need that are specific to binge eating. This book presents a brain-based intervention, but it's a simple one that allows you to move forward without knowing every detail of the neurotransmitters and neural pathways involved.

Primitive Brain / Reward System = Lower Brain

Before we move on to discussing how recovery will change your brain, I am going to simplify the terms used throughout this book from here onward. Initially, it was important to give you a basic scientific perspective, but keeping the language of recovery in simpler terms will prove exceedingly more useful going forward. Instead of continuing to talk about neurotransmitters, the limbic/reward system, the primitive brain, and other nervous system processes involved, I am simply going to use *lower brain* to refer to the part(s) of the brain and nervous system responsible for driving binge eating, regardless of specific location or brain chemicals implicated.

The term *lower brain* actually refers to all of the automatic functions of the brain over which we do not have conscious control. Most of the unconscious, lower brain processes aren't problematic, but as we've discussed, some are temporarily dysfunctional in bulimia and BED. The term *lower brain* illustrates the fact that the processes that drive binge eating are "below" your conscious, higher self—both physiologically and symbolically—because your higher self (located behind the forehead) can override and change the lower brain processes. I will refer to the part of you that can override the lower brain messages as your *higher brain, higher self,* or *true self,* to illustrate that this is the part that feels like "you" and that is independent of the urges.

The higher brain, which will be covered in more detail in later chapters, contains the *prefrontal cortex,* which gives you the ability to choose what to focus on and which actions to take based on the information coming from the lower brain. The higher brain is often called the "mind,"[71] which is the seat of our conscious awareness. To take the two parts of the brain down to their basic functions: The lower brain receives information from your external and internal environment (including bodily sensations and feelings) and processes that information in a rote way, without rational thought. Once the lower brain processes the input, it submits this information to your conscious awareness—your higher brain—which has the ability to determine how it wants to use that information.[72] As it relates to binge eating, you have the power to decide—with your higher brain—what you will ultimately do when the binge urges arise from the lower brain.

[3]

How the Two-Goal Recovery Framework Changes the Brain

It's by repeated "no" responses that diminish the intensity of the urges that we can eventually move forward and look to embrace a "normal," healthier version of ourselves.

~Helen

NOW THAT WE KNOW the basics of how urges work in the lower brain and that the brain processes behind those urges are temporary and can be changed, we can learn about the two-goal recovery framework that will allow you to make that change. In our brains, change is not the exception—it's the rule. Our brains are constantly in flux throughout life, and sometimes it takes only one alteration to one small input to change the whole system. With our higher brains, we can direct that change.

The brain learns based on past experience, and it physically changes based on where attention is focused and what actions are taken. This is a well-established concept known as "neuroplasticity"—a property of the brain that allows neurons (nerve cells) in the brain to adjust their activities in response to changes in the environment, new situations, one's actions, and where one focuses their attention.

Leading neuroplasticity researchers Jeffrey Schwartz, M.D., and Rebecca Gladding, M.D., explain this concept well in their book *You Are Not Your Brain: The 4-Step Solution for Changing Bad Habits, Ending Unhealthy Thinking, and Taking Control of Your Life*:

> The mind is involved in helping you constructively focus your attention. Why is this important? When you learn how to focus your attention in positive, beneficial ways, you actually rewire your brain to support those actions and habits.[73]

Because of neuroplasticity, our habits, even our mental habits, are not fixed, permanent brain states.[74] If we don't use our habits, then the neural pathways that support them weaken and fade; in other words, when it comes to the brain, "what you no longer use, you lose."[75] The science of neuroplasticity shows that through the choices we make and through guided practice, we can create real, lasting change to the very neural pathways in our brains

Right now, you have strong, organized neural pathways in the lower brain that drive the urges to binge, and there is no way to turn off the urges except to retrain the brain. The two goals of recovery—dismissing urges and eating adequately—allow you to do just that. When you dismiss urges, you teach the lower brain that the habit is no longer necessary—that eating large amounts of food isn't vital to your survival and that binge eating isn't a behavior you need to be driven toward. In this way, dismissing urges rewires the brain so it no longer supports the binge eating habit. When you eat adequately along with dismissing urges, you teach your lower brain that there is no food shortage and that it no longer has to drive you to eat as if there is. In effect, eating adequately tames the survival instincts.

If you do both—dismiss the urges and eat adequately—you take care of both factors that drive binge urges (survival instincts and habit), and the lower brain pathways that compelled you to binge will gradually quiet. You will also simultaneously be strengthening the parts of the higher brain responsible for overriding lower brain messages, so that it becomes easier to dismiss urges over time. This is not just a quick fix that will stop your behaviors only to have them return; it's a fundamental change in the way you respond to urges that fundamentally changes your brain.

Top-Down Self-Control

As discussed in the last chapter, our higher brains are responsible for deciding what to do with the information from our lower brains. Right now, your higher brain isn't doing that job. It is letting the lower brain run the show when it comes to binge eating. This is why you feel hijacked by the urges. Your brain is functioning from the bottom up, meaning you are performing the behaviors called for by your lower brain. The goal in this book is to get you to start operating from the top down, using the higher brain to inhibit the unwanted binge behaviors.

The specific part of the higher brain responsible for inhibition of behaviors is the prefrontal cortex, and even more specifically, the right lateral prefrontal cortex. Research has consistently demonstrated the importance of the right lateral prefrontal cortex in controlling food intake and in sending the "stop" signal to lower brain regions.[76] Again, it matters not that we can pinpoint exactly how the higher brain is able to override lower brain messages, only that it can. Most importantly, the prefrontal cortex has ultimate control over your actions—your voluntary muscle movements. The lower brain cannot move the muscles; it needs your higher brain/prefrontal cortex to *act* on its messages, and your higher brain always has a choice.

Exercising top-down self-control might not come naturally for binge eaters at first. The prefrontal pathways responsible for inhibiting binge eating can become weak with lack of use; furthermore, there is some evidence that bulimics have a harder time with inhibition in general, not just specific to food.[77] This impulsive quality, which may be a consequence of the disorder or a possible risk factor for developing the habit, facilitates the loss of control binge eaters experience.[78] In the research, impulsivity is characterized by a combination of heightened sensitivity to reward and impaired inhibitory control,[79] so it follows that the two-goal recovery framework will affect both the reward circuits in the lower brain and the inhibitory network in the higher brain.

The aim of the two-goal recovery framework is to strengthen the higher brain pathways that inhibit binge behavior and weaken the lower brain pathways that drive the binge urges.

It's important to note here that restrictive dieting is not compatible with directing these brain changes, because restrictive dieting results in the loss of inhibitory control. When you are in a calorie deficit, your body conserves energy by reducing or eliminating functions that aren't necessary for survival. The self-control function of the prefrontal cortex happens to be *unnecessary* for your immediate survival during a food shortage; so the lower brain gets the scarce resources, so that it can drive you to eat.[80] In effect, restrictive dieting puts your higher brain in an energy-depleted state so that you'll feel more out of control and be less capable of resisting binge urges. Recovery Goal 2 ensures that you will have a properly functioning prefrontal cortex that is able to resist binge urges.

WHY THERAPY DOESN'T USUALLY LEAD TO BINGE-SPECIFIC BRAIN CHANGES

Let's take a moment to briefly talk about why traditional therapy might not direct the changes you want to see (namely, stronger higher brain pathways that can easily veto binge urges and, eventually, the dissolution of the lower brain pathways that drive binge urges). As we learn more about the brain, I believe that any form of therapy that addresses underlying psychological issues and difficult emotions as a front-line defense against binge eating will become an old-fashioned practice of the past. Sitting down talking to trained professionals about problems will always serve a purpose as a means to help people improve their lives; however, eating disorder treatments are "highly unlikely to remain 'brainless.' "[81] Treatment *has* to change, considering the dismal success rate of talk therapies.

Recent research shows that psychodynamic therapy, in which addressing the root emotional causes and underlying problems is primary, helps only 6 percent of bulimics stop binge eating after five months of treatment, and only 15 percent after two years,[82] which is unacceptable. I think the reason psychodynamic therapy is not effective is because it doesn't target the parts of the brain that are problematic in binge eating. Talking about problems, or trying to solve them using the brain's rational capacities, does not address the wiring problems in the lower brain that override the higher brain in active bulimia or binge eating disorder; it does not teach someone to better utilize self-control as it relates to binge eating.

Of course, sitting down talking about emotional problems isn't the only way eating disorders are treated today. Cognitive behavioral therapy (CBT), which is considered the best available treatment for binge eating, does actually address the problematic binge eating and purging behaviors. In the same study mentioned above, cognitive behavioral therapy did much better, with 42 percent of people ending their binge eating and purging behaviors after five months of treatment, and 44 percent after two years.[83] CBT will continue to have a place in eating disorder treatment because it encourages active habit change, not just digging into underlying emotional problems.

However, even CBT leaves much room for improvement in terms of being a treatment targeted for the specific problematic brain processes involved here. CBT, like psychodynamic therapy, also relies on a lot of thought analysis, which, again, is not usually a helpful way to direct change in the lower brain. As we will see, you can't reason with the thoughts that come along with the urges—they are automatic and are resistant to change via rational arguments. Furthermore, as Jeffrey Schwartz states, CBT therapists "do not emphatically tell you that these brain-based messages are not representative of who you really are and that you do not have to act on them."[84] CBT gives value to the binge urges—saying that they are symptoms of perfectionism, anxiety, depression, low self-esteem, and so forth. Much time is spent on changing other negative thoughts and negative behaviors, unrelated to binge eating, which can get you a little off track in teaching you to directly resist urges.

A fundamental problem of traditional therapy in its various forms is that it fails to differentiate who you are from the temporary lower brain glitch you are experiencing. It also fails to recognize that you have fundamental control over your actions, without needing to solve a bunch of other problems first. Traditional therapy is sometimes like going to a mechanic because of bad brakes: The mechanic recommends a complete engine tune-up, a paint job, a new air-conditioning unit, and a new windshield, and while all of that stuff is great and will certainly enhance your vehicle, what you really need is to be able to stop the car! Now, eating disorder therapists and programs are not trying to upsell you on services like a mechanic might, but just as the mechanic may truly believe that those other improvements are called for to make your car run more effectively, therapists believe that transforming yourself in other ways will give you the ability to stop binge eating.

If you go to the mechanic to fix your brakes, the brakes need to get fixed—quickly, before you harm yourself or someone else. Then, if you are unhappy with some other things about your car (or yourself), you can go back to the repair shop (or the therapist's office). Therapy or any form of treatment shouldn't begin with someone telling you that you are damaged, that you have a destructive habit for deep psychological reasons, or that you are filling some emotional void. You aren't broken or in need of a complete overhaul; you only have a temporary inability to put on the brakes when urges arise. Working on the two-goal recovery framework day after day will help you do just that.

This doesn't mean other forms of therapy are useless; you can certainly find something appealing in any form of therapy. But if you can stay focused on what you truly need to do to recover—dismiss binge urges and eat adequately—you'll be able to decipher what is truly helpful to you in recovering from binge eating specifically. That's the great thing about creating an authentic recovery based around the two-goal framework: You can incorporate anything that helps lead you toward those goals.

THE BRAIN WANTS TO HOLD ON TO OLD IDEAS

When directing change in your brain, you need to know that, for some time, the brain will still be wired to support all of your old ideas and habits. Even if the above brain-based perspective feels liberating and helps you gain a better understanding of your urges, that doesn't mean your old beliefs will suddenly go away. The brain has a natural tendency to be as efficient as possible; it likes to hold on to ideas that we already have, because changing your beliefs requires more mental energy and your brain is usually trying to conserve that energy—for things like survival.

The higher, rational part of the brain that is responsible for decision making and incorporating new ideas requires much more energy than the rest of the brain, and it has limited resources compared to the rest of the brain (and, as we talked about earlier in the chapter, it's the first part to be compromised during a food shortage). New ideas that provide contrast and dissonance use "loads more energy"[85] in the brain; therefore, the brain is more comfortable finding evidence in your daily life to support already-held beliefs and running on old habits and programs. In this way, we are all primed to "avoid information that goes against our existing belief system."[86]

This whole topic of the limited energy of the higher brain, and of energy efficiency in the brain in general, is one we will return to frequently in this book.

But as it relates to this chapter's focus on shifting to a brain-based perspective of your eating disorder, the takeaway message is this: Just because your brain may automatically default to old belief systems doesn't mean those belief systems are serving you.

Even if information in this book resonates with you, including your own insights as you reflect on the writing prompts, you can always expect some push-back from your brain. For example, if you've spent a long time believing that your eating disorder is a coping mechanism for anxiety, this idea will naturally keep popping up. Don't let the brain's efficiency deter you from moving forward with new ideas that feel like they will serve you better than your old ones. Consider that you might be holding on to old ideas, not because they are facts, but only because that's what the brain is inclined to do.

If your old ideas ultimately end up feeling the most correct to you, then no one is telling you that you have to change your mind; but give new ideas ample opportunity to take hold. Don't expect yourself to suddenly snap out of whatever you currently think about your eating disorder and how to overcome it. But stay with it, and gradually, the new ideas will take root and these promptings will cease. The Recovery Goal 1 section and other areas of this book will help guide you in putting aside ideas that aren't working for you—especially those that tell you that you binge to "cope"—and staying focused on ideas that help you chart your own path to recovery.

THE TWO-GOAL RECOVERY FRAMEWORK BRINGS YOU BACK TO "NORMAL"

As we've discussed, the brain changes resulting from the two-goal recovery framework are specific to *binge* eating. The information in this book is not a cure for all unhealthy eating—it is not going to make you never want to eat sugar again; it is not going to stop you from sometimes, or even often, wanting a few more bites of your favorite foods; it is not going to take away your desire to stop for fast food sometimes instead of cooking at home. The end result of quitting binge eating will not be a you that always makes healthy food choices and never takes pleasure in indulgent foods. Rather, the recovery framework is designed to bring you back to "normal" (understanding that there is a lot of subjectivity attached to that word).

This is not a method to give you perfect self-control around food or to make you view food as fuel and nothing more. That would actually be detrimental, in my opinion, because it could throw you right back into dieting and also restrict your social life so much that it would be unhealthy for your mental state. The sooner you accept that your eating after recovery won't be perfect, the less you will doubt yourself and overthink every bite. Your "cured" brain will not urge you to *binge*, but you will not be banishing your healthy appetite or desire to take pleasure in food; nor will you be ridding yourself of every impulsive occurrence of mindlessly grabbing a snack or convenience food. Nevertheless, if you want to keep tuning up your eating habits after you've ceased binge eating, you will be in a *much* better position to do so once you've recovered.

PART II

RECOVERY

SECTION 1
RECOVERY GOAL 1:
DISMISS URGES TO BINGE

YOU KNOW NOW WHERE we are headed: focusing on practical solutions to correcting a temporary brain-wiring problem, using a basic two-goal framework to get there, and empowering yourself to make choices along the way that feel authentic to you. The first goal in the framework is learning to dismiss urges, which will be the theme of this whole first section of Part II. As mentioned in the Introduction, dismissing urges is the only goal that some people will need to achieve recovery. To work toward this goal, you'll first go through some preparation work and then learn what I call the "Five Components of Dismissing the Urges to Binge."

The Five Components of Dismissing the Urges to Binge are the same as what I called the "Five Steps to Quit Binge Eating" in both *Brain over Binge* and its accompanying workbook. I believe the new language more accurately describes how you will be using these concepts—not necessarily in sequential steps, but instead all working in conjunction to lead you to view your urges in a new way and give you the ability to choose your own actions. As you go through the Five Components, I encourage you to answer the prompts in writing rather than just musing on them in your head. When dealing with binge urges, the act of writing about them can immediately make them feel less threatening and facilitate a perceptual mental shift that allows you to view your urges differently.

Before proceeding with Recovery Goal 1, it bears repeating that restrictive dieting isn't compatible with dismissing urges. This doesn't mean you have to eat anything and everything—trying to eat healthy is okay; but if you are depriving your brain of necessary calories and nourishment, you will not be successful in consistently dismissing binge urges because your survival instincts will stay in high gear, depriving your higher brain of energy. Do your best to put aside restrictive dieting right now, knowing that more help for you in this regard is contained in the second section of Part II: Recovery.

[4]

What Urges Are You Trying to Dismiss?

When I binged, it felt as though I was outside my body looking at myself doing those things. I felt like a bystander even though I was the one shoving food into my mouth. Food like salad dressing straight from the bottle, frozen foods straight out of the freezer, food from the trash, etc.

~Carla

TO DISMISS BINGE URGES, you will start by getting a clearer picture of what those binge urges are, to you personally in your life. To identify the *urges* to binge, you need to first identify the binges themselves.

DESCRIBE YOUR BINGES FIRST

Binge eating is subjective. If you intuitively know what your binges are, then you don't need to spend much time here. For me, my binges were unmistakable—they were big, and I always felt out of control. Sometimes I'd have what I called "mini-binges"; they weren't quite as big, but the loss of control was still present. When I quit binge eating, I quit the binges and the mini-binges at the same time. My mini-binges did not consist of eating a few cookies or a big piece of cheesecake. Instead, I felt driven to eat something in substantial quantity, like half a loaf of bread with butter or twenty-five Oreos, then I felt nearly as distressed as when I would consume 6,000–8,000 calories during a "real" or "full" binge.

You may also find your binges easy to identify or define—there is often an unmistakable mind-set and way of eating, where you know on an intuitive level what you consider a binge. Or maybe your binges are not so clear-cut to you. After all, there is no calorie rule, where anything above that limit is a binge and anything below it is not a binge. Take athletes, for example: Some can consume thousands of calories in a single meal, and it's not at all abnormal or out of control for them (in fact, it's necessary to fuel their activities), whereas someone else might eat six cookies and feel like it was undoubtedly a binge.

The people who might have to analyze their binges a little more are those whose binges aren't necessarily "episodic," but more like excessive grazing that is spread throughout the day. If this is the case for you, the questions in this chapter will help you get a better sense of how you think and feel before, during, and after binges—and how the binges are different from your more normal eating habits. If you don't feel like you have "normal" eating habits right now, that's okay as well, just define your binges the best you can at present, and as you regulate your eating in Recovery Goal 2, you'll have a much clearer picture of your problematic eating habits.

A good way to start thinking about how to define your binges is to ask yourself what "quitting binge eating" means to you. I'm not talking about all the ways in which your life would be better or the relief you would feel to put your eating disorder behind you. I'm talking about something much simpler. I'm talking about deciding what exactly you would stop doing if you stopped binge eating. Contemplate and then complete this statement:

If I never binged again, I would never ...

_____

_____

_____

_____

_____

_____

_____

_____

Now let's go into a little more detail about your binges. Your answers to the following questions will help you create your "personal binge definition" on page 46. This definition will help you clearly see the behavior you want to stop, which will then allow you to start noticing the urges to perform that behavior and learn to dismiss them.

What are the specific behaviors that you personally classify as binge eating?

_____

_____

_____

_____

_____

_____

_____

_____

What do you think and feel *before* you begin a binge?

_____

_____

_____

_____

_____

_____

_____

What do you think and feel *during* a binge? Describe the experience:

_____

_____

_____

_____

_____

_____

_____

How much and what type of food do you typically eat during a binge?

_____

_____

_____

_____

_____

_____

_____

What do you think and feel *after* a binge?

_____

_____

_____

_____

_____

_____

_____

Is there anything else you think, feel, or do before, during, or after binges that you do *not* do when eating normally—things that can help you set your binges apart from your regular eating habits?

_____

_____

_____

_____

_____

_____

Do not analyze your answers or try to solve any of this right now, and don't be ashamed of what you've written. You are simply describing what *is*, without judging it.

REFINING YOUR BINGE DEFINITION

To get an even clearer picture of your binge eating, it can help to read some diagnostic criteria for binge eating. Currently, "official" diagnoses of binge eating disorder and bulimia are made using the *Diagnostic and Statistical Manual of Mental Disorders*, Fifth Edition (DSM-5). The criteria for diagnosis is always in flux and open to interpretation, and I use it here only as a guide—to give you an idea of how binge eating typically presents itself in a clinical setting. The specifics of your problem may substantially differ from these criteria, but according to the DSM-5, a binge eating episode is characterized by these common elements:

1. Eating a larger amount of food than normal during a short period of time (i.e., within any two-hour period)
2. Lack of control over eating during the binge episode (i.e., the feeling that one cannot stop eating)

The DSM-5 also says that binge eating episodes are associated with three or more of the following:

1. Eating until feeling uncomfortably full
2. Eating large amounts of food when not physically hungry
3. Eating much more rapidly than normal
4. Eating alone because you are embarrassed by how much you're eating
5. Feeling disgusted, depressed, or guilty after overeating

After reading the diagnostic criteria, what descriptions apply to your binge eating?

_____

_____

_____

_____

_____

_____

More important than the diagnostic criteria is how a binge *feels* to you on an intuitive level. Without judging or censoring yourself, take a minute to write down a few adjectives or phrases that immediately come to mind when you think about your binges.

Intuitively, I view my binges as:

_____

_____

_____

_____

_____

_____

Don't Overreach in Defining Binges

A lot of people with eating disorders have perfectionistic personalities and might get caught up in trying to maintain an ideal diet. If this is the case for you, you may find yourself wondering if all "non-hungry eating" should be considered binge eating or if all junk food should fall under the umbrella of binge eating. My best advice is: When you define your binges, tone down your inner perfectionist.

Does ordering fries with your meal instead of salad as a side qualify as a binge? Is picking up fast food for dinner a binge? I don't think so by any stretch of the imagination. I do value health and eating well, but eating less-than-healthy food is a legitimate choice sometimes—based on financial considerations, taste, time constraints, and social situations. Even eating when not physically hungry can be perfectly normal (I doubt anyone who has dessert after a meal is truly hungry for that dessert).

When you first quit binge eating, it is very helpful to not put so much pressure on yourself to get your non-binge eating exactly right. When I first quit, I would have driven myself crazy if I'd treated every craving for junk food and every instance of non-hungry eating as an urge to binge. I think it was helpful that I defined my binges by what I knew them to be, not by overanalyzing and creating a lot of rigid rules for myself.

Even when your binge eating stops, you may be left with some imperfect eating habits, like most normal eaters, and you can then define which ones you are okay with keeping and which ones you want to change. Connecting all of your less-than-ideal eating habits to your binge eating can complicate recovery, so don't try to tackle every food issue right away.

PUT ASIDE OTHER LESS-THAN-IDEAL EATING HABITS

Just because you aren't overreaching in defining your binges, that doesn't mean you are going to ignore your other less-than-ideal eating habits for the rest of your life. After you quit binge eating, you will be better able to tackle other eating challenges you may have, such as overeating, eating too much processed foods, grazing, or putting too much emphasis on your body size.

It can help to keep a running list (below) of your less-than-ideal eating habits, so you can download them from your mind and stop worrying about them for now. Essentially, when you add a less-than-ideal habit to the list, you are fully acknowledging it but disconnecting it from your binge eating recovery. This will help you stay focused on dismissing the binge urges themselves. You may actually find that many of the food issues you think you have now simply go away after binge eating stops and you are eating normally again; or you may not see the eating issues as *problems* anymore, but as only minor imperfections that everyone deals with.

I have trained myself to eat a dessert or snack every night after dinner, which for me is really frustrating. It may not be a binge, but I feel like my higher brain doesn't want to have this habit.

~Ellen

What are some eating habits that you aren't completely satisfied with—that you might like to improve *after* binge eating stops? (You can add to this list over time as you encounter situations where you eat in a less-than-ideal way.)

_____

_____

_____

_____

_____

_____

_____

_____

Simply recognize and accept that you may need to address some things on your list at some point after binge eating stops. Don't dwell on these eating habits; don't put yourself down because of them; and most importantly, don't think that less-than-ideal eating leads to binge eating.

YOUR PERSONAL BINGE DEFINITION

Now that you've described your binge eating in detail, read diagnostic criteria for binge eating, analyzed your binges on an intuitive level, and learned that you should *not* include all of your less-than-ideal eating habits in your binge definition, it's time to write your "personal binge definition." You may want to go back through this chapter and/or spend a little time observing your own behavior before writing your definition.

There is no right or wrong answer. Remember that this is the behavior "you" want to be free of, and no two answers will be exactly the same. Once you are ready, try to capture below what a binge means and feels like to you.

Your personal binge definition:

_____

_____

_____

_____

_____

_____

_____

_____

Throughout this section on Recovery Goal 1, when "an urge to *binge*" is referred to, you will now have a clear picture of what that means. This is the behavior that your urges drive you to do. And now we are going to move on to learning about, recognizing, and ultimately dismissing those urges.

[5]

Focus on the Urges

When the urge takes over, it's like going into a trance, or becoming a different person. I can now recognize when this is happening, but at times the urges still seem convincing and real.

~Evan

SO FAR, YOU'VE LEARNED that urges are the true cause of your binge eating, which you clearly defined in the last chapter. In this chapter, you'll zero in on what your urges feel like and how they present themselves in your life. Getting to know your urges allows you to better identify them when they occur. You don't want to be caught off guard and begin a binge before even realizing that you had an urge prior to taking the first bite.

ZERO IN ON YOUR URGES

Your urges encompass all of the thoughts, feelings, physical sensations, and cravings that make you feel compelled to binge. The urges have a "voice," which the author who helped me recover, Jack Trimpey of Rational Recovery®, calls the "Addictive Voice."[87] You hear a voice in your head trying to convince you that binge eating is a good idea, and sometimes the reasons can seem very logical. This voice is not your own in the sense that it's not indicative of your true desires—it's a product of the faulty signals coming from the lower brain. It only sounds like your own voice because the primitive brain has no language of its own; instead, it "uses your language to enlist your voluntary muscles to get what it wants."[88] Said another way, the higher brain centers translate the messages from the lower brain to make them more complex and nuance-filled,[89] more appealing to your conscious, reasoning self.

Take a moment to think about your urges and how they get you to binge. In answering these questions, you are not trying to solve anything; you are only getting to know your urges a little better. You can add to these answers over the next several days as you observe how your binge urges operate.

What do binge urges feel like to you?

_____

_____

_____

_____

_____

_____

What physical symptoms do your binge urges create?

_____

_____

_____

_____

_____

_____

_____

When do your urges arise? How often? Are there any patterns to when your urges surface?

_____

_____

_____

_____

_____

_____

Do the urges have a "voice" that encourages you to binge? What does that voice sound like? What does it tell you?

_____

_____

_____

_____

_____

_____

_____

Does the voice of the urge use logical reasons to get you to binge? List as many of those reasons as you can:

_____

_____

_____

_____

_____

_____

_____

What does the voice of the urge promise you? What payoff or rewards does it say you'll get if you follow through and binge?

_____

_____

_____

_____

_____

_____

_____

Write down anything else you notice about your urges:

_____

_____

_____

_____

_____

_____

_____

Urges to binge can sometimes be subtle, and if you are just beginning to recognize your urges to binge, it can be helpful to read your answers to the above questions on a daily basis, so you know what to look for prior to a binge.

You may be someone who feels like they immediately go into a binge without much prior thought; but this is never the case. There is always an urge beforehand, you may just need to spend a little more time learning to recognize it. Don't worry about dismissing the urges right now, just set your sights on being able to identify an urge when it arises. That ability to be aware of the thoughts, feelings, and sensations that prompt you to binge will help you realize that, even though the urges are automatic, the behavior is not; there is always at least a moment when you have the ability to choose differently.

[6]

Focus on Why You Want to Quit

I have spent up to $3,200 per year on binge foods and laxatives when I could not pay rent or my student loan. I have missed family gatherings, Christmas Day, dates with men, important events, social events, days of work, interviews, helping others, volunteering, being a good friend and daughter, I have missed LIFE for bulimia.

~Lauren

I WANT YOU TO READ just as much of this book as you need to achieve recovery, then get on with your life. However, if you don't desire recovery, you can finish this book and then read ten more recovery books without being any better off. Wanting recovery doesn't mean you feel like you want to quit every single moment; but it means that, on the whole, you have a desire to be free of this problem. You have to know that your current behavior is holding you back from living the life you want. You don't have to try to convince yourself that life will be great after you recover, because there is certainly no guarantee of that; but you do have to believe that what you have now isn't what you truly want. What you have now feels appealing sometimes—because of the primal wanting and primal liking that stem from the lower brain—but that's different from being who you truly want to be and doing what you truly enjoy doing.

You will inevitably have mixed feelings about recovery. To help you observe your mixed feelings, fill out the chart below and then answer the two questions that follow. As you complete this cost-benefit analysis, keep in mind the ideas of primal wanting and liking from the lower brain and see if you can distinguish the thoughts that feel more like they're coming from your higher self. As you fill out the chart, don't list costs and benefits you think you "should" have—you aren't trying to convince yourself of anything here; you are simply observing that you have mixed feelings but that ultimately, you *do* have reasons why you want to move beyond binge eating.

Benefits of Quitting Binge Eating	Benefits of Continuing to Binge
Costs of Quitting Binge Eating	**Costs of Continuing to Binge**

Based on the chart above, and on your introspection and intuition, answer the following questions.

Why do you want to *keep* binge eating?

_____

_____

_____

_____

_____

Why do you want to *quit* binge eating?

_____

_____

_____

_____

_____

_____

_____

As you look at your answers above, do some of your responses feel more like "you" than others? Do some feel more like they are a product of your lower brain?

_____

_____

_____

_____

_____

_____

_____

Can you recognize primal wanting and liking versus your true desires and pleasures in any of your responses?

_____

_____

_____

_____

_____

_____

Look at your answers in the chart above and ask yourself:

Are the costs of continuing to binge *greater than* the benefits of continuing to binge?

_____

_____

_____

Are the benefits of quitting binge eating *greater than* the costs of quitting binge eating?

_____

_____

_____

For most people who have come this far in a recovery book and have taken the time to do this analysis, the answers to the two above questions are usually "yes" and "yes." Yes, the costs of binge eating are greater than its benefits, and yes, the benefits of quitting are greater than the costs of quitting. For some people, both answers are not "yes" or there is some ambiguity there. If that's the case for you, that doesn't mean you can't move forward. As long you feel like some part of you wants to recover, you can build on that. There will be more information throughout this book that can help you grow that desire and also realize that the part of you that doesn't want to quit is just a function of the habit.

KEEPING YOUR ATTENTION ON WHY YOU WANT TO QUIT

The more you can direct your focus on the benefits of quitting, the less your lower brain will remind you of the benefits of continuing to binge. Accept that you will have some hesitations about quitting and that you will sometimes feel that you have valid reasons for continuing your behavior. You won't believe your reasons for quitting all of the time; but as much as you can, keep your attention on why you want to be free of binge eating.

If you didn't want to rid yourself of the habit, you wouldn't be reading this book and you'd be happy continuing to binge. When you find yourself thinking about a benefit of binge eating or the cost of quitting, don't try to argue the point or try to make the thought go away. Instead, just observe the thought without judging it, then gently refocus your attention on one of the reasons you do want to quit.

REMINDERS TO REFOCUS

Rather than let your thoughts automatically remind you of the reasons you shouldn't quit, take control of how you think about recovery on a daily basis. Posting reminders for yourself can help with this. You can write a reminder for each of the items you listed on the cost-benefit chart that support your desire to recover and post these reminders wherever you will notice them. Also, when you wake up each morning, you can bring to your mind or write one benefit of recovery. Don't worry if negative thoughts arise, just notice them and keep bringing your attention back to why you want to move forward with dismissing urges.

How will you use reminders to keep your attention on why you want to stop binge eating?

_____

_____

_____

_____

_____

_____

_____

[7]

You Don't Binge to Cope or for True Pleasure

My therapist wanted me to journal when I had the urge to binge and categorize it under "anxiety," "stress," "sadness," or whatever. But sometimes the urges to binge came out of NOWHERE. There was no anxiety or stress or any deeper feelings. I could get the urge anytime. I went to this therapist for about a year (she was a psychologist specializing in eating disorders), but I felt like the whole thing was just not adding up. Figuring out all your life problems in order to quit bingeing felt like an impossible task, not to mention there were far too many times that I felt my life was perfectly fine, I was happy and had no stress, yet I still had urges.

~Tracy

SOMETHING THAT OFTEN HOLDS people back from dismissing the urges to binge is clinging to the idea that they "need" to follow the urges to fill some sort of emotional void or to "cope." This is an idea perpetuated by traditional therapy, as well as by pop culture. This chapter will help you understand why this theory may not be helping you.

WHAT DOES IT MEAN TO COPE?

Dictionary.com lists the definition of *cope* as: "to face and deal with responsibilities, problems, or difficulties, especially successfully or in a calm or adequate manner."

When was the last time your binge eating helped you deal with a problem, responsibility, or difficulty successfully? Temporarily zoning out while binge eating is not facing that problem successfully. The common response from traditional therapy is that binge eating is a *faulty* coping mechanism, one that developed when you seemingly had no other options available to you. In this popular theory, what you need to be able to let go of your behaviors is to develop better coping strategies. Then, supposedly, you won't want or "need" to binge anymore.

This advice actually felt a little insulting to my intellect when I was bulimic. I knew my options for coping with problems and difficult emotions; but when I couldn't successfully avoid a binge by trying to cope better, or when the urges were too overwhelming for me to even try to do something other than binge, it made me feel so personally inadequate to follow the urges, because in theory, all I had to do was handle my problems better, right? How hard could that be? My friends and family seemed to be able to choose any number of behaviors to help themselves when facing a difficult problem, even if they didn't always cope perfectly. Yet, somehow, I couldn't bring myself to do something as simple as take a bubble bath instead of binge?

The problem is, coping better with problems does nothing to quiet binge urges once the habit is in place. The difference between me and my friends/family was not that my problems were bigger or that I was somehow too inadequate to choose an alternative coping behavior; it was that I had urges to binge and they didn't. The only thing a binge eater successfully copes with by acting on a binge urge is the urge itself. Binge eating makes all the thoughts, feelings, and sensations that were strongly driving you toward binge eating go away. Once you act on an urge, you no longer have to be tormented by it, you don't have to fight it anymore, you don't have to experience all the troublesome thoughts and uncomfortable feelings that go along with it.

Your stress level drops and you feel a sense of relief when that happens, but those temporary good feelings aren't a result of you having dealt with whatever problem you happened to have in the background of your life at the time. Your other problems remain after binge eating, and binge eating creates countless additional problems; however, during and after a binge, one big problem—the urge—is gone. More support for the urges being the primary problem is that some people actually don't have a strong connection between difficult emotions/stress and binge eating. Plenty of binge eaters feel urges during happy times and actually experience appetite *reduction* during stressful times. There were countless times I experienced and succumbed to urges to binge when I was feeling good otherwise.

Some of you may have indeed developed binge eating behavior during or following a time of stress or emotional turmoil, and we'll talk about that in the next chapter, but that doesn't mean the binge eating actually helped you cope then or that it helps you cope today. This is not to be insensitive to your other problems, because they are no doubt very real and possibly even overwhelming. However, the reasonable you, while not experiencing urges to binge, knows that binge eating is not what you truly want to do to cope and knows that it doesn't work. The following questions will help you reflect on this.

If you had no desire to binge whatsoever, would you choose to binge anyway—just to cope with feelings/problems in your life? Why or why not?

_____

_____

_____

_____

_____

_____

_____

If you had no desire to binge whatsoever, would you choose to binge anyway—just to [insert any reason you think you may binge, such as "deal with stress," "avoid intimacy," "be emotionally numb"]? Why or why not?

_____

_____

_____

_____

_____

_____

_____

Without the urges making you feel so compelled to binge, binge eating is not something you would choose to do to cope. There are just too many consequences.

Think Back to Before Therapy or Exposure to the "Coping" Theory

I've heard from so many people who describe the very common, simple beginning to their binge eating: a diet, which led to binge eating, which formed a habit. Then they go on to explain all of the deep reasons for their behavior that they discovered in therapy and through guided self-analysis. The truth is, without the influence of these pervasive ideas about binge eating, most people would naturally view binge eating as something that doesn't help them deal with any of their problems, but instead as just a very bad habit that makes their problems worse.

You likely didn't make the "coping" connection when you first started binge eating. It was only after the habit took hold, or after you heard or read traditional ideas about binge eating being an emotional crutch, that you began to have a desire to "cope" mixed up with all of the physical and mental components of your binge urges. In response to this, you might say that you simply didn't understand your problem when it first started, but you do now—in a deeper and more complex way. You might say that the "real" (emotional) reason you binged was hidden from you in the past, and now you have a better understanding of your underlying issues.

If that's the case, if solving and coping with those underlying issues is helping you avoid acting on binge urges, then there is no reason to change course, because you are already making the necessary brain changes. However, if it's not helping, then it's time to put aside those ideas. To do this, it can be helpful to think about how you felt about your binge eating problem prior to hearing any mainstream ideas about the disorder, whether that means before therapy or any other form of self-help, online learning, or media consumption. Using myself as an example, I can look back over my old journal entries from my days of binge eating and notice that there is a marked difference between how I talked about my binge eating before and after I started therapy.

There was one entry in particular that was telling. I wrote it in October 1999 at age 18, about a week or two before my first appointment with a therapist regarding my binge eating. I had been binge eating for about seven months by then, and the binges had been steadily increasing in frequency and quantity of food. It was evident that, at the time I wrote this entry, I had not yet been introduced to the idea of binge eating as a coping mechanism:

> I'm out of control. I can't stop eating or thinking about food. [At lunch], I was doing my best to eat slow and be normal, but I really just wanted to dig into everything. I'm like this almost all of the time now, and I don't know why. Last night it was like I almost <u>wanted</u> to binge. After the first part of the binge, I actually felt good. But then, when I kept getting up at night and after lunch today, I just feel like a big failure.
>
> Do you think my body is just trying to tell me something? Or am I just crazy? Sometimes I feel like if I had a choice of what I wanted to do, I would choose to just sit in my room and stuff myself. I've actually gotten to the point where I enjoy it. After I binge, I just lay in bed and go to sleep. It's sad but sometimes I would rather eat than do anything. Every time I do it, I swear to myself that I'm never going to do it again, but I always do. Right now, I'm feeling so nauseous and sick, but if I were alone in my room, I know I would eat more.

I just want to be normal. I just want to eat and forget about it. I don't want to think about food all day long.

From my raw intuition at the time of this entry, it seems I had a couple of clear ideas of my own about my binge eating: (1) It was out of control; and (2) I thought I actually "liked" to binge in the moment, even though I hated the consequences. At the time I wrote this entry, my abnormally strong food cravings and urges to binge were the result of my survival instincts—the binges were a natural and adaptive response to my extended and extreme dieting. However, all I knew at the time was that I couldn't seem to control myself around food, and I hated myself for it.

I didn't realize that the part of me that "liked" binge eating wasn't really me at all, but my lower brain, which was driving me to protect myself from starvation, rewarding me for it with pleasurable effects, *and* steadily building a habit. Each time I binged, I reinforced the pattern a bit more, and my body and brain became dependent on large amounts of the very foods that were initially so attractive to my survival instincts—the ones high in sugar/unhealthy fats/carbohydrates that might be good for short-term survival but are impossible to thrive on in the long term.

I think this entry is very important because of my honesty—admitting that I found a sense of pleasure in the binges. This type of honesty was extremely rare in my journal entries after therapy, when I became convinced that I binged for complicated emotional reasons. In later entries, I attributed the binges to bad feelings, negative events in my day, issues rooted in my past, conflicts with friends or family. Rarely did I say what I said here, which was basically: *My cravings feel out of control, but you know what? It actually feels good—temporarily—when I give in.* It only made sense that it felt good: Of course there was great pleasure in the relief from self-imposed starvation!

This entry is also telling in that I said I wanted to be "normal." I didn't want binge eating in my life, and I was therefore receptive to help—to therapy—which I began shortly after writing this. Once I began therapy, I didn't need to learn that all of this was a symptom of underlying emotional and psychological issues and spend years searching for and trying to resolve those issues. I needed to learn that I was healthy, albeit food-deprived, and that my body and brain were reacting to try to protect me.

The next two questions will help you remember how you came to view your binge eating as a coping mechanism, if applicable.

If you think you binge to cope with emotions/problems, how did you come to that idea? Did you discover it on your own or through some form of therapy or self-help?

_____

_____

_____

_____

_____

_____

Prior to learning that binge eating is a coping mechanism, what did you think your bingeing was all about?

_____

_____

_____

_____

_____

_____

COPING AS ONE OF THE "LOGICAL" REASONS TO GIVE IN TO THE URGE

Binge eaters often try to fight the urge until they have a thought that seemingly gives them a "logical" reason to give in. Since the lower brain cannot act without our conscious consent, because it cannot control voluntary muscles, it uses whatever thoughts appealed to your reasoning in the past to get you to binge again. For example, when your binge eating first began, you may have been on a restrictive diet. Your urges to eat a lot of food were so strong that you rationalized giving in by thinking something like, *I've already slipped on my diet, so I'll eat as much as I can right now and get back on my strict diet tomorrow.* You really believed this thought at the time and tried to get back on your restrictive diet; but your urges eventually overpowered you, and so again you thought, *I'll start over tomorrow* to excuse giving in to the urge.

It doesn't take long for any rationalization to take hold as a habitual thought—a mental rut that your lower brain will trigger again and again. Your lower brain connects the dots between the thoughts that propel you to perform the habit and the rewarding properties of the habit itself. Even though the rationalization in the example above may have started out as your conscious thought, it becomes a conditioned pattern. This is simply learning—training our brains to do things without our conscious input; and it works just fine in most areas of our lives, but it works against us when thoughts habitually encourage destructive behaviors.

This all has to do with the "coping" theory because it provides countless rationalizations to binge that can become unhelpful, habitual thought patterns. If you are experiencing an uncomfortable urge, and you remember what you learned in therapy—that a binge eating episode is a way to relieve stress or deal with your problems—then it's easy to bring a problem to mind and then think something like, *I'll give in just this once because I've had a hard day*. When the urge is so uncomfortable, it only makes sense that you'll look for a logical reason to give in. You know you aren't a weak or gluttonous person, but you don't feel like you can fight the urge; so deciding that you are doing it for a deep and meaningful emotional reason is appealing.

If you link your binge eating to your emotions and problems a few times, then your lower brain will begin automatically triggering thoughts about your problems and negative feelings, along with producing the physical sensations and cravings that accompany an urge. The lower brain will start automatically suggesting binge eating in times when you feel the need to "cope." In effect, popular ideas about binge eating unintentionally encourage more conditioned thought patterns that rationalize binge eating and connect the behavior to many aspects of your life. Even if you are working hard to solve problems in therapy, you are creating a bigger one—a strongly conditioned lower brain that habitually promises you a way to cope, but doesn't deliver. Instead of emotional stability, you are left with shame, pain, guilt, regret, and even more problems and difficult emotions in the long run.

Do you tend to rationalize giving in to an urge? What are some of the common "logical" reasons for binge eating that the voice of your urge gives, especially ones that are linked to "coping"?

_____

_____

_____

_____

_____

_____

_____

Can you remember the first time you had some of these thoughts? Did you learn any of the rationalizations in therapy or from another source?

_____

_____

_____

_____

_____

_____

Prior to a binge, what do your urges say a binge will do for you?

_____

_____

_____

_____

_____

_____

After a binge, what does the urge actually do for you?

_____

_____

_____

_____

_____

SEPARATE OTHER PROBLEMS

To avoid being taken in by thoughts telling you that binge eating is a way to cope, it's necessary to break the link between your other problems and your binge eating. This does not mean you will be indifferent to your other problems and difficult emotions; the problems in your life are real and deserve your attention. However, to more easily dismiss the urges, you can't hold on to the idea that binges are a viable choice to help you cope.

Some of the problems you have are actually the result of binge eating; so those problems will naturally go away after binge eating stops. Moreover, without binge eating, you'll have an easier time coping with any other problems you may have, always remembering that how well you cope has no bearing on whether or not you binge.

List below the problems and difficult emotions in your life that you will keep separate from binge eating. These could be emotional issues from your past, daily stressors, relationship problems, anxiety, depression, low self-esteem, and so on. The point of doing this is to allow you to fully acknowledge the other problems (as you did with your less-than-ideal eating habits), but at the same time, confirm that these issues are not reasons to binge.

Your *other* problems that you want to avoid linking to binge eating recovery are:

_____

_____

_____

_____

_____

_____

_____

As you look at your list, remind yourself of all of the people in the world who have these same problems but do not binge. Also remind yourself that you likely had some or many of these problems before you started binge eating and that you'll likely have some or many of these problems in your future binge-free life.

If you ever hear the voice of the urge connecting any of these challenges to binge eating, tell yourself: *That is a separate problem with a separate cure. It's not why I binge.*

You Don't Need the Secondary Benefits of Binge Eating

Ingesting large amount of foods filled with sugar and fats creates temporary side effects that you may view as positive, including but not limited to: the immediate primal pleasure of the food, a brain-chemical-induced dreamlike state, a distraction from your life, a feeling of emotional numbness, an excuse to avoid your responsibilities, or a reason to avoid social settings. I call these temporarily positive side effects "secondary benefits," with the "primary benefit" you receive from binge eating being relief from the urge to binge. The lower brain's job is to reward the behaviors it deems necessary for survival, so those temporary, secondary benefits are all part of the habit too.

Without the urges making you feel compelled to binge, you would never choose to binge as a way of getting those secondary benefits, just as a nonsmoker would never pick up a cigarette in order to relax or focus, even though smokers commonly cite these positive side effects. The secondary benefits of binge eating can certainly become addicting, and you may very well start to crave whatever side effects the binge may have, but please don't assume that you are binge eating because you somehow "need" these secondary benefits. Everyone needs pleasure and comfort, and distraction is nice sometimes too; but in the form of binge eating, these "benefits" are just an illusion, perpetuated by the urges.

> It became like a drug that gave my mind a little vacation. It was like I was indulging myself secretly in my apartment and treating myself, and it felt a bit like pampering at times. At the time I wasn't allowing myself any other kindnesses or pampering. Then I think that in itself became a habit and addiction.
>
> ~Felicia

The secondary benefits become fuel for your lower brain. *You've had a stressful day; you should just eat and forget about everything*, the voice of the urge will say. The way you can tell this isn't a valid thought is that other avenues to achieving the same benefits (i.e., "forgetting about everything," "being numb") aren't appealing. If the secondary benefits were what you truly wanted, you'd be open to other options. After a binge is when it's easiest to tell that tempting thoughts like this are from the lower brain, because you realize then that the effects of the binge weren't as good as your urges promised and that the temporary benefits you experienced weren't worth the cost of the binge.

Traditional therapy makes too much of these secondary benefits when they are related to emotions, framing them as deep and meaningful. If you enter an emotionally numb state after a binge, it is assumed you must have feelings you can't face. If you become distracted from the rest of your life during and after a binge, it is assumed you must have problems that you can't handle. Even if you binge on a relatively problem-free day, it is assumed there must be a hidden emotion or problem that was under the surface—that you needed to escape. This is not the case at all: Your lower brain is just rewarding and reinforcing its habit, ensuring that you keep repeating it.

What are the secondary benefits of your binge eating?

_____

_____

_____

_____

_____

_____

_____

_____

How does the "voice" of the urge use the secondary benefits to get you to binge?

_____

_____

_____

_____

_____

_____

_____

_____

_____

Spend some time thinking about whether or not these secondary benefits are worth it to you. Do you feel you truly need these side effects? Or do you only temporarily feel you need them when you have a desire to binge?

_____

_____

_____

_____

_____

_____

_____

Once you've binged, do you think the secondary benefits were worth it? Why or why not?

_____

_____

_____

_____

_____

BINGE EATING IS THE *ONLY* THING THAT GIVES YOU PLEASURE

If binge eating were the only thing you enjoyed and had to look forward to in your life, then you likely would not be reading this book. You'd be doing it without wanting to change. If you feel enough remorse or uneasiness about your behavior to read a recovery book, then you know there are better options out there for you; you know there is something to live for besides large amounts of food.

We all deserve some fleeting, temporary, even shallow pleasure at times; and some forms of normal pleasure may even give you a little guilt—the kind of guilt that says, *Well, I probably shouldn't have done that.* You may stay up late watching a movie you love, for instance, and then feel tired at work the next day. But you aren't reading a book about quitting late-night movie watching. Good forms of pleasure taken slightly too far will produce fatigue, a nagging feeling that you shouldn't do it, and usually a natural inclination to make better choices. They don't ruin your life like binge eating does.

If—at this point—you honestly can't think of anything that brings you pleasure besides binge eating, it's probably just because binge eating has gotten in the way of your life so much that you are no longer seeking more from your life. You may be feeling too ashamed to go out and find things that you enjoy. This is understandable, but encourage yourself to move forward anyway, knowing that once the binge eating is over, you can begin to discover things you enjoy. Don't use a lack of fulfillment in your life as an excuse to continue your behavior, because binge eating is likely the main thing preventing fulfillment. Once binge eating is no longer an option, you'll naturally seek things that bring you pleasure.

For a moment, pretend your urges to binge are gone. Imagine that you no longer feel driven to eat excessive amounts, that you eat normally. Now imagine that your binge-free self is looking for something pleasurable to do and answer the following questions.

What do you imagine a future self, free of urges to binge, enjoying?

_____

_____

_____

_____

_____

_____

If you had no desire to binge whatsoever, would you choose to binge—just for pleasure? Why or why not?

_____

_____

_____

_____

_____

_____

After recovery, you will certainly still enjoy food and you may choose a piece of cake or something else that is indulgent just for pleasure sometimes; but impulsively eating the whole cake or several chocolate bars at once will seem like the opposite of true pleasure.

[8]

The Indirect Connection to Emotions and Stress

I no longer use being upset as an excuse. My lower brain had conned me into eating when I was angry or sad, but I'm onto it now.

~Lana

FOR SOMEONE WHO BEGAN binge eating in response to dieting or who hasn't spent years in mainstream therapy, it can be easy to see that binge eating isn't truly about coping with emotions or about true pleasure and that your other problems are separate. If you already see this, then you can go on to the next chapter, which begins the Five Components of Dismissing the Urges to Binge. This chapter is for those who need to spend a little more time learning about emotions as they relate to binge eating, realizing any connection you may notice is only indirect.

AN EMOTIONAL HOOK DEVELOPS OVER TIME

I'm not saying that there is no absolutely no link between binge eating and emotions, because there is an emotional aspect to nearly everything we do in life. You follow your urges to binge in the midst of life—with all its ups and downs, fears and failures. Anything you do repeatedly can eventually have an emotional hook for you. Again using smoking as an example, think of someone who lights a cigarette for the first time as a teenager, just to try it; then, over time, it starts to feel like they have to smoke to relax. In reality, having a cigarette helps them relax primarily because it quiets the incessant urge.

Nevertheless, quieting the urge *is* actually a form of stress relief; so the smoker's brain develops a link between smoking and stress relief. *Smoking = relaxation* becomes the default program in the brain, so that all the aspects of the smoking habit will become associated with relaxation—such as going outside away from stressful situations, doing something with the hands, talking to a trusted friend while smoking, and, of course, having the chemicals from the cigarette enter your system. Since all of this becomes linked with relief from stress, soon other forms of stress will automatically bring up thoughts of smoking.

It is the same with binge eating. Lifting the stress of the urge by binge eating allows you to feel temporarily relaxed, so that your brain will associate binge eating with stress relief. Then, of course, the brain chemicals released by eating temporarily bring down stress levels as well, strengthening that mental connection between the binge and the state of reduced stress. Once this connection is made, you may indeed crave binge eating more in times of stress than non-stress because of conditioning.

Think about how your binge eating became connected to stress relief over time, then write about any insights you have:

_____

_____

_____

_____

_____

_____

We Naturally "Want" Rewards More During Stress

Another reason for the link between binge eating and stress is simply that it's during times of stress that stress-*relief* (pleasure) seems the most appealing. Studies have shown that negative mood and emotional distress increase the "reward value"[90] of food for binge eaters, meaning that through a lower brain process, the reward of a binge becomes more enticing. This is not specific to binge eating; stress increases the consumption of a variety of rewards, not limited to food.[91] It's important to note, however, that the reward doesn't actually become any more pleasurable during times of stress.

Remember that "primal wanting" and "primal liking" are independent lower brain pathways, and it seems that it's only the "wanting" that gets amped up during stress. A recent study showed that stress caused participants to "want" rewards more and to work harder for rewards, but not to experience increased pleasure.[92] This is useful information as you prepare to dismiss binge urges because it will help you avoid the trap of thinking that the reason you want to binge during stress is significant to your higher self. It's an automatic and ancient lower brain process, with survival and avoidance of pain as primary objectives.

STRESS AFFECTS THE HIGHER BRAIN TOO

A binge is not what your higher brain wants during stress; but unfortunately, if this process is not understood, the higher brain can seem absent in times of stress. Just like when you are food-deprived and more resources are allocated to the lower brain, when the brain senses that you are physically, mentally, and emotionally stressed, the higher brain's functions aren't deemed as necessary as the lower brain's, so it can be in an energy-depleted state.[93] This doesn't mean your higher brain isn't capable of dismissing urges; a little awareness goes a long way in keeping the higher brain in control.

In the development of your disorder, the fact that the self-control functions are weakened amid stress further explains how an indirect stress-binge connection can form. You were more likely to give in to the urges during trying times, so a stronger link may have developed between binge eating and stress than between binge eating and non-stress. There is nothing you have to do to resolve this situation, except know that the link is only temporary. There is nothing wrong with your inherent ability to cope, and those connections will fade in time.

WHEN BINGE EATING STARTED FOR EMOTIONAL REASONS

If dieting led to the development of your binge eating, it's easy to realize that you simply acted on the survival instinct urges more during stress, so a link developed. On the other hand, you may be someone who feels that the association between binge eating and stress didn't develop over time; instead, you feel that the relationship ignited binge eating in the first place. Maybe your binge eating developed right after a period of extreme stress or sadness in your life, or maybe it's been going on since childhood and you can remember a strong emotional link even back then. To address this properly, it's necessary to talk about the concept of *emotional eating*, which is not the same as binge eating but can be interrelated.

First and foremost, we are never void of emotion, we experience it in everything we do, so any activity can be an emotional one. You can engage in emotional shopping, emotional dancing, emotional driving, and emotional teeth brushing. What people usually mean when they use the term *emotional eating* isn't just *experiencing* emotions during eating or bingeing, but *using* food to deal with uncomfortable emotions. So, with that logic, emotional teeth brushing would be using oral hygiene to deal with sadness, stress, boredom. To some extent, everyone uses food and other behaviors as a way to deal with emotions, which can have a healthy place in our lives and in culture as a whole.

I do not believe that food has to be viewed as fuel and fuel only. In our culture, food is present in celebration, in mourning, in family gatherings that are often abounding with emotion. I remember hearing from several sources during the course of my eating disorder that suggested something was wrong with people eating in emotional situations—as if it is one of many flaws in our country that helps contribute to the development of eating disorders. However, in other cultures and throughout time, food has been an accepted and welcomed part of emotional life, without eating disorders being a serious problem. The fact that humans seem naturally drawn to emotional eating is likely due to the fact that stress makes rewards, including food rewards, more enticing.

Today, we live in a culture that makes emotional eating risky for some people who are susceptible. The highly processed, highly palatable foods that are available can quickly become reinforcing; coupled with that, the higher brain has more limited resources during times of stress—both factors that explain how emotional eating can gradually or quickly increase until binge eating results.

The reward networks become dysfunctional, and the habit becomes deeply rooted in your lower brain circuits. You land in the same position as someone who began binge eating in response to a diet. Regardless of which pathway you took to binge eating, once the habit is established, any emotional factors that contributed to the development of your habit no longer drive the binge eating. Gillian Riley, author of *Eating Less* and *Ditching Diets*, explains it this way:

> It's a common idea that those who overeat carry some deep wound that needs to be healed, but that isn't necessarily the way to see it. Sometimes people start to overeat because of some difficulty in their lives, but when the difficulty has passed—and perhaps completely resolved—the addictive relationship with food persists, simply because the addictive desire continues to be fed and reinforced.[94]

Even if there was some clear, but temporary emotional link at the outset, now you primarily seek relief from the urges. It can also help to remember that any emotional relief you think you experienced in the past or perceive that you experience now is not *truly* helping you cope or even feel better. Riley says, "Your biggest breakthroughs will occur when you discover that difficult emotions don't get any worse when you don't overeat."[95] This is supported by research, which shows, for example, that a negative mood will naturally improve whether or not someone eats what they believe are "comfort foods." In other words, comfort foods don't actually speed up the process of feeling better and, in fact, are more likely to make things worse. A review of around eighty studies concluded that comfort eating—specifically chocolate in this particular research—usually made negative moods last longer instead of stopping them.[96] There is certainly pleasure and distraction in the moment of eating chocolate or other delicious foods, but as a strategy for coping with emotions, comfort eating is not actually comforting. These studies addressed moderate forms of emotional eating, not binge eating, which—as you know by now—always makes you more uncomfortable in the long run.

As we will talk about in the discussion of Recovery Goal 2, to recover doesn't mean that you will never "emotionally" eat again, even if you took a stress-induced, non-diet path to binge eating. Even though emotional eating isn't going to solve your problems or take negative moods away, you still might feel drawn to going out for ice cream with a friend to lift your spirits after a breakup, to going out for a big meal at your favorite restaurant to celebrate a promotion or anniversary, or even to curling up on the couch when you are feeling hopeless and eating a few cookies and milk. No, these things might not resolve your negative moods, but this type of moderate emotional eating is completely understandable and no big deal. Choosing pleasure in the moment isn't something we can or should completely avoid as a human. There is certainly a point at which emotion-motivated eating becomes unhealthy even after binge eating is no longer involved, but you will learn to remain in control and enjoy eating without taking it too far.

What was the emotional situation or source of stress that you believe prompted the onset of your binge eating?

_____

_____

_____

_____

Did emotional eating gradually develop into binge eating? What was the point at which you realized it was abnormal and out of control?

_____

_____

_____

_____

_____

_____

Looking back, can you identify a time when the urges became the driving factor of your binges?

_____

_____

_____

_____

_____

_____

Insights about comfort eating not actually being comforting:

_____

_____

_____

_____

_____

_____

_____

_____

THE STRESS-BINGE LINK WILL DISSOLVE

In this chapter, we've discussed two indirect links between emotions/stress and binge eating: (1) emotions becoming linked to binge eating over time; and (2) emotional eating taking a bad turn and developing into a binge eating habit. One or both of these factors could apply to you. As you learn to dismiss urges, remember that it's not a big deal if you mostly want to binge when you are experiencing negative emotions or stress—it's just your automatic programming based on your past history and some natural brain mechanisms. It's like when a child mostly wants a pacifier when they are upset. They aren't different or more emotionally needy than other children; the link between stress and sucking has merely developed over time, or the parents offered the pacifier for comfort when negative emotions were present and then a habit formed (or a little bit of both).

Either way, the solution to quitting the pacifier habit is the same: to stop sucking the pacifier—not to make sure to meet the child's emotional needs in other ways or to make the child happier so he or she will stop wanting the pacifier. The child will certainly still want the pacifier at times, no matter what you do; and there is, of course, no way for a child (or an adult) to avoid every negative emotion. But if you stop giving the child the pacifier, if you stop binge eating—in every situation—then the desire for it will go away, regardless of the emotions involved.

There might be some extra fussing at first when the child is dealing with unmet desire, just as the lower brain will "tantrum" a bit when you stop your habit; but one day the child will get upset or stressed and their lower brain will not prompt them to seek a pacifier, and the habit will be broken. Likewise, one day you will be anxious or sad or lonely, and you will not have one thought of binge eating. To get there, you only need to start with learning how to dismiss one urge to binge. In the next section, you'll get started on doing just that.

Write about any insights you've had about the connection between stress and binge eating and about the new ways you've come to view that link in this chapter. How can you remind yourself that the urges are now the true problem, not the stress?

[9]

Component 1: View Urges to Binge as Neurological Junk

THE FIVE COMPONENTS OF Dismissing the Urges to Binge all work together to help you view your urges differently and respond to them differently. You will work through them one at a time, letting the ideas sink in before moving on to the next one; but ultimately, you will use them all each time you have a binge urge. As you progress through the Five Components, use your "personal binge definition" from page 46 to focus on the specific behavior you want to stop. You are not applying these components to all of your less-than-ideal eating habits. This would create too great of a focus on eating, when what you really want is to rewire the brain to stop being so fixated on food.

The first component is learning to view your urges to binge as "neurological junk." To properly understand neurological junk, we need to briefly talk about thought. Most people go through life hearing thoughts in their head and assuming they are real, assuming they are their own, assuming they have validity and truth; and even when the thoughts are harmful, we assume there are deeper reasons for those destructive thoughts. The truth is that most of us would be better off if we took many of our thoughts less seriously. Just because we hear a thought in our head doesn't mean we have to give it value or attention or credibility; it doesn't mean the thought is worth listening to or acting upon.

The "voice" that encourages binge eating sounds very much like your own voice, but as we've learned, it's not. Right now, you cannot make the urges to binge go away, but you can begin retraining your brain so it will no longer be dependent on binge eating. You do this by not allowing the urges to lead you to action. To avoid acting, you will learn to experience any thought, feeling, or sensation that encourages binge eating as rubbish from the lower brain—what I call "neurological junk." Viewing the urges as neurological junk means:

- You will view the urges as worthless, faulty brain messages.
- You will not give the urges any consideration, attention, or value.
- You will view urges as not coming from "you."
- You will not fight or argue with the urges.
- You will not try to decipher the meaning of the urges.
- You will not try to make them go away.

RECOGNIZING NEUROLOGICAL JUNK

The ultimate goal of Component 1 is to deprive the urges of attention, because neurological junk doesn't deserve attention. However, before doing that, you'll need to briefly turn attention to them, so you can learn to label them as neurological junk. The questions below will help you examine the way your urges present themselves in the form of *thoughts*, *feelings*, and *physical symptoms*, and help you recognize that the urges do not represent truth to you (in your higher brain).

Urge Thoughts:

Name one thought that the "voice" of your urge tells you to get you to binge:

_____

_____

_____

_____

_____

When you are between binges and feeling rational (and *not* experiencing an urge), do you truly believe that the above thought warrants binge eating? Explain:

_____

_____

_____

_____

_____

Urge Feelings:

Name a feeling that you have prior to binge eating (anxiety, excitement, sadness, fear, etc.) and why it makes you feel compelled to binge:

_____

_____

_____

_____

_____

_____

When you are between binges and feeling rational (and *not* experiencing an urge), do you truly believe the above feeling warrants binge eating? Explain:

_____

_____

_____

_____

_____

_____

Physical Symptoms of Urges:

How does a binge urge make you feel physically? Name one or more physical symptoms that encourage you to binge:

_____

_____

_____

_____

_____

_____

When you are between binges and feeling rational (and *not* experiencing an urge), do you truly believe the above physical symptom(s) warrants binge eating? Explain. (It helps to think about whether or not a doctor would recommend binge eating as a remedy for the physical symptom[s].)

_____

_____

_____

_____

_____

_____

NEUROLOGICAL JUNK IS MEANINGLESS, POWERLESS, AND HARMLESS

The following three words best describe neurological junk:
- *Meaningless* (the urges have no significance to your higher self)
- *Powerless* (the urges have no ability to make you binge)
- *Harmless* (the urges aren't there to hurt you; they aren't your enemy)

To get the hang of viewing your urges as neurological junk, you will be thinking and writing about other things in your life that you view as meaningless, powerless, and harmless. When you begin seeing the urges as meaningless, you don't feel the need to give them any attention. When you begin seeing the urges as powerless, you no longer feel like you have to obey them. When you begin seeing the urges as harmless, you no longer feel threatened by them. You can have them without anxiety or fear or worry that you'll do something you'll regret.

Viewing urges as nonthreatening has another benefit: It keeps you in a brain state that is more conducive to dismissing urges. When you become anxious and fearful as urges arise, the brain senses a threat; and as we discussed earlier, stress draws resources from the rational parts of the brain responsible for self-control and defers them to the survival-oriented lower brain pathways. This is obviously not an ideal state to be in when resisting urges. When dismissing urges, you don't want to be operating from automatic, habitual, fight-or-flight responses. Viewing urges as meaningless, powerless, and harmless can keep the brain in a state where you can better access your self-control. The following questions will help you begin to conceptualize urges in a nonthreatening way.

What is something that is meaningless to you? When you think about it, how do you feel? (Do not choose something you dislike; choose something you have absolutely no interest in. Examples: a trivial political issue that doesn't affect you, a sport you don't care about.)

_____

_____

_____

_____

_____

_____

If you felt the urge to [insert something you would *never* consider doing], would you give this urge any consideration? Why is this urge powerless to make you act? Is it difficult to avoid acting on it? (Examples: dance on a table at a restaurant, drive on the interstate without a seat belt, smoke.)

_____

_____

_____

_____

_____

_____

Think of something or someone who is harmless to you and describe what it feels like to think about this person or thing. Does it bring you any anxiety or fear? (Examples: a brush, a pet in a yard in another city.)

_____

_____

_____

_____

What would it feel like if you could view your urges to binge as meaningless, powerless, and harmless? Would you still feel compelled to act on them?

_____

_____

_____

_____

_____

_____

_____

One important thing to consider is: If you can view urges as meaningless, powerless, and harmless, they will no longer feel like urges. The word *urge* signals intense wanting and feeling strongly compelled to do something. But if you view the urge as just junk, then it ceases to be an urge. For simplicity and continuity, you will continue to see the word *urge* in this book, but you may want to choose a new word to replace it—to diffuse its power in your mind.

How might you refer to your urges to underscore that you will now be viewing them as meaningless, powerless, and harmless? (Example: *I could call my urges "suggestions."*)

_____

_____

_____

_____

_____

SHIFT YOUR PERSONAL PERSPECTIVE

To view the urges as neurological junk, there isn't anything you actively *do*. You only need to change your mind-set, so that you can let the urges come and go without turning attention to them or acting on them. When it comes to shifting perspective surrounding urges, you will learn much more from your own experience and insights than from listening to advice from others. Keep track below of anything you learn or experience that helps you view your urges as meaningless, powerless, and harmless neurological junk. You can refer to this chart often as you move forward through Components 2–5.

Insights That Help You View Urges as Junk
Example: *If I relax my face when I'm experiencing a binge urge, it helps the urge feel more harmless.*

[10]

Component 2: Separate the Higher Brain from Urges to Binge

YOU NOW KNOW THAT your urges are neurological junk from the lower brain and that "you"—your higher self—is distinct from your urges and fully capable of dismissing them. Component 2 will help you fully understand and experience the separation between yourself and your binge urges. Separation reduces the intensity of binge urges in a way that makes dismissing them come much more easily and naturally. Begin separating yourself from urges by answering the following two questions.

What are the goals you have for yourself that are inconsistent with your eating disorder?

_____

_____

_____

_____

_____

_____

_____

_____

_____

Do you feel like you freely choose for binge eating to be part of your life? If you could push a button and make the binge urges go away, would you? Why?

_____

_____

_____

_____

_____

_____

EGO-DYSTONIC URGES

The part of you that has goals inconsistent with the eating disorder and wants the binge urges to go away is your higher brain/higher self (more specifically, your prefrontal cortex). This is the executive of the brain and gives you your identity, reason, and the ability to choose your own actions. When not experiencing an urge, it's usually rather easy for bulimics and those with binge eating disorder to see that their urges are separate from their true selves, or ego-dystonic. *Ego-dystonic* means not in line with what the true self wants. When an internal state or behavior is ego-dystonic, it feels intrusive and unwanted. However, urges can temporarily convince us that binge eating is ego-*syntonic*, meaning in line with what the true self wants.

At an OA [Overeaters Anonymous] meeting, I was instructed to introduce myself as, "Hi, my name is Olivia and I am an overeater/ compulsive eater." And I thought: No! No! This is NOT what I am. I am so much more than this ... everyone in this room is!

~Olivia

To avoid falling for this and to remain aware of the fact that you are separate from your lower brain, it can help to spend some time contrasting your higher self with the urges and disassociating from the neurological junk you've been experiencing.

In the following chart, you can write words or phrases to describe your urges, as well as to describe "you" (your sense of who you are apart from the urges). The list describing you can include personality traits, hobbies, interests, beliefs, even problems and flaws. This is not a good-self-versus-bad-self exercise; it's an attempt to determine how you see yourself without the binge eating. You don't need to become your "ideal" self to be able to separate your higher brain from your urges; all you need is to see that your urges are not consistent with who you perceive yourself to be and who you want to be in the future.

You	Your Urges
(who you are apart from urges)	

Separating from Urges Is Not Active

Since writing *Brain over Binge*, many people have asked me if there was anything specific I "did" to separate from the lower brain—as if there had to be something missing from the passive process I described. Besides briefly reminding myself of what I'd learned about the brain and the fact that the urges weren't truly *me* the first few times I tried this technique, there wasn't anything I actively did to disengage the lower brain. Feeling separate from urges is a mental shift that either comes right away with new understanding or comes with time and practice. It's a mental shift that you have to experience for yourself to truly comprehend. Someone can tell you that you are separate from your urges a thousand times, but until you feel it for yourself for the first time, it's not going to make a difference in your life and you will still feel at the mercy of your urges. But if you can sense even one moment of being disconnected from an urge, you will begin to feel capable of dismissing them.

Write about a time when you felt apart from an urge. How did it feel? What did you learn? Use as much detail as you can, so that you can better internalize your experience.

_____

_____

_____

_____

_____

_____

_____

_____

Keep track of all you learn as you practice separation from binge urges:

_____

_____

_____

_____

_____

_____

_____

LOOK TO YOUR INNER STRENGTHS

Analyzing the darkness in your life and personality to try to figure out why you are binge eating, as is done in traditional therapy, is ineffective because your urges aren't from "you" at all. When you realize the urges aren't a reflection of your imperfections and negative experiences, it's easier to separate yourself from them. So, rather than focusing on what's wrong about you and how that might contribute to urges, you are going to start focusing on what's right about you and how you can use that to your advantage when dismissing urges.

You are undoubtedly successful in other parts of your life, and you can use your inner strengths to your advantage while you are trying to recover. You can choose to focus on areas of your life where you do use self-control very effectively and build from there. There are countless times each day when you are tempted by something inconsistent with your long-term goals, but you don't give in to those temptations. The self-control function in the prefrontal cortex is like a muscle, and focusing on the times when your self-control is working well helps strengthen it even more.

Write down all of your strengths you can focus on and use to your advantage while recovering. In other words, what is right about you that you can focus on instead of dwelling on your weaknesses?

_____

_____

_____

_____

_____

_____

_____

As you go through your day, write down all the times when you don't follow a desire to do something harmful, no matter how insignificant it may seem. (Examples: ignoring a desire to text while driving, ignoring an urge to check social media when you should be working.)

_____

_____

_____

_____

_____

_____

_____

Write down what you learn by dismissing other desires. What does it feel like? How do you avoid acting? How can these measures help you when you experience binge urges?

_____

_____

_____

_____

_____

_____

_____

_____

BE A "COMPASSIONATE OBSERVER" OF YOUR THOUGHTS

Our brains run on autopilot much of the time and produce most of our thoughts beyond our conscious awareness; this doesn't only apply to binge eating. In any given moment, you (your higher self) can choose which thoughts to focus on and which thoughts to dismiss. The more comfortable you can become with the idea that you are more than your thoughts, the better you will be at separating from the binge urges.

Learning to observe even your non-eating thoughts will give you practice for when the harmful binge thoughts arise. To do this, you need to become a compassionate observer of your thoughts—listening to them with curiosity and without judgment—and realize that you don't have to identify with the harmful ones. Below, keep a running list of any thoughts that feel intrusive and harmful in your life. Do this without trying to solve the problems that might be connected to these thoughts, and don't try to change them. Simply observe.

Thoughts I've observed that feel harmful:

_____

_____

_____

_____

_____

_____

_____

_____

When you have any of these harmful thoughts, practice kindly ignoring them. It's as if you are telling your brain, *No thank you*, then just moving on with your day.

What have you discovered from being a compassionate observer of your thoughts?

_____

_____

_____

_____

_____

_____

_____

_____

Your Urge Voice and Your Own Voice

Everyone's urge voice sounds like their own, but there are often subtle differences in the voice of the urge and the voice that feels like it's authentically yours. This also goes for other thoughts that are harmful in nature—there is often a distinctive quality to these thoughts that can make hearing your own voice in your head feel uncomfortable to you. Sometimes the voice is demanding, sometimes harsh and critical, sometimes alluring (but not in a pleasant way), sometimes urgent, sometimes repetitive.

Sometimes the difference between helpful thoughts and habitual harmful thoughts is very obvious; for example, your urge voice may talk *to* you, not for you, addressing you in the second person to plead its case for a binge: *You should ...* or *You want ...* However, it's usually not this cut-and-dried, and everyone's urge voice follows a different pattern. The voice will almost always attempt to appeal to your reasoning, and sometimes it sounds like it only wants to take care of you. Remember that you want to separate from *any* thought that encourages binge eating, regardless of exactly how the voice of that thought sounds; but it can be helpful to explore how your unique lower brain delivers messages during binge urges, so you can better separate from it.

Write down anything you notice about how your urges "talk to" your true self. Is there anything that sets the voice of the urge apart from what you perceive to be your true voice?

_____

_____

_____

_____

_____

_____

_____

_____

_____

WHEN THE HABIT IS NOT AN OPTION, THE URGES ARE EFFORTLESS TO DISMISS

There are certain things "you" would never consider doing, because of a strong moral conviction or simply because the actions would be absurd or too dangerous. These actions are simply not an option in your mind. The more you can move binge eating into the category of "not an option," the easier it will be to feel your power over the urges. Know that, if it weren't for the urges, you would naturally view binge eating in the same way that you view absurd or dangerous activities that you would never do.

Complete this sentence: If I ever had an urge to [insert any action that is simply not an option in your mind], I would never act on it.

Now really try to create—in your mind—a desire to do that thing. Try to think of all the benefits of doing it, try to create feelings of wanting. You'll find that you simply *can't* take those feelings seriously. This is because your higher brain has already determined that you will never do this, regardless of what you may think or feel at any given time. You'll also see that no thought in your brain can make your body take action to perform that behavior. What you've just experienced is the feeling of being more powerful than your harmful thoughts. When you specifically think of binge eating as not an option, it may create some uneasiness; but the uneasiness you feel viewing binge eating as not an option is from your lower brain, not from you.

When you think about binge eating as "not an option," how do you feel? How can you remind yourself that any uncomfortable feelings aren't your true feelings?
(Example: *My lower brain wants to hold on to the habit, but binge eating is not an option for me. I always feel bad afterward, and I do not want to do things that make me feel bad.*)

_____

_____

_____

_____

_____

_____

Before you developed binge urges, did you ever consider binge eating? Likewise, when your urges go away, would you ever entertain binge eating as an option?

_____

_____

_____

_____

_____

_____

A Quick Note About Separating from the Dieting Voice

As you know, in order to quit binge eating, it's vital to stop depriving yourself of necessary nourishment. If you are having trouble eating enough food, it could be because the harmful dieting mind-set has also become wired as habit. Once you spend enough time on restrictive diets, or engaging in calorie counting or excessive exercise, the voice encouraging those behaviors can be intrusive and habitual as well. It's usually easier for a binge eater to see that the binge urges are not from their higher self, but they hold on to the belief that the voice encouraging restrictive dieting is their true voice.

We will discuss this further in the Recovery Goal 2 section, but here it's worth mentioning that you can start to separate from that dieting voice as well—viewing dieting as a destructive habit and learning to see restrictive dieting, too, as "not an option." Even if you truly feel you need and want to lose weight, know that depriving yourself of necessary nourishment is not an effective way to do that. You can eat normal amounts of food, despite that programmed voice in your head telling you that you need to restrict food intake.

[11]

Component 3:
Stop Reacting to Urges to Binge

A COMMON REASON FOR uncomfortable feelings during a binge urge is: your reaction to the binge urge. The binge urge is a given—it's automatic. However, the way you react to the urge is not a given. Most reactions are mental: You feel the desire to binge, so you start trying to argue with it in your head or trying to force yourself to think of other things. Some reactions can be physical, such as tensing up your body or clenching your teeth. Some mental reactions and physical reactions to binge urges pop up seemingly without your conscious control. But you can learn to minimize many of your counterproductive reactions.

Some counterproductive reactions to binge urges are:
- Talking back to or arguing with the urge
- Engaging in any mental dialogue with the urge
- Judging the urge instead of simply observing
- Trying to figure out why you are having an urge
- Trying to stop thinking about binge eating
- Tensing up your body

Think about how reactions such as these can lead to uncomfortable feelings. If you argue with the urge, you may begin to feel anger that it is there interfering with your life. If you start analyzing why you are having the urge, you may become frustrated that you can't find a reason—or worse, find a reason that gives you an excuse to give in. If you try to push urge thoughts out of your mind, you may become anxious when they don't go away. If you label the urge as dangerous, you will start to feel fear that you'll give in. If you change your posture, muscle tightness, or facial expressions in response to binge urges, you are allowing the urges to have control of your physical body, creating a feeling of powerlessness.

In other words, your reactions can make your urges feel much worse than they actually are. When the urges feel worse, you are more likely to give in to them, just to make all that discomfort go away. But if you can stop reacting to the urges, you won't feel desperate for relief from the urge, allowing you to ride it out.

Write about some of the ways you react to your urges, physically and mentally:

_____

_____

_____

_____

_____

_____

_____

_____

_____

_____

Can you see how these reactions lead to negative feelings during binge urges?

_____

_____

_____

_____

_____

_____

DETACHMENT: THE HEATED ARGUMENT EXAMPLE

A good example of nonreaction is thinking about being in a heated argument with someone, and then mentally checking out of the argument. When you are in an argument, and internally and externally reacting to the other person—listening intently to them, judging their words against what you already know, thinking critical thoughts in your head, calculating your responses while they are talking, tensing up your body, hardening your facial expression, and arguing back—you undoubtedly experience many negative feelings and internal discomfort. All of these mental and physical reactions cause you anxiety, and they really wear you out. You'll instinctually feel the urge to get rid of these uncomfortable feelings by fight (arguing back and "winning" the argument) or flight (getting away from that person).

Now imagine that you realize the argument is futile and not worth your time. As a result, you just quit letting the person's words affect you. You just stop reacting, whether through your words or through your thoughts or through your physical movements. You stop thinking how wrong the other person is, you stop thinking of counterarguments in your mind, you soften your expression, you let your arms hang loosely, and you stop listening intently—you stop focusing on their words. Once you have stopped paying attention, the experience dramatically changes. You may still hear what the other person is saying, but it makes no difference to you and you no longer feel upset or experience that fight-or-flight instinct. You could theoretically stand there all day and not be bothered much at all—maybe just bored.

Whether it relates to a heated argument or binge urges, this type of nonreaction can also be called "detachment."

> *Detachment is when you aren't involved in what you are experiencing.*
> *Even though the internal and external factors are still there, you are no longer*
> *personally invested.*

When you are detached, you are steady and unmoved by what's going on around you; and in the case of binge eating, you are unmoved by what's going on in your lower brain. We all detach naturally from experiences sometimes, but detachment is also a practice and a skill that can be trained. Detachment is a common concept in Eastern philosophy and religion; a goal of many forms of meditation is to detach from thoughts and sensations of the body in order to experience a deeper reality.

If you can experience binge urges with detachment, it will change the quality of the whole experience. Detachment from your urges isn't trying to convince your lower brain that it is "wrong," because that will just engage it even more. You don't need to criticize neurological junk—it has no malice against you and no power to affect you. If you don't let your lower brain bother you, if you just let it do what it's been conditioned to do without reacting at all, it's going to fall silent.

Imagine the heated argument scenario and write about how it feels to detach from the argument. (You can also reflect on an actual experience you've had detaching from a conflict.)

_____

_____

_____

_____

_____

_____

Imagine what it would look and feel like to detach from your binge urges and experience them without reacting. What would that look and feel like?

_____

_____

_____

_____

_____

_____

REAL-LIFE EXAMPLES OF DETACHMENT

Thinking of examples of reacting versus detaching in real life can help you conceptualize what you are trying to accomplish when binge urges arise. I'll provide two examples, and then you can think of a few of your own in the chart below.

The first example of reacting versus detaching is watching your own kids misbehave as opposed to watching kids you don't know misbehave. If you are a parent, it's likely that your kids acting poorly is going to elicit a reaction in you—often a frustrated one. It's only natural. They are your responsibility, and it's up to you to take control of the situation. But if you don't know the misbehaving kids and they are under another adult's care, you will experience the situation in a different way. Besides briefly thinking, *That's annoying* or *I'm glad those aren't my kids*, you won't have a strong reaction to their outburst. Even though you might think a couple negative thoughts about the parents or kids, it's not your problem. You aren't going to get the same anxious and uncomfortable feeling as when your own kids are embarrassing you and making your job much harder, and you aren't going to feel primed for action. We react to things in our life that mean something to us—when we are personally invested.

The second example of reacting versus detaching is listening to a televised political debate about an issue you care about (whether you agree or disagree with what's being said) as opposed to hearing a politician talk about an issue that has no significance to you. If you care about the issue, you will judge each politician's words, think about how the issue will affect your life, and have critical thoughts about the other side of the issue. All of this can make you feel quite attached to the preferred politician's message and upset or angry at the people who don't agree with your point of view.

If you don't care about the message, however, you will simply ignore the debate. Even if you have the TV on in the background, you will move on with your life despite the background noise. This isn't about being insensitive, because we can indeed react strongly to issues that affect others; the assumption here is that the issue is a trivial one.

Neurological junk is trivial as well—it doesn't have a deep meaning to you or anyone else—so don't fuel it with reactions. Below, list your own examples of reaction and detachment in real life.

Experiences That Cause You to React and Your Typical Reactions to These Experiences	Things You Experience with Detachment and Why You Don't React

PRACTICE NONREACTION TO BINGE URGES

Neither of my examples of nonreaction is a perfect parallel to detaching from binge urges, because the urges come from within, whereas the examples I gave (and probably yours as well) involve reacting to something outside of yourself. Not reacting to something originating from your own brain and body is a little different—but not too different—because the lower brain isn't part of "you" in your higher brain. To get used to not reacting specifically to harmful messages in your own head, it's helpful to practice detachment from the tempting thoughts that often convince you to binge.

In the next writing prompt, your job will be to write out and actively think thoughts that encourage binge eating ... then feel your ability to not react to them. You can't actually force a true binge urge (nor would you want to), because a true binge urge arises automatically, whereas you'll consciously be thinking these thoughts. But this is a useful practice nonetheless, because it will help you realize that your thoughts will not cause negative and uncomfortable feelings if you detach from them.

Write down two thoughts that typically encourage you to binge. (Examples: *No one is home tonight, this is your only chance* and *Just this one last time, then you can start over.*)

1._____

_____

_____

2._____

_____

_____

In a safe place where you know you will not follow through on your thoughts, close your eyes and think the first thought you wrote. Now practice not reacting to it. Hear your own voice in your head saying that urge thought, but don't engage in any mental dialogue with it. If other thoughts come up automatically, that's fine; simply observe them. Focus on keeping your internal state and physical body steady and unaffected by what you hear in your brain. Repeat this practice with the second thought. The more you do this, the more you will realize: Just because you hear something in your head or feel something in your body, you don't have to let it affect your subsequent reactions or actions.

IT'S OKAY TO HAVE SOME NEGATIVE FEELINGS DURING BINGE URGES

Once you stop reacting, that doesn't mean you'll never experience negative feelings during a binge urge. The lower brain has a significant role in generating emotions, so you can't always control them. Remember that the goal of this step is to *minimize* uncomfortable feelings that the urge creates, not necessarily banish them. Even if you are able to detach, it's possible for you to suddenly feel grumpy, annoyed, or sorry for yourself when you want to binge. There is no need to try to change the negative feelings that come up—simply remain as unaffected as you can until the urge passes.

DON'T REACT BY WORRYING ABOUT PREVIOUS OR FUTURE URGES

Not reacting also means that you aren't going to be reminding yourself of your past failures in dismissing urges and you aren't going to be thinking about or worrying about the next urge you may experience. If you just deal strictly with that urge in that moment, detachment becomes a more pure experience and feels much more manageable. Try envisioning a blank slate every single time you have an urge. When each urge is treated anew, one at a time, there is less sense of feeling overwhelmed, less exhaustion, less thinking that you can't do this *again*. There is only now. When the weight of countless past urges is lifted, when you don't pull up all of your "reasons" for following the urges in the past or why you may follow them in the future, it allows you to detach from just *this* one urge in *this* one moment.

You Aren't Detaching from Your Lower Brain Altogether

It's important to realize that when you practice nonreaction, you aren't detaching from all of your inner experience and external circumstances. When you are operating from your rational, higher brain, it *can* be helpful to analyze thoughts and feelings, or even change your circumstances to affect your behavior. It can be good to think constructively about your thoughts and even dispute them. However, when reasoning and analyzing don't work (as is the case with binge urges), nonreaction is a very effective strategy. In fact, detachment is useful for all harmful thoughts that are reason-resistant and automatic/habitual.

As a final note to this component of recovery: Don't try to detach from your lower brain as a whole, but just as it relates to binge eating (and other destructive habits and thought patterns you may want to correct in the future). When it is functioning properly, the lower brain gives you desires that serve you well—the drive to eat, drink, avoid danger, stay alive, find pleasure, reproduce, and perform countless helpful habitual behaviors. The lower brain also gives rise to many of your strong emotions that protect you and guide your actions in a productive way. Be thankful for its vital functions, but ignore its junk.

[12]

Component 4: Stop Acting on Urges to Binge

REPEATEDLY FOLLOWING YOUR URGES to binge has created strong, organized, but dysfunctional neural pathways in your lower brain that support your behavior. The goal of dismissing urges is to correct those dysfunctional lower brain pathways, and you do this by not acting on urges to binge. When you stop binge eating, the neural connections that supported the destructive behavior will fade and the urges will go away. Each time you don't act on an urge, you are utilizing neuroplasticity to rewire your brain. In this way, Component 4 is the cure for binge eating, made possible by the three preceding components.

Also in this way, recovery is vastly simplified. I realize that—out of context—telling someone that the *cure* for binge eating is to "stop acting on the urges to binge" sounds ridiculously simple; but I hope it makes sense to you now. In this chapter, you'll see how the concepts you've learned in the three previous chapters come together to allow you to avoid binges. You'll keep track of what works best for you and learn from your successes, as well as determine how to manage any discomfort you may have with this step.

"DON'T ACT" FAST

It is wonderful to have new ideas—it revives us, energizes us, and we feel primed for change and hopeful for the future. New learning actually releases adrenaline, which leads to an excitement for applying new ideas.[97] Utilize these energizing effects to your advantage by putting the concepts you've learned so far to use right away. Don't let yourself get bogged down with *preparing* to stop acting on urges, or thinking you need to analyze the Five Components further, or believing you need to sort out something else in your life before you are ready to begin. This can cause your motivation to fade. The most important thing you can do to get your recovery going is to dismiss one binge urge and see that it works, then success will breed more success, until brain changes take root.

There is no doubt that your lower brain will argue against quick action. *One last time*, the voice of the urge will say, *then you can stop.* You'll hear tempting thoughts telling you to give yourself more time for these ideas to *really* sink in or to put off recovery until a major date—or at least until tomorrow. That's all neurological junk, and the more you give it value, the more your lower brain will keep convincing you to put off quitting. The lower brain calls for instant gratification, and to get it, it tells you that the "you" of the future will be perfectly capable of quitting, whether that's tomorrow's you, next week's you, or even New Year's you.

This can go on forever if you let it, because once the future becomes now, the lower brain will still call for instant gratification, will keep postponing your recovery. When you hear those thoughts encouraging you to binge today and quit tomorrow, know that you'll only have those same faulty brain messages tomorrow—along with stronger neural pathways that support the binge eating habit. Know that resistance to change is normal and natural, and anyone who has ever changed anything in their life has also had the desire to delay that change. The only way to move forward is to take that first brave step, using your new ideas to dismiss the very next urge you experience.

Write about what you will do when you experience your very next binge urge, and commit to using the components thus far to try to avoid acting on it.

INACTION, ALTERNATIVE ACTION, OR STILL OBSERVATION

To avoid acting on the urges, there is nothing you have to "do." However, there are three simple strategies you can try while you are experiencing an urge:

- **Inaction:** Just go about your day as if you were not experiencing an urge to binge. (Example: You are unloading groceries and you begin to feel an urge to binge. You simply continue unloading groceries and then do whatever you had planned next.)

- **Alternative Action:** Pick any alternative activity to perform while you are experiencing an urge. It can be the same one each time, or you can pick from a variety of activities. (Example: Every time you have an urge to binge, go for a short walk, or garden, or make art, make phone calls, or even do something less enjoyable but productive, like laundry or dusting.)
- **Still Observation:** Sit or lie down and observe your urges with detachment. (Example: Since this strategy is best used at home, pick your favorite spot to relax and just observe the experience.)

These strategies are not going to shut off the urge; your job is simply to avoid acting on it until the urge fades on its own. You can try all three options and keep track of your experiences below. This will help you determine what works best for you, which could be a combination of options. As long as you are avoiding acting on the urge, there is no wrong way.

What did it feel like to use *inaction* when experiencing an urge to binge? Were you able to avoid acting on your urge? About how long was the urge present?

_____

_____

_____

_____

_____

_____

What did it feel like to use *alternative action* while experiencing an urge to binge? Were you able to avoid acting on your urge? About how long was the urge present?

_____

_____

_____

_____

_____

What did it feel like to use *still observation* to experience an urge to binge? Were you able to avoid acting on your urge? About how long was the urge present?

_____

_____

_____

_____

_____

_____

After you've tried all three strategies for experiencing urges, write about which option, or combination of options, may be best for you and why. (You are trying to find what feels most comfortable and is most successful for you.)

_____

_____

_____

_____

_____

_____

_____

_____

_____

SETTING THE PROPER EXPECTATIONS (WILL NOT ACTING ON URGES BE EASY?)

You've committed to put your ideas into action right away; now you need to set the proper expectations for when urges arise. If you think it will be too easy to dismiss urges, you may get frustrated if the going gets a little rough. On the other hand, if you think it's going to be too hard, you may be too intimidated to get started. You of course want to be hopeful and confident that you can dismiss urges, but it's also important to realize that no two people are the same.

You may have instant success that snowballs into complete recovery, or dismissing urges may prove to be uncomfortable at first, and you may give in to some more urges before getting the hang of dismissing them. In my first book, I shared that it was relatively easy for me to avoid acting on binge urges. It was by far much easier than anything I'd ever tried, but it *was* tricky at first. Sometimes I got pulled into believing that I wanted what the lower brain wanted, and in those times, it took more effort not to act. But within a few weeks, dismissing urges felt natural, and after a few months passed, it was effortless. Your experience could look similar to mine, but if it doesn't, that's okay and I'm here to help—that's why there are so many pages left in this book.

I found it insanely easy. It seemed bizarre to me it was so easy once I made the conscious choice.

~Rita

It was soooo hard!!!! Your experience sounded easy, and I finished Brain over Binge *thinking I would be like that too. But the reality for me was very different.*

~Lillian

Take a minute to evaluate your expectations. Do you expect not acting on urges to be easy, extremely difficult, or somewhere in between? Why?

_____

_____

_____

_____

_____

After you use Components 1–4 to try to dismiss a binge urge, write about how your experience lined up with your expectations. Did you find dismissing the urge to be easy, extremely difficult, or somewhere in between?

_____

_____

_____

_____

_____

_____

_____

DISPELLING THE DISCOMFORT

Dismissing urges shouldn't be *painful*, but knowing that you may not feel great while binge urges are present goes a long way toward helping you set the proper expectations. If not acting on your urges feels uncomfortable, here are some suggestions:

- Go back through Components 1–3 and make sure you understand how to separate yourself from the urges and not react to them. Often, the reason for feeling uncomfortable is that you are still trying to fight the urges.
- Realize that any discomfort you feel is a product of the habit and only temporary. Your lower brain's job is to make you feel uncomfortable so you'll give in.

The lower brain is good at producing feelings of discomfort—especially when you first quit binge eating and the neural connections supporting the habit are strong. The way to overcome this is to *view the discomfort in a new way*. To gain a new perspective on discomfort, think and write about the following questions.

What discomfort do you have during a binge urge, when you are *not* acting on it? Describe in detail what exactly is uncomfortable.

_____

_____

_____

_____

_____

_____

_____

_____

Now write about the discomfort you have *after* a binge? Describe in detail all of the uncomfortable physical and emotional symptoms you have post-binge.

_____

_____

_____

_____

_____

_____

_____

_____

Look at your answers to the two previous questions and ask yourself: Which discomfort would you rather have? The temporary discomfort you have while *not* acting on an urge or the post-binge discomfort? Consider which lasts longer and which is more painful.

_____

_____

_____

_____

_____

_____

Rationally, most binge eaters know that the temporary discomfort they feel while not acting on an urge is much less painful than the post-binge discomfort. The post-binge discomfort lasts much longer and is more difficult to deal with in the long run. It's only during the binge urge that you may temporarily think that the urge discomfort is worse and must be stopped immediately.

Remember that the discomfort of an unsatisfied binge craving goes away rather quickly; but post-binge discomfort lingers and grows and affects all parts of your life. It's important to recognize that you *do* have a choice of which discomfort you'd rather have; but make a genuine one—don't be swayed by the false promises of the lower brain. Discomfort is part of most beneficial changes in life, and you sometimes have to go through it to become the person you want to be.

When you feel uncomfortable not acting on an urge, remind yourself of this: The lower brain prefers comfort, in the moment, without regard to long-term consequences—it's a normal survival mechanism; but you aren't willing to live with the discomfort and pain that acting on the urges cause.

"You" are actually much more comfortable *dismissing* urges. Anytime you experience some temporary discomfort during an urge, it means that "you" are on your way to becoming free of an extremely uncomfortable habit.

Focus on Success

Earlier in this chapter, I explained the benefits of putting your ideas into action right away, in order to utilize the energy of new learning. There is another benefit to beginning to dismiss your urges now: Our brains learn best from success.[98] The brain "doesn't know exactly what to retain from most failures to safeguard against future failure, it doesn't exhibit the same type of neuroplasticity as it does with successes."[99] This means that if you can take a leap and dismiss just *one* urge, that can propel you forward more than reading the rest of this book. Your success will solidify knowledge and allow you to experience fully what it means to view urges as neurological junk and detach from them.

Throughout my binge eating and therapy, I was told to learn from my failures in resisting urges. I was told that binges were wonderful learning opportunities to figure out "why" I was binge eating. After I gave in to an urge, I was told to go back and try to determine what difficult events led up to the binge or what emotions I was either trying to cope with or stuff down. In the theory of traditional therapy, this could help me identify the areas of my life where I needed to cope better, so that I would be less likely to binge. Unfortunately, I was analyzing the wrong factors, as well as bringing attention to all the problems in my life and connecting them to binge eating.

When I finally did have success in 2005 with the new perspective shared in *Brain over Binge* and in this book, my success built upon itself quickly. Once I dismissed one urge—then two, then three—and observed how I was able to do this, my recovery gained a force of its own. There is a science behind this—taking the first step toward a goal and seeing success with it has a profound impact on the brain. Then, each subsequent success is actually processed more efficiently and leverages neuroplasticity more than trying to learn from failure.[100]

With this in mind, use the chart on the following pages to keep track of your successes and what you learn from dismissing urges. If there are times that you *do* act on an urge, don't dwell on it; simply come back to this chart and read about how you succeeded in the past, so you can move forward with renewed focus on what works.

Date/ Time	Urge Description (physical sensations, thoughts, feelings)	What You Did While the Urge Was Present	What You Learned (what worked)

Date/ Time	Urge Description (physical sensations, thoughts, feelings)	What You Did While the Urge Was Present	What You Learned (what worked)

How Long Will It Take for Urges to Go Away?

Understandably, you want your urges to go away as soon as possible. But, ideally, you should get to the point where you view them in such a way that they don't bother you anymore and you no longer feel in a hurry for them to disappear. Everyone's urges will fade at a different rate. Commonly, the urges seem to take about three months to one year to go away completely, although this is not a scientific study, only a timeline based on other binge eaters I heard from after they read *Brain over Binge*. This doesn't mean you will be struggling with powerful urges for a year. After some time goes by—and everyone's experience with this is a little different—it will be effortless to ignore any remnants of binge urges. What used to be urges will simply become insignificant thoughts and feelings that pop up from time to time that don't bother you. In fact, those thoughts and feelings may even serve to remind you of your success; you'll be excited when you hear that old urge voice, knowing that you no longer consider giving it attention.

In my experience, even after the first few weeks of being binge-free, I noticed a significant reduction in the intensity and frequency of my urges. It took about nine months for all remnants of binge urges to go away, but after a few months, it became completely natural not to binge. Automatic thoughts/feelings would still arise very infrequently, but it just wasn't a big deal. Although my urges gradually diminished over time, it didn't always seems like a linear process; and I've found that to be the case with most other recovered binge eaters I've spoken to. Some days during the first several weeks, the urges wouldn't arise much at all; but other days, I would have more persistent urges.

The nonlinear diminishing of binge urges may create some anxiety for you. If you feel your urges gradually going away, and then a strong urge suddenly pops up, it's understandable that you will be worried that you haven't made any progress. You have, but for some reason, your brain sensed that it needed to send a strong urge—it doesn't mean anything significant to you. Sometimes you will be able to identify what may have triggered the urge, such as experiencing a situation in which you frequently binged in the past or accidental undereating for a few days; but sometimes what activates those old neural pathways is rather unpredictable.

Be patient and don't get worked up about your urges going away quickly—you are perfectly capable of detaching from each urge as it comes up, even if some urges are stronger than others. Remind yourself that the neural pathways didn't become wired for binge eating overnight, and it is going to take some time for your brain to change. Trust that this process will unfold exactly how it is supposed to for you, and stay committed even if you can't see change every day.

To help you see that you are indeed improving over time, you can use the chart below to keep track of the fact that your urges are fading. Every 10–15 days, record your urge frequency, intensity, and description, along with anything else you notice about your urges to binge. It can keep you motivated to see progress over time. It's important not to write in this table too often because of the nonlinear nature of the brain changes you'll experience. You likely won't see a change in your descriptions day to day, but over the course of weeks and months, you'll be excited to see that the urges aren't affecting your life like they used to. Also, after the chart, space has been included for you to reflect on and write about what helps you cultivate patience while brain changes take place.

Date	Urge Frequency	Urge Intensity & Description	Other Notes About Your Urges

Keep track of what helps you stay patient and stay the course of dismissing urges without becoming anxious about urges going away:

_____

_____

_____

_____

_____

_____

_____

_____

_____

[13]

Component 5:
Get Excited
(About Dismissing Urges and
Recovery Itself)

COMPONENT 5 IS A bonus; and for most people, it's a very *natural* product of Component 4. When you have success dismissing binge urges, you *are* excited. However, as the days and weeks go by, it's possible to lose that initial excitement. The goal of this step is to keep the initial excitement alive and in focus, and use it to your advantage.

Excitement about recovery isn't just about feeling good; it actually has a useful neurological function. Celebrating a new discovery or skill increases the likelihood that it will be remembered and repeated. Praise, including praise from within, cements that learning on a physical level in the brain.[101] Sometimes the idea of getting excited or praising yourself for dismissing binge urges will seem scary, because you feel you've failed in the past and you don't want to risk another disappointment. That's completely understandable, but know that taking a risk and feeling excited about your initial success will increase your chances of future success.

CELEBRATE TO STRENGTHEN YOUR HIGHER BRAIN

Brain functions that are given attention and significance strengthen;[102] therefore, it only makes sense to find ways to focus positive attention on your higher brain's accomplishments. This will serve to strengthen connections in the prefrontal parts of your brain as the old ones that supported your habit weaken. You can turn attention toward your higher brain's success in many ways. You can verbally congratulate yourself, reward yourself in non-food ways, announce it to a trusted friend or mentor, or simply focus on the feeling of pride and joy whenever you avoid the shame of a binge. Below, write your own ideas of how to congratulate yourself.

How can you turn attention toward your higher brain's success in dismissing urges, cultivating excitement for recovery and strengthening your higher brain?

_____

_____

_____

_____

_____

_____

_____

CELEBRATE OTHER PARTS OF YOUR LIFE

As you have more and more success dismissing binge urges, you'll notice other parts of your life that are worth celebrating as well. Without binge eating, you have the opportunity to do other things—whatever you may enjoy or whatever you need to do—without binge eating getting in the way. Although doing other things won't magically take your urges away, focusing attention elsewhere can actually help the faulty brain pathways change faster. You can focus on the people, activities, and interests in your life that are already there, or you can add some positive elements to your life. Below, you can keep track of things in your life to get excited about.

What is already in your life that you can focus attention on and get excited about?

_____

_____

_____

_____

_____

_____

_____

Is there anything positive you want to add to your life to focus on, now that you'll no longer be binge eating? (Think about some hobbies, experiences, volunteer opportunities, service projects, and/or personal projects that you'd like to explore.)

_____

_____

_____

_____

_____

_____

GET EXCITED ABOUT YOUR RECOVERY REALITY

Your "recovery reality" is what your day-to-day life is like without binge eating. No doubt about it, there will be positive aspects of that reality, and it is helpful to focus on and get excited about those things. Some of the reasons you had for wanting to quit may become evident right away. For example, if you wanted to quit so you could devote more time to your family, you may notice immediately that you are able to be more fully present in your relationships. Other reasons you wanted to quit might not materialize in the way you think they will. For example, if one of your reasons for quitting was so that you could eat only healthy food and lose weight, you may find yourself disappointed.

If you do find yourself feeling let down because life after binge eating isn't perfect, remind yourself that this is reality and life can be hard; but it's better to live a real life than one clouded by binge eating. Don't dwell on the fact that life without binge eating might not be everything you hoped it would be; instead, bring the benefits of recovery to the front of your mind and revisit them often. This can help keep you on the path to complete freedom from binge eating and help you avoid the temptation to fall back into old patterns. As you go about each day, take note of the positive results of recovery you experience and write about them below. These results may be what you expected when you envisioned the benefits of recovery—or they may surprise you.

Positive results of recovery (every time you add something to this list, get excited about it!):

_____

_____

_____

_____

_____

_____

_____

_____

✻   ✻   ✻   ✻   ✻   ✻   ✻   ✻   ✻   ✻   ✻   ✻   ✻   ✻   ✻   ✻   ✻   ✻   ✻   ✻

Moving on After Learning the Five Components

You now have the information you need to allow your urges to come and go without reacting to them or acting upon them. You may already be dismissing your urges and experiencing a reduction in their frequency and intensity. You may already sense on a deep level that you don't need to act on the urges ever again. If that's the case, you can put this book down and get to living your life.

Alternatively, you may understand the Five Components intellectually, but that understanding is not yet leading to behavioral change. That is okay, and it doesn't mean this approach is not going to work for you. For the Five Components to affect your life, you have to truly understand them on an insightful level, not just an intellectual one. *Learning* that the urges are neurological junk that you don't need to act upon is different from *knowing* and *experiencing* that same information and feeling at your core that you are separate from the urges.

This perceptual shift is what allows the Five Components to create lasting change for you. In the next chapter, Amy Johnson, Ph.D., is going to talk about facilitating insight surrounding the binge urges and what that might look like for you. Amy will share some stories from clients about how the Five Components worked in their lives. The timing and nature of habit change is different for everyone, but you can create a mind-set that will allow change to occur more naturally.

After Amy's discussion, I will talk about maintaining your progress in Chapter 15, then address the three main challenges that binge eaters have with Recovery Goal 1 in Chapters 16–18. Chapter 19 provides additional tips for those still having trouble dismissing binge urges. Then, before transitioning to Recovery Goal 2, Amy Johnson will talk to you again—this time about the concept of detachment on a deeper, spiritual level, for those who want to tie their recovery to a bigger picture.

[14]

The Power of Insightful Understanding
by Amy Johnson, Ph.D.

SOME OF THE BIGGEST questions people have upon learning the truth about urges are: *How do I detach from my urges? How do I sit through the urge and simply dismiss or ignore it? How do I come to view the urge in a brand-new, nonthreatening way when it feels anything but?*

The answer is simple: You have a deep personal insight that leads you to view urges as neurological junk. From there, you feel less attached to and taken down by them. There is a separation between you and your urges that provides the opportunity to not act on them.

When you come to see that urges are powerless, harmless, fleeting thoughts on which you do not have to act—that without you acting upon them, they fade on their own and their connection in the lower brain is weakened—it's as C. S. Lewis says: "Nothing changes, but everything is different." There is nothing you actively have to do to change things, but everything changes by virtue of your new perspective.

So, the answer to the "how" questions is overwhelmingly simple: You come to deeply, insightfully see a new truth. But as simple as the answer is, insight doesn't come on demand. It's not something we have control over. The good news is that humans are wired for insight. We're designed to evolve and grow to see more and more about life as we move through it, and those insights we pick up are just what you need to stop binge eating permanently.

HAVING INSIGHTS OF YOUR OWN

If the only thing needed is personal insight about your habit, your innate health, and the nature of your urges, the obvious next question is: *How do I have those personal insights?*

You become open-minded and curious.

You set aside everything you've heard before (the best you can, anyway) and everything you think you know about habits and urges and yourself, and you stay open to everything that's being shown to you in this book.

You take on "beginner's mind," as they call it in Buddhism, a place where you're soft, open, curious, and you let what you're reading wash over you without trying too hard to mentally understand it.

You learn that the lower brain's messages are old and habitual, but meaningless.

You learn that urges fade when you fail to act on them. Although it may feel as if giving in to an urge is the only way to quiet it, there is a better way: Do nothing. Urges fade on their own when you do nothing. The more nothing you do, the faster your brain is rewired and your binge eating habit dies out completely.

Insight is passive. It can't be forced, but it doesn't need to be. Your job is to simply see what there is to see about the fact that urges are safe, healthy, harmless, passing human experience, to stay open to a new understanding, and to not give up.

FACILITATING INSIGHT

Sometimes, especially in the beginning, relating to your urges as neurological junk and allowing them to fade can feel difficult. It makes sense that it would not always feel easy. Interacting with your urges in a detached way is foreign and unusual. If you are used to quickly giving in to urges, not doing so will mean you more fully experience the physical symptoms that accompany those urges. If it feels difficult for you, know that you're in good company and that it will feel easier with time. As you continue to see your experience as safe and temporary and you sit with your urges without acting on them, your brain takes notice and change begins to take root.

Despite the fact that there is nothing you can actively do to produce a deep insight on the spot, there are factors that facilitate insight. First, be open to a new understanding of your habit and yourself. The biggest obstacle to insight is mental rigidity. Unfortunately, black-and-white, all-or-nothing thinking is very common among people with eating disorders, and that way of thinking can keep you feeling stuck in unhelpful ways of seeing things. The type of all-or-nothing thinking that convinces you that if you're not adhering to a strict diet you may as well binge is a perfect example of mentally holding to rigid rules or beliefs that, when looked at in an easier, more flexible way, aren't rational at all.

The mind loves certainty. It loves to settle into a way of thinking that it can label "right." The truth is that there are very few objective rights and wrongs in life. Much of what our minds call "truth" is not inherently so; these beliefs may be our personal truths, but they aren't right or true in any objective sense. To facilitate insight, consider that you might be "wrong" about much of what you thought you knew.

You very well may be wrong about where your binge eating originated, why it's an issue for you, and how you'll recover from it. You might be wrong about what will lead to weight gain or what you need to do in order to reduce or maintain your current weight. You might be wrong if you have inflexible beliefs about the impact particular foods will have on you or if you swear by or completely avoid some foods. I certainly was innocently wrong about all of those things, and much more. Things are not black-and-white, and our personal beliefs are very biased. If you're feeling stuck or hopeless, you're innocently holding on to a lot of biased opinions and mistaking those opinions as truth.

A second way you can facilitate insight is by allowing things to be easy. Truth tends to be earth-shatteringly simple, and the truth about your binge eating is no exception. The "complex problem" of an eating disorder can actually be quite clear-cut when you see it accurately, from a clear state of mind. Many people have put years of hard work into recovery, believing they were dealing with a complex puzzle that required years of hard labor to solve. When shown a much simpler way, they have a difficult time allowing things to be that simple. Be open to the idea that this is much more straightforward than you previously believed.

A third way to encourage your own deep insights is to think less. This may sound counterintuitive, but remember that viewing your urges to binge as neurological junk and choosing to not act on them is not something you *do* as much as something you simply *see*. There is nothing to actively, mentally figure out.

Try to take the information here and notice how it feels and where it resonates as truth, without overanalyzing it or comparing it to everything you believe you already know. If what you hear resonates with you on some level, stay with that feeling. Allow this new perspective to feel right without needing to have a full intellectual understanding of it right away. When you analyze, compare, and contrast, you're holding the information in your intellect at a thought-based, conceptual level. That level of analysis can actually prevent deeper insight.

Cognitive scientists who study insight often talk about the phenomenon of "walking away." Walking away essentially means you release ideas and concepts from your logical, thinking mind and allow them to work for you in a deeper part of your mind.

These researchers find that most insights occur when people are doing things such as driving, taking a shower, waking up from a nap, or being on vacation. Those activities do not promote insights directly (there is no need to add additional showers to your day!), but those are times when your thinking, analytical mind is relaxed and the deeper parts of your mind can work on your behalf. You aren't responsible for creating an insight—your only job is to be open to new perspectives and let your wise mind do the rest. Simply read the ideas in this book and then (metaphorically) "walk away."

INTELLECTUAL UNDERSTANDING VERSUS INSIGHTFUL UNDERSTANDING

The "do nothing" approach in *Brain over Binge* creates a struggle for some people, especially early on when they haven't yet experienced a deep, personal insight that changes their relationship with their urges. Understanding is often intellectual first—you intellectually and rationally see that urges are nothing to act upon, but you still feel compelled to act on them.

This is a very common and normal part of the recovery process. Intellectual understanding often precedes insight. That rational—but not yet visceral—understanding is a great sign that true insight is not far behind.

During this time, you may be tempted to push away or try to forcefully ignore urges, which unfortunately gives them a lot of unnecessary attention. Attention reinforces your thoughts and urges, actually making them *more* likely to return.

The deeper your personal insight around the nature of your urges, the easier and more naturally you will simply allow your urges to pass without stepping in. Deep insight, to the point where you find yourself effortlessly dismissing urges, comes in time, and that timing is different for everyone.

HOW YOUR EXPERIENCE MIGHT LOOK

Since *Brain over Binge*, in which Kathryn published her story of recovering from bulimia almost immediately after learning about the lower and higher brain, many readers have hoped to follow in her footsteps. Some do. Some people learn the truth of how their binge eating is innocently wired in their brain and experience a profound personal insight that leads them to stop binge eating almost immediately, as Kathryn did.

Others do not. Recovery looks different for everyone, and the path of your recovery is unpredictable. It can't be stressed enough that any length of time it takes for you to have your own insights is perfectly normal and okay. There truly is no "right way" for recovery to look. Believing there is a right way is just another example of black-or-white, all-or-nothing thinking that will set you up for disappointment and frustration.

In my discussions and coaching with women who have read *Brain over Binge*, I've noticed that some of them assumed these tools wouldn't work for them because they didn't experience an instant insight that led them to suddenly stop binge eating. They compare their experiences to Kathryn's or to the experiences of other readers and conclude that they won't recover. Nothing could be further from the truth.

The best thing you can do is to continue exploring this information about the truth about your binge eating habit ... and then relax. Yes, that sounds incredibly passive, especially if you are a take-charge go-getter who is accustomed to making things happen in life. But remember, this is different.

SOME READER EXAMPLES

To illustrate that the timing and nature of insightful understanding are different for everyone, below are some examples of how *Brain over Binge* readers came to view their urges as neurological junk and chose to no longer obey those urges. These examples are meant to show the wide range of paths that recovering from binge eating might take, and yet these examples only scratch the surface. Your recovery may resemble one of these stories or it may look completely unique.

RACHEL

Rachel had been binge eating for the greater part of ten years. Before reading *Brain over Binge*, she knew that her urges to binge served no physiological need, but she felt completely powerless in the face of them. She had a very basic understanding of the brain, and she sensed that if she did nothing, her urges might eventually fade—but doing nothing in the midst of an urge felt far too difficult to attempt for very long.

Rachel had been in therapy several times to get help with her binge eating, but therapy never made a significant impact on her behavior. In fact, after spending an hour talking about her eating issues and what she assumed triggered her binges, she often left therapy feeling more hopeless than ever.

When Rachel read *Brain over Binge*, she had several insights immediately. The idea that the lower brain was linked with her survival instincts really resonated with her and explained why she felt so hijacked when an urge would strike. Despite knowing that not bingeing was—in theory, at least—an option, she rarely felt able to exercise that option.

Learning about the lower and higher brain helped her understand the conflict she experienced when she felt taken over by urges. A very real and very significant part of her knew that binge eating was the last thing in the world she truly wanted to do. Hearing that the lower brain was loud but powerless to act was an enormous aha moment for Rachel. She immediately saw that as the way out. Because acting on urges required conscious choice, she realized she was never truly hijacked.

The other piece of the puzzle that made a significant difference was recognizing that the urges would subside and actually retreat for good when she stopped acting on them. Rachel had experienced ignoring other urges in the past (urges to overwork and to smoke cigarettes), and she knew firsthand that those urges faded and retreated when she failed to act on them. She had never really connected those urges with her urges to binge eat, perhaps because her urges to binge felt stronger and more disastrous or perhaps because she formerly believed they signaled some deeper psychological issues. Once she realized that her urges to binge were no different than those other urges, not acting on them became infinitely easier.

It wasn't information that helped Rachel stop giving in to her urges, it was coming to see these things insightfully, as a deep truth.

Rachel had a few very small binges, if you can even call them that, after reading *Brain over Binge*, but they were different than before. She now knew that she could sit with the urge and wait for it to pass; when she did follow through with those minor binges, she was aware that she was choosing to do so. In each case, the binge didn't feel quite right—without the feeling of urgency, there was no instant wave of relief when she began eating. Without that instant relief, the binge felt unnecessary.

Rachel considered herself recovered from binge eating within a couple weeks of reading *Brain over Binge*, and she's now been binge-free for nearly two years.

CATHY

The first time Cathy read *Brain over Binge*, she had several deep insights about the simplicity of recovery, and she stopped binge eating immediately. She saw how she had been thinking of her binge eating as a profound mental health issue with deep roots, a problem she had to "get to the bottom of" in order to recover. Cathy assumed she might be in treatment for much of her life. But when *Brain over Binge* showed her that perhaps her eating disorder was only a brain-wiring problem and that her brain really would rewire if she stopped obeying urges, she simply stopped. Cathy didn't binge for nearly four weeks—that was the longest she had gone without binge eating in several years.

Then thoughts about binge eating began to come back. At first, Cathy dismissed them as old neurological junk, and they faded. But when thoughts about her old habit didn't completely disappear as they seemingly had in the past, Cathy began to question her recovery. Thoughts like *Maybe it's not so simple* and *I knew it was too good to be true* and *My binge eating is too serious for these tools to work* ran rampant, and rather than recognize those thoughts as common fears or the voice of addiction at work, Cathy took them as truth and began to binge eat again.

Cathy didn't overthink things the first time around. She didn't think much at all, actually—she simply began to see things differently after her initial reading of *Brain over Binge*, and so her behavior changed.

What later derailed her was taking her thinking seriously. When Cathy's binge-related thoughts revved back up, she could have dismissed them as neurological junk or the addictive voice, but she innocently took them as truth.

Cathy's progression from quick insight to later doubt is not uncommon. Her experience shows us that recovery is much easier when you're not overthinking things, when you follow feelings of truth and simplicity. Any thoughts that tell you that recovery is too good to be true or that your recovery should look a particular way are products of the lower brain. You can dismiss those thoughts and carry on.

Cathy's story has a happy ending. She eventually realized that she was entertaining a lot of thoughts that made recovery appear more complicated than it really was. She put the tools in *Brain over Binge* back to work and has now been binge-free for nine months.

LESLIE

Leslie had been binge eating and obsessively dieting for fifteen years when she found *Brain over Binge*. Upon first learning about the two brains and that urges to binge—as well as urges to diet—were neurological junk, Leslie immediately felt as if she had stumbled upon an answer. The material resonated with her deeply, and she knew that this approach was different from anything she had ever tried. Leslie experienced a slight letting up of her urges without doing anything at all. She wasn't deliberately putting the tools to work, but her urges naturally lessened to some degree. Although she felt less out of control than previously, she continued to binge eat, diet, and overexercise. Leslie says she didn't feel ready to give up her eating issues just yet and she doubted that it could be as easy as it sounded.

When Leslie finally felt ready to put the *Brain over Binge* tools into action, she found herself doing so very forcefully. When she experienced an urge to binge, she immediately jumped into action trying to convince herself that her urges were neurological junk and that she didn't have to give in to them.

For example, Leslie would go for a long run, in an attempt to distract herself in the middle of an urge to binge. At other times she would pace her living room repeating, "It's just an urge. It's just neurological junk." Sometimes in the middle of an urge, she'd pull out her copy of *Brain over Binge* and attempt to re-read some passages she had highlighted.

Needless to say, Leslie's urges rarely faded into the background when she behaved this way. Her approach resulted in more—not less—attention placed on her urges. She wasn't treating them like junk at all; instead, she was acting as if they were serious threats to be reckoned with. Leslie was relying on sheer willpower and resistance to make it through her urges, which was unintentionally strengthening their connection in her lower brain. It's no surprise that Leslie ended up feeling worse, and binge eating even more, than before she made the decision to stop.

Leslie was a self-proclaimed "go-getter." She was very successful in many areas of her life, and she strongly believed that success was the result of hard work and effort. Accordingly, Leslie approached recovery as a task over which she needed to take charge. She was determined to make it happen rather than allow it to happen, and that approach held her back from recovery.

That is not to say that the *Brain over Binge* tools can't be employed deliberately to some extent—they certainly can. But viewing urges as neurological junk and allowing them to fade is very different than trying to push them away.

Leslie recognized that she viewed her urges as harmful threats to her weight and her well-being. Until she came to see them as harmless, she would continue to white-knuckle her way through them.

By continuing to learn about the way her eating issues were wired in her brain and staying very open-minded about what her recovery might look like, Leslie gradually developed deeper insight about her binge eating and dieting. She saw how fear and judgment of her urges were actually fueling them, and she began to let go. She met urges with increasing calm and clarity and a peaceful, not forceful, resolve to wait them out. Her mind was more at ease the second time around.

When Leslie wasn't scaring herself with thoughts of how disastrous a binge would be and jumping into action to overpower her urges, they felt much less threatening. From there, she slowly and steadily began to see that acting on an urge was her choice.

Recovery felt tenuous for several months—Leslie feared she might lose her perspective and binge at any moment. But Leslie stuck with it, and the process became easier with time. Feeling her urges fade on their own—something Leslie had rarely experienced in fifteen years—helped to convince her that not acting on urges was always a viable option.

Although it felt like a slow and winding path that took nearly seven months, Leslie has now been binge free for almost three months.

JANE

Jane had been caught up in the binge-diet cycle for nearly twenty years. She had been a dancer and actress from the time she was eight years old, and she was hard-pressed to remember a time when she was not either dieting or binge eating. She was determined to change her patterns for good, and when decades of therapy and alternative healing modalities didn't help, *Brain over Binge* gave her the knowledge and the tools she had been looking for to make the change.

Similar to Leslie, Jane's biggest difficulty was that when she felt an urge, rather than seeing it for what it truly was and doing less, she instinctively tried to do more. In her words, she "freaked out" anytime she felt even the hint of an urge. She gave in to her urges almost immediately, rarely letting them fade naturally on their own.

Jane saw that what she really needed was to slow everything down and live less in her head, lost in thought, and more in the moment. If she could notice her urges with some degree of separation, remembering that they were not "her" but her lower brain speaking, she knew she could dismiss them and wait for them to fade. But much of the time, Jane didn't feel that separation between herself and her lower brain urges. She would dive into action (binge eating or restricting food) to quiet the urges, without remembering that waiting was an option.

Jane worked on becoming aware of all of her thinking as a way to practice separating herself from her inner dialogue. She began to take all of her idle thinking less seriously. She realized that because she could observe her lower and higher brain at work, "she" must be something apart from her mind entirely. This insight helped Jane immensely when urges arose. She could finally identify her urges with a bit of distance before reactively and automatically obeying them.

In the beginning, Jane simply stopped binge eating as soon as she was able to. Sometimes that was mid-binge or even near the end of a binge. The more she was able to separate herself from her urges and see how she was choosing to give in to them, the sooner she could stop. After several months of gradual improvement, Jane was able to detach from her urges when they arose, before she began binge eating.

Jane quit binge eating for good about one year after her initial reading of *Brain over Binge*. For her, it was a matter of slowing down the stream of thoughts (urges to binge are just one type of thought in that stream) enough to view them in a more detached way. It took Jane longer than it takes many people to insightfully know that she was not her urges. Today, Jane is binge-free and extremely proud of herself for having the patience and open-mindedness to stick with this process.

If there is one thing to take from these examples, it is that everyone's experience is different. The only thing required for a full recovery from binge eating is the ability to view urges as neurological junk and thus not act on them. That ability comes via insight, but insights vary as widely as people vary. Insights are not always instant or profound, like a lightbulb going off. More often than not, insights grow slowly and gradually. In the end, all that matters is that you begin to dismiss rather than give in to your urges to binge. Any form that takes is perfectly okay.

Beginning Again After a Binge

When people binge again after a period of being binge-free, they often ask something along the lines of "How do I get back on track?" or "How do I begin again after a relapse?"

The answer is always that you do the same thing you did before, which is the only thing there is to do. You reconnect with the fact that your urges are neurological junk that signal no actual need, know that they will fade if you choose to not obey them, and choose to not obey them. When you do not give in to the urge to binge, you don't binge. The rest takes care of itself.

The process is the same whether you are using the *Brain over Binge* tools for the first time or the fortieth time. The approach is no different if you've been binge eating for a month or for twenty years, whether you are going through a divorce or if the circumstances of your life are wonderful. With insight into the nature of your experience, it's extremely simple.

If you successfully stopped binge eating for some period of time but then began binge eating again, you might be tempted to believe some defeatist thoughts that interfere with looking at these truths again. As you saw in the case studies above, those stories in your head often sound like, *See, I knew I would never recover* or *It is not really this easy* or *I can't pull it off long-term*. Those are simply untrue thoughts. They may seem very convincing, but they have no objective validity.

Treat those doubts, fears, and defeatist thoughts as neurological junk because that is exactly what they are. They serve no purpose and are not helpful in any way. They don't reflect reality, and they are mere biased speculation, not fact. Any thought that tells you that you won't or can't stop binge eating is just a passing thought, just part of the habit. Dismiss those defeatist thoughts and let them pass on their own.

[15]

Maintaining Progress

Initially, I found it very easy. The first month after I read Brain over Binge, *I was able to apply the methods to overcome the urges to binge and felt great. However, once I felt it was under control and an urge would come, I wouldn't recognize it right away because I hadn't been bingeing. Then, I would kind of forget what I'd learned, and it was just tougher at that point. Basically, [the Five Components] are something I should keep in my phone so I won't forget them in detail!*

~Kayla

WHILE YOU CULTIVATE A mind-set that invites insight, you may benefit from some additional things to reflect upon; and even after you feel like you truly get that the urges are not "you," you may still have some uncertainty moving forward. Wherever you are in the process of understanding the nature of your urges, it can be helpful to be aware of some common issues that come up in the first several weeks and months of resisting urges—that way, you can feel prepared and confident. This chapter gives you additional ideas to keep your initial progress going.

THE FALSE APPEAL OF THE HABIT

As you experience urges with detachment, your brain will no doubt send some convincing arguments to go back to binge eating. To gain perspective on this, remember that feeling drawn toward old habits doesn't mean you are weak or have a defective or malicious brain. Rather, your brain is simply being economical. Remember that the brain tends to resist new ideas or change because change takes more mental energy than maintaining the status quo.[103] Once brain changes take root, however, and being binge-free is your new normal, you'll no longer feel that pull back toward the habit. But you have to give it time. Until then, writing those thoughts down as they come up can help defuse their power.

Here, keep track of any thoughts that encourage you to go back to the habit:

_____

_____

_____

_____

_____

_____

_____

_____

With these thoughts in mind, remind yourself of three things:
- The appeal of the old habit is *false*. Your brain is being energy efficient, by default.
- The false appeal of the old habit is only temporary (you won't always feel you want to binge).
- If you don't allow yourself to be swayed by the false appeal of thoughts about your habit, your brain will change, and those habits will stop being appealing.

COMMON TEMPTING THOUGHTS

There are four general thoughts that are common in recovering binge eaters, all of which can hinder progress if given attention:
1. *Just one last time.*
2. *You deserve a break from dismissing urges.*
3. *Binge eating wasn't a big deal anyway.*
4. *My case is different.*

Just One Last Time

This seems like the lower brain's favorite tempting thought. Early on in your binge eating, you likely latched onto this thought, because taken at face value, it can seem to make logical sense. If you promise never to binge again after this one last time, it gives you an excuse for giving in to an uncomfortable urge *now*. The problem is, this thought quickly becomes habitual, and the lower brain will use the "just one last time" reasoning again and again ... indefinitely. This type of thought is certainly not specific to binge eaters; it can derail anyone who wants to make positive changes in their life.

The lower brain's job is to convince you to do what it wants—*now*. Buying into this automatic "one last time" tactic just passes off quitting to your future self, but your future self will have this same exact thought. This is because, once the future becomes *now*, your lower brain's job will remain convincing you to binge *now*. In *Rational Recovery*, Jack Trimpey says that, to the lower brain (the "beast" brain, as he calls it), it is always now.[104] You aren't failing to keep your promise when it doesn't really turn out to be your "last" binge, because it wasn't really *your* promise—it was from the lower brain.

Another aspect of "one last time" thinking is a resolution to quit in the future. If you are having an urge, you may find yourself contemplating a more "appropriate" time to quit. You may hear thoughts like, *It makes more sense to quit on the first day of the month* or *Tomorrow is a new week—just start recovery then*. Resolving to quit is a pattern in most binge eaters, and this "logic" from the lower brain can be appealing to your higher self. If you are going to quit "tomorrow," "next week," "next year," it provides an immediate excuse to binge "today," "this week," "this year."

The higher brain latches onto resolution thoughts because, again, they provide an immediate excuse to surrender control to the lower brain. After the binge, you snap out of it and realize you truly didn't want to push off quitting; and once you have a new "quit date," you feel you have to try to make yourself stick to it. You truly make an effort to honor that resolution, but the next time you have an urge, you have those same automatic resolution thoughts—with a later quit date—and you believe them again. To prevent this from continuing to happen, you have to stop giving resolution thoughts any value.

Have you believed your lower brain's "just one last time" or "resolution" thoughts in the past? Keep track of any insights and ideas that help you remember that these types of thoughts are junk:

_____

_____

_____

_____

_____

_____

You Deserve a Break from Dismissing Urges

Although success breeds success, your lower brain may sometimes try to use your success to *justify* a binge. You may hear thoughts like, *You've done so well that you deserve a break.* You may notice that after a certain number of binge-free days, your lower brain starts producing those thoughts, telling you that you've done enough recovering for now. Your lower brain may argue for rewarding yourself for your success in dismissing binge urges ... with a binge. This is obviously faulty logic, but in the moment of a binge urge, it can be convincing.

Not acting on these thoughts is vital to your success. It is important for you to remember that you *will* often feel justified in binge eating for one reason or another—it's normal. Everyone who has ever quit a bad habit has felt justified in keeping it going at times. Remind yourself that your success doesn't mean you deserve a binge; it means you are one step closer to solidifying new neural pathways that no longer support binge eating. You are one step closer to what you truly deserve, and that's a break from binge eating—forever—and a life completely free from any desire to do so.

Write down any insights you have about detaching from "you deserve a break" thoughts:

_____

_____

_____

_____

_____

_____

_____

_____

Binge Eating Wasn't a Big Deal Anyway

As you dismiss more urges, you may begin hearing thoughts like, *Binge eating didn't really interfere with my life too much* or *When you compare binge eating to other habits, it's pretty mild* or *Quitting isn't really necessary because my binge eating wasn't really too bad.* When thoughts like these arise, it isn't necessary to remind yourself of all the ways binge eating was a big deal in your life. Just remember to detach from this form of neurological junk. You know it was a big deal, but your lower brain doesn't remember pain too well when there is a reward to acquire.[105] This is one reason why women have more than one child: Removed from having a baby, they think that it wasn't such a big deal after all. They forget how painful labor was, how debilitating morning sickness felt; they forget what it's like to be sleep-deprived for months or even years. This selective memory is a good thing when it comes to parenting, but it's detrimental when it comes to bad habits. Don't let this natural brain reaction trick you into thinking that binges weren't terribly painful.

Write down any insights you have about detaching from thoughts that tell you that your binge eating wasn't that big of a deal:

_____

_____

_____

_____

_____

_____

_____

My Case Is Different

Some people think that just stopping the binge eating habit may work for others, but not for them. They think that their lives are more complicated, that their binge eating developed for deeper reasons than others, or that they have too many struggles in their lives to quit. If you feel this way, first of all, know that you don't have to quit right now if you don't want to; but also know that you are not alone in thinking that your case is different. Everyone can find at least one unique problem in their life that they think may prevent recovery, but most people can move forward despite that.

We are all guilty of thinking we are somehow different and have a tougher road, even in other parts of our lives. If someone else's life looks better than yours on the surface, remember that you have no idea what that person is going through. When I quit binge eating, I didn't have major trauma going on—I was recently married, I generally enjoyed my job; but there were still countless problems under the surface, and my life was far from being easy. The truth is, we can all find an excuse.

There *are* things that make you different, that is correct; and that is why not everyone will recover on the same timeline. But whatever you are facing, you can make recovery work despite that. If you feel like you can't stop acting on binge urges right now because there are unique issues holding you back, then get to work on those issues if you feel it will help; but know that the "my case is different" thoughts will likely still be there afterward—and at *any* time you attempt to quit. The best course of action is to stop giving these thoughts any attention and to continue to dismiss urges even in the face of them.

Does your lower brain tell you that "your case is different"? Do you truly believe this? How can you remind yourself that everyone's case is different, but this doesn't have to prevent recovery?

_____

_____

_____

_____

_____

_____

_____

_____

No Need to Count Binge-Free Days

What's important to recovery is that you don't follow the current urge to binge, not how many days you've been binge-free. Unless you have noticed that counting binge-free days motivates you in a powerful way, I wouldn't recommend putting too much emphasis on a number. A central benefit of not counting binge-free days is that you don't have to start again at "Day 1" if you do binge. Starting all over again can feel discouraging, so much so that it often causes people to act on thoughts that call for a full-blown relapse. Acting on an urge doesn't mean your habit has control again; it only means you've acted on *one* urge and quite possibly just failed to detach from *one* destructive thought. You don't have to start over at Day 1! You can learn from the experience and keep moving forward, dismissing the very next urge, without the overwhelming feeling of having to start recovery all over again.

Keeping track of the days you haven't binged causes you to focus attention on the habit, when you'd otherwise be able to get on with your life and direct your attention elsewhere. It can cause you to wake up in the morning and go to bed at night thinking about binge eating; it can lead you to view your calendar in terms of when you last binged instead of when you have other events going on in your life. Your lower brain may also send messages like, *It's been twelve days, you deserve a binge* or *You've been binge-free for two weeks—just binge one more time and you can easily get back to two weeks again.*

How has counting binge-free days affected you in the past? Does your lower brain use that number against you (by thinking, for example, *It's been ten days, you deserve a binge*)?

_____

_____

_____

_____

_____

_____

How can you remind yourself to focus only on the current urge? Even if you decide to continue counting, how can you resist putting too much emphasis on that number so you can avoid the "starting over" mentality?

_____

_____

_____

_____

_____

_____

_____

_____

A Slip Is Just a Failure to Detach from One Urge

I binged one time two weeks after I resolved to quit and another time about two months after that. If I would have taken those two binges as evidence that I'd failed and that I had to start all over again, it's unlikely this approach would have worked for me. If you binge, simply try to figure out which thought you didn't separate from or which feeling you didn't recognize as neurological junk, and move forward with increased awareness of those faulty messages. Use the space below to keep track of any thoughts or feelings that have led you to act on urges and practice detaching from them.

Neurological junk that you did not detach from and will not react to in the future:

_____

_____

_____

_____

_____

_____

_____

_____

_____

As you continue to utilize the Five Components of Dismissing the Urges to Binge and the above tips for maintaining your progress, some challenges may arise. From talking to women and men who read *Brain over Binge*, I've noted that these challenges seem to fall in one of three categories: (1) Not Wanting to Dismiss Urges; (2) Fearing Quitting; or (3) Too-Powerful Urges. The next three chapters will address these challenges.

[16]

Challenge 1:
Not Wanting to Dismiss Urges

IT'S BEEN ESTABLISHED THAT a desire to stop binge eating is absolutely necessary for success. If you continue to binge after learning and trying to apply the Five Components, it can be easy to think that maybe you don't *want* recovery after all. This chapter will offer additional guidance if you are doubting your desire to quit.

FALSE, PRIMAL WANTING

You've learned that there is a difference between feeling like you want something—temporarily—because of the lower brain's reward system, and truly wanting it with your higher brain. Temporary feelings of desire for things that aren't good for our bodies, our pocketbook, our marriage, our kids, and our spirit occur every day. Mostly, we say "no" to this form of primal wanting; but sometimes we say "yes" and have to deal with whatever consequences ensue. We are human, and we aren't always going to make perfectly rational choices when faced with desire.

But when we have the same desire for the same detrimental action over and over again and that action is causing us pain, as is the case with binge eating, we need to learn to defer to our higher brain. We need to realize that those habitual feelings of desire aren't representative of our true wants and needs—they're just a lower brain glitch. The primal wanting could also be called "false wanting," because your lower brain tricks you into believing that you want something that you really don't. To begin seeing this, it's important to consider *when* you feel that you *want* to binge. Is it in the moments leading up to a binge, or is it afterward and between binges when you are feeling connected to your true self?

When do you feel like you truly want to binge?

_____

_____

_____

_____

_____

_____

_____

Keep track of any insights that help you separate false, primal wanting from your true desires:

_____

_____

_____

_____

_____

_____

_____

Most of the time, you'll only think you want to binge beforehand; and after a binge, you'll realize that "you," in fact, didn't truly want to binge at all. However, binge urges aren't always neatly compartmentalized into one specific time period. You don't have to be in the midst of a full-blown, powerful urge to experience false wanting. You might be going about your daily life with full conviction of your desire to recover, and then a thought about binge eating pops up that elicits false wanting. Remember that when we're talking about "urges to binge," it means any thoughts or feelings that encourage the behavior, not just the all-consuming cravings.

For me, the excitement and amazement I felt at finally being able to control my behavior seemed to quickly override any of those nagging tugs of false wanting. I tried to experience thoughts and feelings of "not wanting to quit" as just part of the habit as well. I knew I wasn't depriving myself by not giving in to my false, primal wanting; I was only depriving my lower brain of a life-draining habit. I knew I was getting stronger with each conquered urge, and once I got some traction, my true desire to put binge eating behind me forever eclipsed any illusions of wanting to binge.

CONVINCING URGES

The lower brain can sometimes be deceptive in convincing you that you truly want to binge. In my case, the most intriguing reason my lower brain gave me was that it didn't matter what part of my brain generated the urges—I wanted to follow that part nonetheless. It only made sense that my lower brain would try to convince me that I really did like and want to binge. My lower brain sensed I was threatening my own survival, because I'd conditioned it to react as if binge eating were truly necessary. When this happens, your job is only to experience any of that false wanting, longing, and desire with detachment and without acting on your thoughts/feelings. Those feelings will pass, and your true desire to recover will resurface.

To recognize your thoughts of false wanting so you can detach from them, it's helpful to identify them.

What thoughts make you feel you want to binge?

_____

_____

_____

_____

_____

_____

WHEN YOU REALLY *DO* WANT TO BINGE

If the desire for recovery doesn't resurface between binges, and if you identify with the urges all of the time, and if you don't regret your binges, then you do actually *want* to keep binge eating. I think this concept is best illustrated by the example of smokers. Some smokers have no or very little guilt about what they do, and they don't give much thought to the health risks. They simply enjoy their cigarettes, without any plans to stop enjoying them. Other smokers resolve to quit daily or at least from time to time, because they know at some level that what they are doing isn't what they truly want.

Habit is at work in both types of smokers, producing automatic urges to smoke, but the smoker who doesn't want to quit identifies with his or her urges so much that smoking feels like his or her true desire—not just in the moments of smoking urges, but always. This person doesn't have the motivation to start viewing the urges any other way. If the smoker who does not want to quit were given all the tools needed to quit, it wouldn't do any good because there would be no desire to use those tools. But the second type of smoker would welcome and benefit greatly from those tools.

If you are the type of binge eater like the first smoker in this example, this book is unlikely to help you, which was cautioned from the outset. However, there is also a third type of smoker and a third type of binge eater: a person who doesn't feel he or she *desires* to quit, but still feels the *need* to do so out of a sense of obligation—maybe to be a better mother, father, wife, husband, daughter, friend. Or perhaps that sense of obligation comes from spiritual convictions, financial constraints, or health concerns. This is still a form of desire for recovery, although it might be better described as a *need* to recover or a feeling that one *should* recover. If this is the case for you, there are three options.

1. Take a leap and quit. It takes courage and strength—and it can initially feel like a loss—but you will soon realize that you are better off without the habit. Accept that you want to binge, but tell yourself that it's no longer an option. Feel sorry for yourself for a while, if you need to; it's human nature to have desires. But those desires can't always be realized, and they shouldn't always be realized. It's noble and brave to put your desires aside for the sake of someone else or for something greater than yourself.

Even if giving up binge eating feels like a sacrifice at first, once some time passes without binge eating, the true desire to recover can suddenly appear. You'll realize how much time and money you wasted by being caught up in binge eating, and as the urges fade, you'll realize that the pleasure you got from it was never worth it anyway. It's like walking away from an abusive relationship even though you truly love the person. It hurts; but you soon realize that you are better off without that source of pain in your life.

2. Cultivate the desire to quit within yourself. Finding things you enjoy that are incompatible with binge eating can help you find reasons for giving it up. Volunteering to help those less fortunate than you can help you see a bigger picture; reflecting on your life and creating goals for the future can give you a desire to let go of your problem. You can also seek counseling, coaching, or therapy to support you in finding reasons to recover.

Keep track of ideas for cultivating your desire to quit within yourself:

_____

_____

_____

_____

_____

_____

_____

3. Realize you have free choice. If you decide to continue to binge because you want to, then *own* your choice. I would never recommend that someone continue to binge, but I do not agree with labeling people "disordered" or "diseased" when they actually have no desire to quit and are exercising free choice. The book that helped me quit binge eating, *Rational Recovery*, taught me that "self-intoxication is a basic freedom, an individual liberty."[106] *Rational Recovery* told me what I needed to hear at the time—namely, that if I wanted to keep doing it, I could, but I could no longer hide behind a "disease" label or the idea that I needed to sort out a lot of other problems before I could quit.

There were countless eating disorder resources that told me otherwise—that told me it wasn't a choice, that I was justified to continue binge eating because it was serving a purpose in my life and fulfilling my unmet emotional needs. When I believed those things, it did make me feel a little better about myself for continuing to binge because I felt less culpable, but what did that get me? It was better to take a one-time ego hit and realize that I was responsible, then accept accountability for quitting.

BELIEVING THAT BINGE EATING IS ALL YOU HAVE

There are some who feel that binge eating is all they have to hang on to; they feel binge eating is the sole relief from crippling sadness or trauma. Of course we all have our own burdens to carry, but some people are convinced that without binge eating, they would fall apart. It's certainly true that a side effect (secondary benefit) of binge eating and other addictions and habits is temporary distraction from pain. In some cases of severe trauma or emotional distress, this secondary benefit can seem worth it. Even though binge eating doesn't make pain go away, the temporary distraction is what some people feel they absolutely need.

However, most people who have severe emotional pain, trauma, or a history of abuse don't begin trying to get help for binge eating until they realize, at least at some level, that it's actually making the pain worse. By that time, binge eating has become a well-worn habit, one that no longer has much to do with whatever they've been through. In fact, clinging to the idea that binge eating is all you have will tighten the grip binge eating has on you and cement the neural pathways even more. In the moment of an urge, yes, it might be true that binge eating is the only thing that will help you feel better, but consider that this is only because it will temporarily quiet the urges—not because it actually helps you with your sadness, even if you feel like, at one time, it did.

This doesn't mean that you have to just suck it up and quit regardless of what's happened to you. If you've been through trauma or experienced great loss, be kind to yourself above all. But also think about what self-kindness truly means. When you picture yourself in ten years, do you see yourself coming through whatever pain you've endured as a stronger person? Or are you still choosing to binge as a means of distracting yourself? Reaching out to others for help, trying to find joy in small things, searching for spiritual comfort in whatever form that may take, allowing growth to happen after pain—these are all examples of true expressions of self-kindness.

Healthier forms of distraction can be beneficial as well. Trying to zone out and not think about the pain in your life is completely understandable, and it can certainly have a place, provided that your zoning out is not damaging your life even more. Watching a favorite movie, taking a long walk or drive, reading a good book—activities like these aren't going to take away the urges to binge, but they can fulfill your need to escape your pain temporarily.

If you are someone who truly believes that you are choosing to binge because it's all you have, then no one can take that away from you. Sometimes just knowing that you can choose it if you want to makes it suddenly seem less desirable. If the appeal doesn't fade and you still feel you absolutely "need" the distraction of binge eating, then I would advise you to seek professional support until you feel the desire to move beyond your habit.

When Recovery Isn't All You Thought It Would Be

After you stop binge eating, you will certainly be excited and full of hope for the future. You will have a chance at a real life; you'll have your freedom. But most people feel the weight of reality as well, especially during the first few weeks and months after becoming binge-free. All that you lost to binge eating can really sink in, and the months following recovery can be filled with regrets about time wasted or relationships lost. Without being fixated on food, problems previously ignored might come to the surface. None of this means that you in fact binged for a deep reason or that you truly wanted to binge to distract yourself from these problems. You've simply been preoccupied for a while, and it can take some time getting used to focusing on matters other than food and weight.

Another reason for negative feelings after binge eating stops, which was addressed in Component 5, is that life without binge eating might not be everything you'd hoped for. If you've been trying to recover for a long time, you may have had a vision of your recovered self—losing weight quickly, eating effortlessly and naturally, enjoying satisfying relationships, and feeling relatively at peace. Some people are surprised when they find their life still difficult, their binge weight not coming off as fast as they'd like, or their eating habits not falling into place right away.

The illusion that life will be perfect, including your weight, after you stop binge eating is false. The same problems that are there before will still be there. You just have more brain space to deal with those issues now.

~Stacey Cohen,
Integrative Nutritionist

Don't become discouraged by whatever you may face after you stop binge eating; just put one foot in front of the other and get through the early days in the best way you can. You don't have to know where you are going right now; you only have to keep moving away from binge eating because you know it was getting you nowhere. It's okay to feel some regret, but as often as possible, keep your mind on the present and what you need to do to solidify your new neural pathways. Don't be swayed by the neurological junk that says, *Life is too hard, so I want to go back to the habit.*

[17]

Challenge 2:
Fearing Quitting

EVEN IF YOU FEEL like you truly *want* to dismiss urges, you may feel *scared* of recovery. You may have anxiety about what you or your life will be like without the eating disorder. The most important thing to remember is that fear is just a feeling and doesn't have to affect how you act.

RECOVERY IS NOT AS SCARY AS YOU THINK

Before you assume that your fear is real and warranted, consider for a minute that it's an illusion and that there is actually nothing to be afraid of. After you begin dismissing urges, the days will simply come and go, as they always have, but without binge eating being a part of those days. This is not a thing to fear. We can work up things in our minds to be scarier than they are, and whereas some life events actually *do* turn out to be scary, quitting a harmful habit isn't one of those— even though anticipating quitting one can sometimes feel that way.

Fearful thoughts about recovery encourage binge eating; therefore, it follows that fearful thoughts about quitting qualify as neurological junk as well. You don't need to "fight the fear," analyze it, or try to control it; instead, you can begin viewing fear as just another aspect of your habit. To do this, it can help to write down some of your frightening thoughts so you can begin to detach from them.

What fearful thoughts can you treat as neurological junk?

_____

_____

_____

_____

_____

_____

_____

These thoughts don't reflect reality, because in reality, continuing to binge—and a potential lifetime of addiction to the habit—is much more frightening than any temporary apprehension about quitting. You know how much binge eating has taken from you; you know the dangerous health effects you may face; and you know there isn't much hope for the future if you keep it up.

If you think about your life and what you want it to be, what do you fear more: quitting binge eating or continuing to binge? Why?

_____

_____

_____

_____

_____

_____

_____

_____

The lower brain sends messages telling you that life without binge eating will be a scary thing, but "you" know that a life spent binge eating is a much greater thing to fear.

DECONDITIONING THE FEAR

No matter how much you "know" fear is an illusion, it sometimes doesn't feel that way. People with phobias may understand rationally that there is nothing to be afraid of, but their bodies react as if there is. So you may indeed have to deal with some automatic feelings of anxiety welling up as you move forward with dismissing urges. Avoiding the change only perpetuates the fear and prolongs the problem. As you dismiss urge after urge, the fear will become less and subside.

I'm going to share a personal story of overcoming a specific anxiety, which is not food-related but which has implications for those who have palatable fear when starting recovery. It involves a fear of driving: For about five years, I was extremely afraid of driving on expressways. I rarely drove on expressways, and by "rarely," I mean maybe twice a year. I had no problem riding with someone else driving, but every time I tried to drive myself, I became extremely anxious. I found it easier on my nerves to just stick to the surface streets. During those five years, I lived in Phoenix, Arizona, which is probably the best city for someone afraid of expressways because you can get anywhere you want to go via surface streets, provided you are willing to spend the extra travel time.

Because avoiding expressways never prevented me from going anywhere I wanted to go, I didn't have much motivation to overcome the fear. Then, in 2011, we moved to another city, where it wasn't at all practical or possible to always avoid the expressways. In addition, our move brought us within a six-hour interstate drive to close family, and I wanted to be able to make that drive whenever possible. It was time to change.

I changed using basically the same concepts I used to overcome my binge eating. I always knew somewhere inside me that my fear of expressways was irrational—even though there is obviously real danger in driving—but somehow my fear still felt like my own. I felt that fear was ego-syntonic, meaning in line with my true self. However, after thinking this way for years, and after becoming pretty complacent about it while living in Phoenix, I realized that just like my bulimia, this too had become habit. There was some initial fear in my past that, for one reason or another, caused me to avoid the expressway the first time ... and the second ... and the third, until the habit was gradually brought to life. Each time I avoided an expressway, I cemented the pattern such that taking expressways began to seem foreign.

It was only when we moved across the country that I snapped out of my complacency and felt a desire to change. It was then that I realized that what had started out as an ego-syntonic desire to be safer had become ego-dystonic, based on my current goals. All the things I told myself to avoid taking expressways were well-ingrained thoughts that had become automatic, just like my urges to binge. Those thoughts discouraging me from expressways certainly weren't going to stop just because I now *wanted* to drive on them. Just like with binge eating, I decided to get those thoughts to go away with *action*.

I didn't bother trying to go back and figure out where the fear stemmed from or what else I could change in my life to help make that fear go away. I didn't read driving statistics to try to convince myself I would be just as safe on the expressways as on the surface streets. I simply began driving on the interstate day after day and hoped those automatic fears would subside like the urges to binge had.

The way I overcame binge eating is certainly not the solution to every problem; but brain plasticity is powerful, and I knew if I stopped giving my fear value and attention, it could go away.

The first few times I entered the on-ramp of an expressway, I felt rather terrified. But I knew that despite the feelings of fear welling up in me, I could control my motor movements—I could check my mirrors and merge left even if my hands were trembling a little. Now, I realize that some people with fears and phobias actually experience a panic reaction that they physically cannot control and may actually lose control of their motor movements. I am not advocating for those people to simply face their fears head-on. But my fear was more of an every-day variety—not a panic disorder—and so I reminded myself that my reactions were harmless and focused on the motor movements I needed to perform to drive the car.

To my surprise, the fear subsided very quickly. Within a couple weeks, I was using the less-busy expressways in our city with ease and with markedly weaker fear reactions. I began challenging myself by driving longer distances, on busier stretches of interstate, and even straight over the Appalachian Mountains (which was not technically expressway driving, but still something I never would have done just months prior). Yes, there was anxiety present in these situations; but taking the interstate began to feel normal again with a few months.

Now, in 2016, I can't imagine why I ever felt the way I did about driving. I'm still nervous every now and then, but usually only when I'm passing wobbly eighteen-wheelers or driving in thunderstorms. I stopped giving my fears any significance and stopped letting them direct my actions, and so they left me alone. The same can happen with your fear of quitting binge eating; it will subside right along with your urges to binge.

Your Fear Is Not Unique

If you asked anyone who has ever recovered from bulimia or BED about their fear, they would tell you they had to face it—whether it was fear of what their life would be like afterward, fear of failure, fear of the unknown, fear of giving up the pleasure, fear of weight loss/gain, and so on. It's not a unique problem that prevents recovery, just like it doesn't have to prevent accomplishment in other areas of your life. Fear simply comes up when a big change is on the horizon.

In a blog post on her website, Amy Johnson shares a dialogue with one of her clients who feared starting a small business; it contains powerful and applicable advice for those who need a push to move forward in spite of their fear:

You get to choose which thoughts you focus on and buy into and replay over and over. When a particular thought feels true to us, we embellish it. We fondle it and expand on it and make it seem very real and powerful. It's not. That's all that's going on here. The fear you feel is the consequence of elaborating on and believing those thoughts.

You are at a point right now that every single human being who has ever done anything in life has visited. You can listen to the fears and choose to do what you want to do anyway, or you can listen to the fears and take them very seriously.

Most people take the second option. They're the same people who wake up at age seventy and wonder why they didn't take more chances in life. ...

You say: I am so scared.

I know, sweetie. That's part of it, too. But you can do scared—you've handled much worse. You are also scared to not start the business, so you are "doing" scared either way, right?

Scared is how you feel but it has zero to do with how to choose to act.

If you think about your life, you'll find that you've overcome fear before—you've acted in a way that took you out of your comfort zone and succeeded. It can help to reflect on that and use what you've learned from prior experiences to your advantage now.

Have you ever been scared of doing something but did it anyway? What did you learn from that experience that could help you move past your fear of recovery?

_____

_____

_____

_____

_____

_____

_____

[18]

Challenge 3: Too-Powerful Urges

YOU ALREADY KNOW THAT not acting on urges can sometimes bring a measure of discomfort, and there may be times when you indeed feel inferior to the urges. This chapter contains information and strategies beyond the Five Components of Dismissing the Urges to Binge to help you overcome urges when they feel very powerful. If the urges are manageable or even easy to dismiss most of the time, but powerful every now and then, then the best course of action during powerful urges is to focus only on what you can control: your motor movements.

I touched on this strategy briefly in the last chapter when sharing the story of my fear of driving. When my fear got strong and I didn't quite feel separate from my internal reactions, I simply focused on the motor movements I needed to perform to drive the car. Likewise, when you lose the ability to experience your binge urges with detachment, try to keep your attention on your extremities and remind yourself that your legs, arms, hands cannot move without your voluntary decision to move them. Then purposely move them in a direction away from food—and focus on another activity or do nothing at all.

Focusing on motor movements is a great tool to help you get through some urges, but it will become tiring if your urges seem to *always* feel powerful and the intensity doesn't decrease over time. Next, you'll learn what to do if your urges do not start to become more manageable, which requires learning why your urges might feel too overwhelming too often. There are three main reasons, discussed below along with solutions.

THREE REASONS WHY URGES FEEL TOO POWERFUL

Reason 1: You Are Not Eating Enough

You already know that urges that arise because of food deprivation are much harder to detach from than urges that arise due to habit and that dieting compromises the higher brain. Ensuring that you are consuming enough food will allow for a properly functioning prefrontal cortex, capable of dismissing urges. Otherwise, you will remain in survival mode, and the urges will overpower you. If you have problems with eating normally or concerns about giving up restrictive dieting, there will be more help for you in the next section, Recovery Goal 2.

Do you think restrictive eating might be a reason you aren't able to dismiss urges? If so, how can you add nourishment to your meals and snacks?

_____

_____

_____

_____

_____

_____

Reason 2: You Falsely Believe That the Urges Are Too Powerful

The thoughts that tell you that your urges are too powerful to overcome are just more neurological junk. Why give these specific thoughts any more credibility than other thoughts that encourage binge eating? Your lower brain will use thoughts that get you to act, and if this one has worked in the past, it will keep coming up. Believing this thought will guarantee that the urges remain strong; to counter this, start believing that the strong feelings and tempting thoughts are nothing you can't handle.

What do you feel that makes urges seem too powerful? What thoughts make you believe that you aren't capable of dismissing the urges?

_____

_____

_____

_____

_____

_____

If you can stop giving these thoughts and feelings value and attention, your urges will automatically lose their power over you.

Reason 3: You Need More Time and Space

Sometimes when people think their urges are too powerful, the actual problem is that they are going from urge to action so quickly that they don't realize they are in fact capable of making a different choice. It might feel like the urge is so persuasive that you can't control your actions, but with a little extra time and space, you might find your own power. To correct this, you need

You can't always be in the perfect situation or the perfect physiological place in your body all the time, but when the urge comes up, you need to have the time and the space to notice.
~Cookie Rosenblum

to work on remaining present when the urges come—staying in the gear of the higher brain and avoiding switching into unconscious action. There are two ways you can do this: (1) temporarily altering your environment and (2) waiting to binge.

1. Temporarily Alter Your Environment: Although you do have control in any situation, there is nothing wrong with trying to give yourself an edge if you are struggling. Engineering your environment to purposefully add time and space between your urges and the action of binge eating is one way to help yourself avoid slipping into unconscious action. This can mean keeping your favorite binge foods out of the house for a short time, changing your schedule or eating locations, or eating with others. If you find that you aren't even attempting to apply what you've learned, then staying away from places where it would be easy to be swept away by an urge makes sense.

Altering your environment doesn't mean you view yourself as powerless; in fact, it's quite the opposite—you are giving yourself the opportunity to learn to utilize your own power. Soon, you'll be able to draw upon that power in an instant. Even once you are confidently binge-free, you may still choose to keep some foods out of the house—not for fear of bingeing on them, but just because you tend to choose those foods over healthy choices too often. Even normal eaters sometimes keep tempting food out of the house.

This extends beyond food—some people find it best to avoid things that are too enticing for them, for the sake of their health, pocketbook, or relationships. I, for one, don't usually buy paper towels because I use too many of them when they are on hand. With four young kids, there are messes upon messes, and it is so much easier to grab a paper towel, wipe the mess, and toss it rather than deal with the trouble of rags. However, if I don't buy the paper towels, I create a situation where I have to carve out the time to wash rags and keep some ready for use at all times (or at least be creative about what I can use to clean up a mess).

Altering your environment is not about placing restrictions on yourself or creating rigid rules, it's about helping yourself have a chance of making good choices. Think of helping a child quit a habit like sucking a pacifier. Would you tell the child that he had to quit, but then still keep the pacifiers next to his bed? Of course, this example is a little different because we all *have* to eat, but if you feel overwhelmed by the urges, consider removing some of the temptation, for now.

Are there specific situations where you don't feel you have time and space to detach from binge urges?

_____

_____

_____

_____

_____

_____

_____

How might you want to alter your environment until you gain more confidence in dismissing binge urges?

_____

_____

_____

_____

_____

_____

_____

What changes can you make that will allow you the time and space to use what you've learned about dismissing urges?

_____

_____

_____

_____

_____

_____

_____

_____

2. Wait to Binge: Along the same lines as altering your environment, you can purposefully give yourself time between urge and action by using a clock. Richard Kerr, founder of bulimiahelp.org and author of *The Bulimia Help Method*, contributed a guest post to my blog in which he talked about this waiting strategy. Richard suggests that, after acknowledging and accepting the presence of a binge urge, you should decide to resist the binge urge for just ten minutes at a time. This is because, he says, "when you tell yourself that you have to make it through the rest of the night (or the rest of your life) without bingeing, the emotional burden of that commitment can become overwhelming."

You are much more likely to succeed with a ten-minute interval, which can give you a great boost of confidence. Tell yourself that if you still want to binge after ten minutes have passed, then that's okay; but try to wait the full ten minutes before making any decision as to whether or not you will binge. During the ten minutes, Richard recommends not just staring at the clock, but instead turning your attention elsewhere. Helpful things to do include physical movements (as simple as going for a walk), anything that takes you away from possible binge foods, and immersing yourself in a project or hobby. In other words, choose an alternative action to perform during those ten minutes. Doing something else won't make the urge go away, of course, but it is hard to focus on two things at the same time, so it should at least lessen the intensity of the urge.

After the ten minutes are up, Richard says to congratulate yourself, because even small steps like this can go a long way toward weakening the urges; but he suggests also challenging yourself to accept the harmless urge sensations and feelings for another ten minutes. You can continue to do this until the urge passes, and it will pass, whether that takes five minutes, twenty minutes, or longer. After each ten-minute increment, give yourself permission to binge if you feel it's too difficult, but always remember that it is your choice to do so and that you are in control. You can repeat this process as many times as the urges arise. As you practice this technique, you may notice the length of time you are able to avoid acting on a binge urge increasing, until the urges fade and disappear altogether.

List some activities you could perform during the ten-minute "wait to binge" intervals:

_____

_____

_____

_____

_____

_____

_____

_____

Keep track of anything helpful you learn or experience while using the "wait to binge" approach:

_____

_____

_____

_____

_____

_____

_____

_____

[19]

Supplementary Ideas for Dismissing Urges

Environmental factors are a big issue for me. For example, when I had to move back with my parents, I relapsed. I have now gained better control by just taking it one day at a time in difficult situations ... and my faith always strengthens me.

~Meg

IT'S WORTH ANOTHER REMINDER that if you are already dismissing urges, you do not need to read further into this section. More information is not always better, but if you feel you need some extra ideas to reflect upon or try, those that follow may help spark success upon which you can then build.

KNOW THE TRIGGERS AND PREPARE FOR THEM

Trigger is a common eating disorder term. In traditional therapy, a binge trigger is something that causes binge eating, such as a certain thought, feeling, or situation. For example, if you typically binge when bored, then boredom is a binge trigger for you. In *Brain over Binge*, I explained how triggers cannot actually cause binge eating, because only urges to binge cause binge eating (to get even more specific, only choosing to act on an urge to binge causes binge eating). This does not mean triggers have no significance.

You'll likely find that urges to binge do in fact arise more often in certain situations or at certain times of the day; this is due to conditioning. Knowing what commonly triggers your binge urges can be helpful because if you know when your urges are more likely to arise, you can become more aware during those times. As mentioned in the previous chapter, you can alter your environment temporarily if you feel it's necessary, and this applies when considering triggers as well.

If you feel like you need to prevent yourself from getting, let's say, too bored, until you become more confident in resisting urges, that doesn't mean you are weak or not using the Five Components correctly. It means you are using what uniquely helps *you* dismiss urges. Try not to avoid triggers for too long, however; you ultimately *do* want to face your trigger situations, because that's how you'll produce the brain changes you want. When you experience a trigger, have an urge, and don't binge, your brain learns to disassociate the trigger from the binge, and it will gradually stop sending the urge in response to that trigger. If you never experience the urges because you somehow avoid all of your triggers, the habit won't be fully deconditioned in those situations. In other words:

To properly utilize neuroplasticity to erase your habit,
*you have to **experience the urges** and **not act on them.***

For example, let's say you are someone who frequently binges in response to eating sugar. If you stop eating sugar, many of your urges may go away, but the moment you decide to have some sugar, an urge could arise. This is because you've never broken the trigger-urge-binge connection, and the lower brain is still running on the old program you've taught it—that a binge follows eating sugar. You don't have to break all of those old trigger-urge-binge connections right away, but you don't want to live a life where you are constantly having to avoid or fear your triggers.

To prepare for facing the urges in trigger situations, you can mentally practice how to handle situations in which you usually binge. Although you can't truly create a binge urge, you can try thinking about a situation where you typically binge—when you are not in that situation—and then tell yourself all of the faulty reasons that you should binge in that situation. Practice detaching from those thoughts, letting them flow through you without giving them any power. This can help you feel more prepared and much less vulnerable in situations that typically trigger urges.

Write down any triggers for binge urges that you have noticed:

Are there any triggers that you would feel more comfortable avoiding for now? How do you envision incorporating those triggers in the future so that you can rewire your brain?

What trigger situations do you want to prepare for mentally? Keep track of anything that helps you recognize neurological junk in trigger situations:

BE AWARE OF THE EFFECT OF ALCOHOL

Certain substances, specifically alcohol, contribute to weaker higher brain (prefrontal cortex) functioning, which is obviously detrimental in moments of temptation. Some people wonder if they should even consume alcohol at all while trying to dismiss urges because they experience a palpable reduction in self-control when they drink, but other people have no issue with it.

I personally did not change my alcohol consumption when I first quit binge eating. I had an occasional drink—a beer or glass of wine, sometimes two—a couple times a month. Since it took only a few months for my binge urges to decrease significantly, there were maybe about six times when I was able to experience the effects of alcohol on my binge urges and my ability to dismiss them. Looking back, I do not specifically remember any marked increase in my binge urges under the influence of alcohol or having more difficulty avoiding acting on those urges. This is not to say that I think drinking alcohol is risk-free when it comes to recovery from binge eating.

When I was in college, prior to quitting binge eating, drinking was indeed one of my binge triggers. I remember that feeling of disinhibition—temporarily not caring about recovery while under the influence of alcohol and not bothering to fight the binge urges. Binge eating under the influence of alcohol took on more of a hazy quality, rather than a voracious one, and it always ended with less regret—until morning, when I had to contend with the effects of both the food and the alcohol.

After I stopped binge eating, I was able to avoid that "I don't care" mind-set that often gets drunk people to do things they regret. This could be simply because I didn't drink very much at the time I quit binge eating. In college, I would sometimes have more than a couple of drinks, and it's very possible that doing that while trying to recover might have ended in binge eating. There is no way to know, but I'd like to think that binge eating was so "off-limits" in my mind that I still would have been able to resist.

For those who drink a little more often and in greater quantities than I did when I quit binge eating, here is some information to help you decide whether it's wise to continue doing that while also trying to dismiss binge urges:

- With each drink, the prefrontal cortex is impaired a little more, making you feel less in control of your voluntary muscle movements and reducing rational thought.
- Alcohol has the opposite effect on the lower brain; instead of impairing it, drinking causes a release in dopamine, which arouses the pleasure/reward circuitry. For some, this could mean an increase in urges to binge, but not necessarily—the feeling could simply be pleasurable in its own right, without triggering a desire for a binge.

Given these effects, alcohol might best be avoided. However, even with altered consciousness, it is still possible to say no to binge eating. Everyone has lines they don't cross even when they have been drinking (like driving a car or dancing on the bar). I'm sure you can think of some outrageous behavior that you can trust yourself not to do even when you've had too much to drink. If you choose to continue to drink while recovering from bulimia or BED, then binge eating has to become one of those outrageous things that you would never do, regardless of your blood alcohol level.

If you find that you are binge eating nearly every time you drink, then it would be wise to refrain from alcohol altogether until you are more confident, then gradually add it back into your life (if you want), starting with very small amounts. As a word of caution, I am talking here to people who don't have a problem with moderate drinking; this advice is not for people who feel they can't control their alcohol intake. Although some of the ideas in this book can certainly apply to excessive alcohol consumption as well, it is beyond the scope of this book.

MEDITATION

Meditation boosts the ability to use detachment from all forms of unproductive desires, primarily because—opposite of alcohol—it boosts prefrontal cortex functioning.[107] Meditation is like strength training for the prefrontal cortex. There are many ways to meditate, and you can find something that works for you. (I've included a short description of a useful meditation technique at the end of this section.)

The use of meditation in eating disorder recovery isn't new. When I was in therapy fifteen years ago, my therapists encouraged me to meditate, but the way they framed it, meditation was supposed to help me relax and make me feel better, which would then supposedly lead to less binge eating. Because of this expectation, meditation often left me worse off than when I started, because I felt like a failure at meditating. As soon as I would begin to meditate, my thoughts would race and I couldn't focus on relaxing for more than a few seconds, it seemed. This would get me upset with myself, and I would worry that my lack of relaxation would cause binge eating.

So here, I'm not recommending meditation as a form of relaxation—although it can certainly serve that purpose as well; rather, what I am suggesting is that you meditate in order to gain greater access to your self-control functions and the ability to be aware of your thoughts without turning attention to them. Instead of trying to meditate with the goal of feeling better, the goal for you will be to notice when your mind wanders and bring it back to a focal point. The breath is an easy focal point, but you can also focus on something physical, like the feeling of your feet or hands, or you can focus on a certain word or phrase that you repeat over and over.

When you notice your mind wandering or a lot of mental chatter in your head, just gently bring your attention back to the sensation of breathing (or whatever focal point you have chosen). This act of drawing the mind back from distraction and habitual thought activates the prefrontal cortex/higher brain. Something I wish I would have known is that you aren't meditating "wrong" if your mind keeps wandering. When unwanted thoughts pop up, that's your opportunity to put your higher brain to use and therefore change your brain. You may have to refocus 100 times during a short meditation when you first start, but if you keep practicing, you will get better—both at meditating and at gaining an awareness of your thoughts that will then carry over through the day.

This can translate into stronger neural connections in the areas of the brain responsible for self-control and self-awareness[108] and a heightened ability to dismiss binge urges. Meditation actually increases blood flow to the prefrontal cortex, and it has also been shown to be one of the most powerful ways to increase willpower. Research indicates that self-control and ability to focus improve after just three hours (not all at one time) of meditation and that visible brain changes can be observed after eleven hours.[109] Just five minutes once or twice a day will add up quickly, and you may start experiencing positive benefits and increased awareness right away.

If you need a little guidance getting started, try this simple meditation from Kelly McGonigal's book *The Willpower Instinct: How Self-Control Works, Why It Matters, and What You Can Do to Get More of It.*[110]

1. *Sit still and stay put.* Sit in a chair with your feet flat on the ground, or sit cross-legged on a cushion. Sit up straight and rest your hands in your lap. It's important not to fidget when you meditate—that's the physical foundation of self-control. If you notice the instinct to scratch an itch, adjust your arms, or cross and uncross your legs, see if you can feel the urge but not follow it. This simple act of staying still is part of what makes meditation willpower training effective. You're learning not to automatically follow every single impulse that your brain and body produce.

2. *Turn your attention to the breath.* Close your eyes or, if you are worried about falling asleep, focus your gaze at a single spot (like a blank wall, not the Home Shopping Network). Begin to notice your breathing. Silently say in your mind "inhale" as you breathe in and "exhale" as you breathe out. When you notice your mind wandering (and it will), just bring it back to the breath. This practice of coming back to the breath, again and again, kicks the prefrontal cortex into high gear and quiets the stress and craving centers of your brain.

3. *Notice how it feels to breathe, and notice how the mind wanders.* After a few minutes, drop the labels "inhale/exhale." Try focusing on just the feeling of breathing. You might notice the sensations of the breath flowing in and out of your nose and mouth. You might sense the belly or chest expanding

as you breathe in, and deflating as you breathe out. Your mind might wander a bit more without the labeling. Just as before, when you notice yourself thinking about something else, bring your attention back to the breath. If you need help refocusing, bring yourself back to the breath by saying "inhale" and "exhale" for a few seconds. This part of the practice trains self-awareness along with self-control.

How can you build short spans of meditation (as little as five minutes) into your daily life?

_____

_____

_____

_____

_____

List any types of meditation you want to incorporate:

_____

_____

_____

_____

Keep track of the benefits you notice as a result of meditation, which can help you stay motivated to continue practicing:

_____

_____

_____

_____

_____

_____

_____

THERAPY'S USEFUL CONCEPTS FOR DISMISSING URGES, FRAMED IN A NEW WAY

Some people can't or don't want to let go of traditional therapy concepts, but if those concepts aren't working in their current form, it's possible that simply viewing some of them in a new way could make them effective. Just like meditation didn't work for me the way therapy suggested that I use it, there are other concepts from traditional therapy that, if given a different context or seen in a new light, could help you dismiss binge urges.

When therapy does help reduce or resolve binge eating, I believe a large part of that is because it can indirectly make the higher brain more capable of resisting urges. Solving other problems and feeling better in general can have a physiological impact on self-control, because the prefrontal cortex, as we've learned, functions better without too much stress. Therefore, less stress—emotional stress included—can result in less default, habitual, survival-oriented reactions. Furthermore, the lower brain is more likely to seek reward during times of stress. So, all around, reducing stress can put many people in a better state to use the Five Components of Dismissing the Urges to Binge.

Traditional therapy does not frame things that way, however, so most people keep working on their inner emotional problems, hoping that it will make the urges go away, which it doesn't. Even if the urges become less frequent because of less stress (although there is no guarantee of this), if you don't have the tools to resist them, you'll still feel compelled to act on them when they do inevitably come up, and the habit will persist. I'm suggesting using therapy concepts to improve your emotional and mental state so that you will be a in a better position to dismiss urges, not because working on your issues takes all urges away.

This is best illustrated by looking at anxiety and depression. If therapy assumes you binge due to anxiety, you are therefore led to learn to reduce anxiety and you might end up bingeing less. It's not that you took away your emotional "need" to binge; it's that reducing anxiety can keep the brain out of that fight-or-flight state that is not useful for dismissing binge urges. A similar brain mechanism is at work when you aim to reduce depression. Depression can make you feel like you can't or don't want to accomplish anything, especially self-control tasks like avoiding a problematic behavior. However, if depression is lifted even a little, you will have greater access to your rational, higher self, and your desire to quit may improve. It's not that when you are happier, you no longer want or need to binge to "cope"; it's that reducing depression makes you more capable and more motivated to dismiss the urges.

All of that being said, I don't think striving to reduce anxiety, depression, or other stressful emotional problems should be a frontline defense against urges (which is why this section comes at the end of the discussion of Recovery Goal 1). It is too inefficient an approach because everyone has numerous problems, and it's nearly impossible to prevent stress altogether. Even if you could, that would result in urge *reduction* at best; urges can and do arise when you are feeling otherwise calm. However, if you view working on other issues that create stress as just one tool to give you an edge over urges, it can serve a useful purpose.

List ways you can work on stressful problems like anxiety and depression to give your higher brain an advantage over the urges:

_____

_____

_____

_____

_____

_____

_____

_____

_____

_____

_____

Another related and useful concept from therapy that I will frame in a new way is seeking identity, meaning, and purpose in your life. Again, this concept is useful not because it will make you stop feeling compelled to binge, but because feeling connected to your deeper goals or a deeper sense of purpose helps you separate from your urges—to see that they are not in line with what you truly want. I've discussed extensively how wanting to recover is absolutely vital, and it's in this area that therapy concepts can do a lot of good.

How can you work on seeking identity, meaning, and purpose in your life to assist your higher brain's desire for recovery and your sense of being separate from the urges?

_____

_____

_____

_____

_____

_____

_____

_____

Based on your own insights, are there any other concepts from therapy that you could reframe to give your higher brain the upper hand over the urges?

_____

_____

_____

_____

_____

_____

_____

_____

_____

If you decide to incorporate traditional therapy concepts into your recovery, remember that you always remain capable of dismissing urges regardless of your other issues. There are other detrimental behaviors that you just don't do—even if you are depressed, anxious, feeling emotionally stressed about events from your past or in your present, or not feeling particularly purposeful—and binge eating must become one of them.

BASIC SELF-CARE (NOT SELF-INDULGENCE) TO BOOST THE HIGHER BRAIN

Self-care is another important component of traditional eating disorder treatment. This is because of the popular idea that an eating disorder is actually a (misguided) way to care for yourself. The theory goes that if you learn healthy self-care, you won't feel the need to binge. What I personally read and learned about self-care while I was in therapy convinced me that I needed to put *me* before others, in order to get what *I* needed emotionally, so that I didn't need to rely on binge eating. Of course, that never worked, and the theory felt all too self-centered, leading to more guilt for trying to put *me* first, on top of all the guilt binge eating already created.

I was in therapy during a time in my life when I didn't have a husband, kids, or a lot of responsibility outside of my schoolwork and part-time jobs; and I actually did have the luxury of putting myself first and even pampering myself sometimes. However, some of you might be baffled at the idea of putting your own needs before those of others—I know I would be today as a mother of four young kids. If you are caring for children, an aging parent, or a sick spouse, or if you are in a highly demanding career or educational path, you likely can't relate to the idea of pampering yourself. So it's a good thing that putting yourself first is not necessary for recovery!

Having demands on your life and your time, along with having a strong desire to help others, does not have to affect your ability to dismiss binge urges. Nevertheless, if you are currently struggling to resist urges, then self-care is one of those traditional therapy concepts that can be viewed in a new way to become a tool to give you an added advantage. You certainly don't need to put your own needs above those of the people you care for; but while you are learning to use the Five Components, the basics of self-care can ensure a properly functioning prefrontal cortex.

When we are exhausted, overworked, or undernourished, our self-control suffers, and the brain is primed to let survival mechanisms and habits—good or bad—run the show.[111] This does not mean you have to get nine hours of sleep a night, take a vacation, or buy expensive vitamin supplements. It only means that if you are currently unable to dismiss binge urges, make sure you are not sabotaging your higher brain by neglecting your most basic needs: a decent amount of sleep, a little relaxation, and adequate food intake.

Being tired, overwhelmed, and exhausted won't be a problem for your recovery in the future when your new habit is to *not* binge. Even though you may not be at your best when you don't sleep well or have worked a long, stressful week, binge eating won't cross your mind. Since recovery, I've had four babies who were awful sleepers, so there were long stretches of time when I got vastly insufficient sleep—I'm talking maybe two to four noncontinuous hours a night for months at a time—and not once did binge eating cross my mind. There are times in life when self-sacrifice is necessary and something you gladly accept, and that won't change just because you have a history of an eating disorder.

What I'm suggesting here is a focus on basic self-care as a short-term tool to help your higher brain during the time when dismissing urges takes up a lot of its energy. Once you get better at dismissing the urges, it won't be as demanding on the higher brain, so even if you don't sleep or your boss or kids drive you absolutely crazy that day, you'll still have the energy reserves in your higher brain to easily say no to the urges.

If you are currently going through a time in your life when you feel deprived of basic self-care, my advice would be to analyze the situation and try to find areas of opportunity for sleep, rest, and nutritional improvements. Even if all you can do right now is to carve out an extra half hour for sleep each night or a ten-minute nap during the day and to force yourself to not skip a meal just to save time, those small steps alone will benefit your prefrontal cortex. Congratulate yourself on the times you are successful, but be patient and forgive yourself if you don't dismiss the urges every time. Try to find small moments of self-awareness in the midst of the difficulty of your life, and that will help you feel more centered and connected to your higher brain when urges arise.

List some ideas for caring for your higher brain through basic self-care.
(Examples: finding time for very short breaks during your workday, rearranging your schedule to allow for more sleep, asking for help with children or household responsibilities.)

_____

_____

_____

_____

_____

_____

_____

_____

SPIRITUALITY

A few months after *Brain over Binge* was published, a family member told me that some of the concepts I talk about in the book tied in to his personal spiritual path. I don't consider myself a deeply spiritual person, although I greatly admire that quality in others, and I frequently read spiritual material and aspire to have some form of personal faith one day. At the time I actually quit binge eating, I did not think I was doing anything even remotely spiritual. In fact, I thought it was the opposite of spiritual, because I was relying on myself—my own will, my own brain—to stop binge eating. I wasn't sure I even believed in God at the time—and certainly not a personal God that could help with my recovery in any way.

However, a year after my recovery, I read *The Mind and the Brain: Neuroplasticity and the Power of Mental Force* by Jeffrey Schwartz, M.D., and Sharon Begley, which helped me understand my own recovery and also showed me that there may have been something spiritual to what I'd done. Dr. Schwartz taught his patients with obsessive compulsive disorder (OCD) to observe their own thoughts in such a way that allowed them to turn attention away from the harmful OCD urges and avoid acting on them, which led to real, measurable brain changes. I found remarkable similarities between what Dr. Schwartz taught his OCD patients and what I'd done to stop binge eating. In the book, Dr. Schwartz makes a connection between his OCD therapy and Buddhist mindfulness meditation, which teaches the person to observe thought and emotion with detachment in order to experience a deeper reality underneath all the brain activity.

The fact that neuroscience shows us that how we choose to think and direct our attention can physically change the brain has profound philosophical, moral, and spiritual implications. This is actually pretty deep stuff. The Five Components are not outwardly spiritual—I have primarily concentrated on the practical application of using the higher brain to resist urges from the lower brain—but you can take the concepts you've learned here to another level to include the human spirit. It's possible that you may benefit from aligning the Five Components with your spiritual beliefs, and that will give more meaning and conviction to your recovery.

Remember, anything that helps you dismiss the urges is useful, whether it's something mundane or holy. A spiritual perspective can come in countless forms, depending on your own beliefs. Some Christian readers have told me they view the lower brain's urges as stemming from Satan/evil and the higher brain's power source as the Holy Spirit or Jesus within them. People of all faith backgrounds can view their "true selves" as who they believe they are in the greater cosmic scheme of life.

In the next chapter, Amy Johnson will delve into the topic of spirituality more deeply for those looking for guidance in this area. She will share her perspective on how spirituality can merge with recovery in a helpful and meaningful way. As Amy will explain, there is more to your "true self" than just inhibiting behaviors and vetoing faulty messages from the lower brain. Grasping a more profound sense of who you are at your core can help give you another level of insight into dismissing urges. In the space below, you can keep track of thoughts and ideas on spirituality gained from this short section and the next chapter.

Reflect on and write about any relationships you observe between your spirituality and your recovery and how your spiritual nature can be an asset to dismissing binge urges:

---

[20]

Going Deeper:
Spirituality and Recovery
by Amy Johnson, Ph.D.

AS YOU NOW KNOW, the lower brain is animalistic, instinctive, habitual, survival-based, and nonthinking. The higher brain, on the other hand, is your thinking brain. It embodies intellect, logic, and reasoning. The higher brain obeys or vetoes many lower brain messages and is capable of overriding old habits, producing behavioral change, and exercising free will.

Given those features of the two parts of the brain, the higher brain is the part you think of when you think about your concept of yourself and your identity as a person. Realizing that your lower brain is not "you," and that the "real you" is much more aligned with the logical and personal higher brain, makes ignoring lower brain messages infinitely easier. That voice urging you to binge is not who you are any more than the voice that recommends you sell everything you own and move to an island after a stress-filled day. Those voices are simply reactive thought, which is emotional and biased. Your higher brain is available to step up and over-ride those emotional, reactive urges, providing you with more rational choices that don't leave you en route to a deserted island.

But while it is clear that urges to binge and other lower brain messages are definitely not who you are, in many ways, it doesn't seem quite right that your higher brain represents the totality of who you are either. When you equate yourself with your higher brain, you're essentially equating your fundamental essence with your physical brain. "You" are your brain? That doesn't feel like the whole story. Your brain is a machine. It's a really amazing one, for sure, but it's still a physical machine with many limitations. You are much bigger than any single organ in your body.

That Which Is Aware

You may have heard something like the following: "You're not a human being having a spiritual experience; you're a spiritual being having a human experience."

This has nothing to do with dogma or religious beliefs, but it's also not like the scientific, research-backed, brain-based content that's been discussed thus far. You may already take a spiritual view of life that assumes that your true nature extends far beyond your physical reality.

On the other hand, you may not espouse these spiritual beliefs. Maybe you've never thought much about it or you aren't sure what you believe. That is perfectly okay. You don't have to see things exactly as presented here in order to benefit from this short discussion. The sole reason for this discussion on the spiritual view of life is because viewing yourself as a spiritual being—something far greater than your physical experiences—can bring enormous comfort, perspective, and insight.

In a spiritual sense, you aren't an organ that simply enacts programmed behaviors and vetoes faulty lower brain messages any more than you are your logic abilities, your intellect, your fine motor skills, or your blood, bones, and muscles. Who you fundamentally, deeply are at your core is not your physical body and its contents any more than it is your eating disorder, occupation, sexual orientation, or relationship status.

Consider this: You've learned to observe, detach from, and dismiss your urges to binge. Experiencing a degree of separation from those urges—where you're able to notice them without a lot of judgment or emotion, simply label them "neurological junk," and not act on them—is what is helping you stop binge eating.

What part of you notices those urges with detachment? Your higher brain does the noticing of your lower brain, right? But you are also able to observe your logic, intellect, and rational decisions. You are able to introspectively be aware of your preferences, wishes, and dreams—the stuff of the higher brain.

What or who is doing that noticing? The higher brain is what is being observed, but who or what is observing it?

Something beyond the brain or the mind is capable of noticing the brain's or the mind's functions in a detached way. As long as philosophy, psychology, and spirituality have been in existence, the question has been asked: *What is it that is aware of the mind?*

Observing the contents of your mind and brain without attachment, from a somewhat distanced, removed place, is often called "being the watcher" or "practicing mindfulness." But what if you had that same distanced awareness from your higher brain contents? Said another way, if you can stand apart from and be aware of your urges, then "you" clearly aren't your urges. If you can stand apart from and be aware of your higher brain thoughts and processes, it stands to reason that the real "you" might be more than those thoughts and processes as well.

YOUR SPIRITUAL NATURE

If the "real you" is something far beyond a collection of lower brain impulses and higher brain choices, what is the nature of that true self? What is that awareness that is the "real you"?

This might be the most commonly discussed topic in the history of the world, and still, probably no one knows for sure. Words clearly cannot describe your true nature, but words are often used as metaphors to point toward the feeling of it. Some of the words used to represent your true nature are *universal energy, soul, spirit, God, oneness, being, completeness, unity, clarity, the nonphysical, eternal, unconditional love,* and *all that is.* Some suggestions for connecting with your true nature are directives such as *Be in the now* and *Look within.*

When you view your urges as neurological junk that are not who you really are, you are able to detach from them in a way that allows them to float by and not drag you down. When you view your entire physical existence as not who you really are, you are not as easily taken down by what occurs in any particular point in time and space.

To catch a glimpse of your basic nature, it is helpful to look at children. Babies are born naturally tapped into a sense of peace. If you've ever been around babies for any extended period of time, you have no doubt noticed that they don't reside in that peace indefinitely. They experience strong emotions and even what look like tantrums, but they experience those emotions in a clean, uninhibited way, and those emotions pass. When they do, the babies bounce back to their innate state of well-being.

Adults are also effortlessly "bounced back" when they do nothing to interfere with the natural process, but adults have a harder time doing nothing. We are raised to feel as if we need to make things happen, including making ourselves feel better and making ourselves well again when we are not. But the true nature of all humans of any age is that we are well. We are fundamentally, mentally, and emotionally healthy. Just like babies and small children, when we simply feel what we feel without resistance and interference, all things naturally pass. This is true for all thoughts and emotions, including, obviously, urges to binge eat.

As seen in the eyes of newborn babies, your default setting is one of infinite well-being and peace of mind. You don't always feel a connection with that underlying peace in your daily life because you are a spiritual being having a human experience. Being a human being means that you have a lot of mental and physical components. You have physical health and the rewards and challenges that go along with having a solid body with which to travel through life. You have an active mind, full of stories, thoughts, memories, urges, instincts, and impulses. And you have rich emotions that stem from all of that mental content. Being human is an amazing gift, and part of the gift is that the mental and physical components sometimes look like they are who you are. They conceal your true nature at times, but they aren't your true nature. Your fundamental essence is untouched by what's happening in your physical life on this planet.

When you are aware of your true nature that always lies beneath your very human goings-on, you can rest in that awareness. You can relax into the peace and well-being that are always there for you, beneath the addictive voice and the concerns about your weight. Beneath the human, brain-based, ego-like concerns are stability, peace, and infinite wellness.

Psychology Versus Reality

This discussion of our true self being something far beyond our physical, mental, or emotional self invites us to look at the difference between psychology, or the more physical side of life, and what we're calling a "deeper reality," or the more formless, spiritual side of life.

If your fundamental nature is health, peace, clarity, and well-being, that means that anytime you're not experiencing those states—when you're confused, suffering, in pain, or lacking well-being—you are not fully in touch with your basic nature. You are caught up in your psychology rather than the reality of who you really are.

Your well-being is always there. Because it's who you are, it's a constant; it never leaves you and you never leave it. You couldn't leave it if you wanted to.

And yet, it often feels as if it's not there when you're living through a thick layer of very dense psychology—when your mind is full and busy and your emotions are heavy and strong. Your true self, the reality of who you are, is always there underneath that surface chaos even when you don't feel it. Knowing that brings a sense of peace.

Remembering in the midst of difficult times that what you're feeling is only psychology and not deeper reality takes the edge off, much like remembering that an urge to binge is only neurological junk takes the edge off. It allows for distance. In the same way that you can dismiss an urge, you can begin to dismiss any flurry of painful thought or emotion as neurological—or psychological—"junk" and simply wait for it to fade. When it fades, it is replaced with new thought and emotion.

Anything that is happening within your psychology—in your lower or higher brain—will naturally subside on its own when you don't act upon it or strengthen it with your focus and attention. You've seen that this is true of urges. Actually, it is true of all thought and emotion.

Your reality is that you are much, much more than your lower brain or your higher brain. You are more than your mind or your body; your difficulties or successes in life; or any arbitrary, physical world labels you might use to describe yourself. Your true self is unending peace and well-being, and it is always there under the flurry of psychology on the surface.

*   *   *   *   *   *   *   *   *   *   *   *   *   *   *   *   *   *   *   *

You've come to the end of the first half of Part II of this book, Recovery Goal 1: Dismiss Urges to Binge. You may already feel like you have everything you need to put binge eating behind you. If you've already quit binge eating (or are fairly confident you can with what you've already read, along with some time to process and apply it in your life) and you feel like you are eating in a normal way, then you do not need to read the next section. Recovery Goal 2: Eat Adequately is for people who do not have a grasp of hunger and fullness, still engage in restrictive dieting, and/or struggle with other bothersome food and weight issues.

SECTION 2
RECOVERY GOAL 2:
EAT ADEQUATELY

YOU DON'T *NEED* TO eat in a particular way to recover. Provided you are not dieting restrictively, the way you eat really doesn't matter. However, not knowing how to approach eating normally makes recovery difficult for some people. Some are determined to continue dieting restrictively, and in so doing, they find themselves unable to dismiss the powerful, starvation-induced urges to binge. Some people decide to try to follow their hunger and fullness only to find that those signals aren't working properly. Others may just need some simple, flexible guidelines to get started eating normally.

This section of the book addresses a variety of topics related to implementing normal eating habits and dealing with weight issues to help you sort out what you need to do to achieve Recovery Goal 2. Let's take a minute to talk about what "eating adequately" means.

The definition of *adequate* is: "satisfactory or acceptable in quantity and quality."[112] So when "eat adequately" appears here, it means you need to consume a satisfactory *quantity* of food that is of acceptable *quality* overall. In short: *You need to eat enough decent food.*

Adequate is not a very inspiring word, I know. However, *ideally, perfectly, optimally,* and even *healthy* are overkill for eating disorder recovery and often set you up for failure. It's so common for those trying to recover from binge eating disorder or bulimia to overthink their eating habits or try to get things exactly right; in the process, they lose sight of the simplicity of recovery. I am not saying you *can't* strive to eat in an ideal way, but recovery does not hinge on that. Aiming for adequate eating best supports recovery for two reasons:

1. Adequate eating ensures that you are getting *enough* food.
2. Adequate eating ensures that you are getting necessary nutrition while also allowing for all types of foods.

Adequate eating doesn't always line up with the way you believe you "should" be eating based on how you think humans were theoretically designed/adapted to eat, but it can. Adequate eating doesn't always line up with instructions you are handed by a nutritionist or an eating disorder expert, but it can. Adequate eating might not always line up with your hunger and fullness levels or your schedule, but it can. Healthy eating, structured/scheduled eating, and intuitive eating all can be adequate ways of eating if you are eating a satisfactory quantity of food that is of acceptable quality overall. Even optimally healthy eating—if that's what you feel is right for you—is, of course, adequate as well. You have freedom to personalize adequate eating to work for you.

This section is not a detailed instruction manual or a set of rules for normal eating; it's a collection of ideas that you can apply as you see fit. Learning to eat adequately doesn't lend itself well to defined steps, and the concepts of *food quantity* and *food quality* cannot be neatly separated, because both work together. For those reasons, this section will not always proceed linearly but is organized in a way that will allow you to gain a general foundation up front, then move on to eating topics that might cause you concern.

In the first two chapters, you'll put aside two major barriers to adequate eating: restrictive dieting and body image obsessions. Then you'll gain information and strategies to help you create your own version of adequate eating. Next, you'll explore topics that commonly come up while working on Recovery Goal 2: "healthy" eating, food cravings, overeating, weight, and night eating.

If you already have a feel for what "adequate eating" means to you, or if you feel you are rather well connected to your sensations of hunger and fullness, then you might not need much of the information in this section. So I again remind you to stop reading when you feel you have the information you need to eat adequately and move on with your life. Overthinking your eating habits can be counterproductive, keeping mental energy focused on eating when you want to divert it elsewhere.

The primary contributor to this section is recovery mentor Katherine Thomson, Ph.D., but you will also hear from master certified coach and weight loss expert Cookie Rosenblum, M.A., and integrative nutritionists Pauline Hanuise and Stacey Cohen. I couldn't have written the pages that follow in this section without the help of these women, who all have great insight on the topic of learning how to eat in a normal way because they have all gone through that process themselves and helped others do the same.

A WORD OF CAUTION

If you have a health condition that requires a special diet, please seek the advice of your physician about food quantity and quality. Of special importance: If you have been severely restricting your calorie intake, or if you have frequently used self-induced vomiting, laxatives, or diuretics, you need to be aware of "refeeding syndrome," which was mentioned in the Important Considerations and Disclaimers section at the beginning of this book. Refeeding syndrome is a dangerous condition involving electrolyte and fluid shifts that can occur not only in eating disorder patients, but in anyone who undergoes more than ten days of undernutrition—examples being cancer and postoperative patients. Refeeding syndrome is preventable with medical supervision. Even if you aren't at risk for refeeding syndrome, increasing food intake to an adequate level *gradually* is a good idea.

[21]

Remove the Restrictive Dieting Barrier

My experience with an eating disorder makes even the idea of a restrictive diet off-limits for me. I can feel when I even start thinking about going on a restrictive diet or strenuous exercise program this resistance forming in my mind. I do not think I could have fully recovered if I had kept restricting and dieting. I had to give up that struggle over controlling my weight completely. I think I would have been swept back into the disorder otherwise. The habit itself of bingeing and purging became so addictive to me, so I don't see how engaging in those activities which led me to start that habit could be safe for me.

~Cori

TO LAY THE BASIC foundation for adequate eating, we need to first remove two barriers that often prevent women and men from even beginning that endeavor: the desire to continue restrictive dieting, which will be addressed in this chapter, and body obsessions, which will be addressed in the next. Giving up dieting can be paramount to eating adequately, and for some people—especially those who have just recently started binge eating during a period of dieting—stopping the food restriction may significantly reduce the binge urges.

Giving up restrictive dieting is not a cure in and of itself for most people. Binge eating can continue even in the absence of dieting,[113] and once habit is a factor, as it is for most people who are looking to recover, giving up dieting won't eliminate the urges. One study showed that 43 percent of patients being admitted into residential treatment for bulimia reported not currently dieting.[114] This is why it is important to learn how to dismiss urges prior to giving up dieting; that way, when giving up dieting doesn't completely eliminate your urges to binge, you'll know how to avoiding acting on them. Furthermore, knowing how to dismiss urges gives you the confidence to give up dieting. Otherwise, you'd probably worry that you'd end up eating adequately *and* binge eating on top of that. After reading the first part of the book, you have a defense against that possibility.

ALLOW THE DIETING OBSESSION TO FADE NATURALLY

Before discussing a lot of scientific reasons to give up dieting, consider that restrictive dieting could be just a *reaction* to the binges themselves—an attempt to counteract the extra binge calories. Once you know how to dismiss urges, you may choose to put restrictive dieting aside without any further advice. This also applies to other eating problems that may just be a *result* of binge eating, such as abnormal cravings or skewed hunger and fullness signals that will be addressed in later chapters. After binge eating stops, the body can gradually regulate itself with no need to "work" on these other problems.

It's understandable that binge eaters feel the need to "diet." When a person fundamentally feels out of control around food, imposing rules and restrictions can seem like a reasonable thing to do. Unfortunately, the rules backfire when it comes to such a basic survival drive like eating. What if you tried to restrict your water intake to only certain times and allowed yourself only a set amount, even if you were very thirsty? You'd likely experience a heightened awareness of your thirst and a more aggressive thirst. Keeping the reins pulled too tightly makes you feel more out of control.

Once you develop confidence in dismissing urges, you are going to naturally feel like you can release the reins and start giving yourself sufficient quantities of food. It doesn't have to look perfect now, or ever; but without binge eating, you'll be in a much better place to genuinely decide how you want to fuel your body, and you'll likely make *healthier* choices than when you tried to impose strict rules on yourself. This can happen without a lot of effort from you. So for now, be open to the idea that the appeal of dieting will wane after you stop binge eating. If it doesn't, or if you are stuck in the mind-set that you *must* diet restrictively to lose weight, then you will benefit from the rest of the information in this chapter.

Do you think your dieting is in any way just a reaction to your binge eating? If so, how?

_____

_____

_____

_____

_____

_____

_____

_____

_____

_____

Insights that help you let the dieting obsession fade naturally:

_____

_____

_____

_____

_____

_____

_____

_____

_____

_____

GIVING UP DIETING DOESN'T MEAN UNHEALTHY INDULGENCE

Changing eating habits to make them more nutritious isn't "dieting," so long as you are not denying your body of needed calories and nutrition and you are not being overly rigid and restrictive. There is a big difference between changing the composition of what you eat so that your food is more nourishing and simply slashing calories to lose weight.

I think when people are truly focused on becoming healthier, it's not just about losing weight or staying under a certain number of calories. It becomes an effort to nourish your body well, to feel better, to gain energy for living, to prevent disease. It ceases to be about how many pounds you can lose or what size jeans you can fit into. And, usually, if you focus on becoming healthier (and if you do have some excess weight), the weight will come off naturally.[115] So when I talk about giving up dieting, I don't mean you have to give up healthy eating as well—provided healthy eating isn't a stressful obsession for you.

Do you fear that letting go of restrictive dieting means letting go of health goals? Write about ways to remind yourself that you are giving up dieting to support your health:

_____

_____

_____

_____

_____

_____

_____

_____

PUT ASIDE CALORIE DEFICITS

If you are in a calorie deficit, your lower brain is going to remain primed to act in the interest of your immediate survival (and primal pleasure) and your higher brain will have a more difficult time championing your long-term best interest. We've already discussed the fact that an energy shortage leads to lower self-control because the brain diverts resources away from the higher brain and its rational capacities, and it energizes the primitive, lower brain for the task of obtaining food.

The fact that your rational behavior and self-control are depleted when you are hungry is something that all people experience. We all get irritable and have more trouble controlling our reactions and actions when we're in need of food.[116] This only makes sense neurologically, because abundant self-control isn't necessary for us to seek food—at least, it wasn't for our ancestors. Now, we do have to exhibit some form of patience when waiting in line at the grocery store or waiting for our food at a restaurant, but our primitive brains are still dominant in times of hunger. This doesn't mean you can never get hungry while trying to recover, but making sure you aren't in a calorie deficit day after day will help immensely in dismissing binge urges.

For years, calorie deficits were the gold standard of dieting, and many weight loss experts and doctors sill recommend low-calorie diets. Low-calorie diets are based on the fact that one pound of fat is equal to about 3,500 calories; so in theory, every calorie deficit of 3,500 calories should lead to one pound of fat loss. The weight loss industry was based around this presumption for years, but it has now become apparent that the 3,500 calorie deficit theory is a drastic over-simplification. The research shows that calories don't interact with the body in this mechanical, mathematical way. Our bodies and the foods we eat are more complex than that; there are numerous biological and behavioral factors that affect energy balance.[117]

Furthermore, not all calories are created equal—meaning they are not all metabolized by the body in the same way, and each unique body can metabolize calories differently. For example, some foods—like fructose—cause hormone changes that increase appetite and encourage weight gain,[118] while others—like protein—promote satiety and boost metabolic rate.[119] The 3,500 calorie deficit myth also doesn't account for metabolic adaptation by the body and brain to cope with a calorie deficit. When you give your body less fuel, it reduces its energy expenditure, even on a cellular level, so you burn fewer calories.[120] Very low-calorie diets can cause the body to suppress its resting metabolic rate by up to about 20 percent.[121]

There are individual and lifestyle factors, such as exercise and age, that may determine the extent of this metabolic suppression and the timeframe in which it happens; but the main takeaway is that the body works to defend its natural weight during calorie restriction.[122] It only makes sense that the body has weight-maintaining mechanisms—they prevent humans from losing weight continuously if there isn't enough food available. Research has measured a decreased metabolic rate after three to six months of calorie restriction,[123] which explains why restrictive dieters may lose weight in a predictable way when they first commence a diet, but after the body gradually makes corrections to conserve energy, the weight plateaus or gaining begins.

Because of metabolic adaptation, after dieting for a period of time, the dieter will require fewer calories to maintain his or her weight,[124] which can make the dieter feel trapped into restrictive eating. This all assumes that the attempts at calorie restriction actually result in calorie restriction—and don't lead to binge eating or lesser forms of overeating. People who are using low-calorie diets to lose weight often end up with *more* disinhibited eating than non-dieters.[125] Through neurological mechanisms involving reward circuitry, a prior restriction experience promotes future behaviors to increase consumption of calorically dense foods.[126]

This usually means that a normal diet without binge eating actually contains *fewer* calories than restrictive dieting and binge eating combined. Let's look at an example, using 2,200 calories as a normal daily intake. Assume you are trying to restrict your calories to 1,600 per day, but then you binge on top of that—let's say you binge ten times per month, at 5,000 calories per binge. If you spread those binge calories out evenly over each day and combine that with your daily "low-calorie" diet intake, you are actually eating about 3,200 calories per day—1,000 calories more than a normal diet per day. Next time you fear giving up a calorie deficit and eating normally, remind yourself that, in reality, that's creating a calorie surplus. Since eating more as part of your daily intake can help you avoid binges, it simply makes sense mathematically to forgo restricting.

You may be thinking right now that none of this applies to you because you don't count calories; however, you could be unknowingly eating too little. Many restrictive dieters do not even know they are in a calorie deficit—or at least not know the extent of it. You may be someone who tries to eat healthy all of the time or tries to eat very small portions for weight loss. The goal for many is simply to restrict and restrict some more until the number goes down on the scale. I've had women tell me they truly believed they were eating enough, but when they actually tracked their intake, they were only getting between 1,100 and 1,600 (non-binge) calories a day, which is not enough. An energy intake that low is going to put the body in "survival mode"—keeping you focused on food, plagued with cravings, and faced with binge urges that are much harder to dismiss.

How have you used calorie deficits and/or starvation diets (with or without actually counting calories) in the past for weight loss? How has this affected you?

_____

_____

_____

_____

_____

_____

_____

What are your reasons for hanging on to calorie deficits?

_____

_____

_____

_____

_____

_____

———————————————————————————————

———————————————————————————————

———————————————————————————————

———————————————————————————————

How can you use the above information to remind yourself that eating enough is actually more effective for dismissing binge urges and for reaching/maintaining a healthy weight?

———————————————————————————————

———————————————————————————————

———————————————————————————————

———————————————————————————————

———————————————————————————————

———————————————————————————————

———————————————————————————————

———————————————————————————————

Aren't There Benefits to Calorie Restriction?

Prolonged calorie restriction increases the life span of rodents, and in recent years, research has begun investigating whether it has the same effect on humans.[127] There is some evidence suggesting that reducing energy intake by controlled caloric restriction or intermittent fasting protects various tissues against disease,[128] although other research purports that there is little evidence to calorie restriction giving health benefits[129] or increasing life span.[130] It's easy to find dieting websites promoting the benefits of low-calorie diets and citing studies to support their cause; it's also easy to find eating disorder websites warning of the dangers and consequences of dieting, citing different studies.

Because calorie restriction *might* prove to be helpful for some individuals with certain health conditions, this doesn't mean it is something that should be recommended across the board. Far from it. Calorie restriction is something that, if undertaken, should be medically supervised so that it doesn't result in malnutrition, and it should never be undertaken by someone who is at risk for an eating disorder. Granted, it's hard to know who is and who is not at risk prior to dieting, which is why I believe that there are better ways to promote health than food restriction. But you *know* you are susceptible to binge eating, which makes the decision easy.

As with anything in life, we have to weigh the benefits with the possible negatives, and right now, for those reading this book, it's not worth the risk involved. The negative impacts have already offset and will continue to offset any health benefits, so just put the idea of cutting calories aside. Far in the future, when binge eating is ancient history for you, if you need to follow a medically supervised low-calorie diet for one reason or another, you can revisit the risks and benefits then. This is true not only for calorie restriction, but for any other type of special eating regimen that you might want or need to undertake for health reasons in the future. Unless there is a pressing health issue for which your doctor deems a special diet necessary, please don't try it right now.

Even if, one day, it is conclusively determined that eating fewer calories lowers the risk of aging-related diseases, remind yourself that stopping binge eating *is* reducing your calories. You are eliminating *excess*, and that will allow you to reap health benefits. If you are bulimic, you are also eliminating health-sabotaging and potentially deadly purging behaviors, a major step on the journey toward a healthy life.

[22]

Remove the Body Obsession Barrier

Years of bingeing and purging had me bloated, anxious, and ... fatter! I was exhausted with hating myself. It may sound silly, but I was too old, smart, and savvy to keep hating my body like a 15-year-old insecure teenage girl. It was time to grow up. It was time to listen to my body. It was time to learn what being kind to my body and loving my body could really do for me.

~Neena

STRONGLY RELATED TO THE dieting barrier to adequate eating is the body obsession barrier. If you are unhappy with your weight and want to be thinner, you may resist adequate eating, or you may tell yourself, *Okay, I'll start eating adequately once I lose weight.* You should know by now why this is a bad idea. Typical advice for binge eaters dealing with poor body image is to learn to accept your body for what it is. That makes sense when it comes to your natural weight—the weight, give or take 5 to 10 pounds, your body gravitates toward while eating a relatively healthy, nonrestrictive diet and exercising moderately.

Each person is thought to have a genetically influenced natural weight or weight range, often called a "set point," that their body innately wants to be.[131] Evidence suggests that we all have a regulatory system for our body weight and that adults who do not try to control their weight stay remarkably stable over time.[132] Research posits that up to 70 percent of the variations in people's weights may be accounted for by genetics, which means that weight has a stronger genetic influence than almost any other condition.[133] This still grants an important role for environment and personal choice in making the best of your unique body, but it also means that your body does have a basic blueprint that you need to accept and even honor.

However, most binge eaters are not at their natural weight, making the advice to "accept your body" hard to put into practice. If my highest weight as a binge eater was, in fact, my natural weight, I would have benefited greatly from learning to accept that and avoiding trying to make my body into something else. Learning to appreciate things about your body (and qualities other than how you look) is a great endeavor for anyone of any age, but it's often too difficult for a binge eater to do. I just couldn't force myself to accept my highest weight when I knew that it wasn't in a normal range for me. I used to get upset with myself for continuing to dislike my body, because I wasn't "succeeding" at self-acceptance. Looking back, I shouldn't have beat myself up over having negative body thoughts. It added an extra layer of guilt and self-judgment that I didn't need.

If a normal eater with a relatively healthy self-image woke up one day and was 15, 30, 50, or even 100 pounds heavier than their natural, healthy weight, they would likely have similar thoughts and feelings. My poor body image was to be expected, and fighting against it didn't do me any good. What I needed to know—and what I'm telling you here—is that it's okay to not be in love with your body right now while binge eating is a factor; and it's actually okay to not love your body ever. The key is to avoid acting on those negative body thoughts with restrictive dieting, and also to avoid letting those superficial thoughts get in the way of a meaningful life. You can let them come and go with detachment, just like binge urges.

The good news is that you likely won't have to use detachment in this way for long. Being larger than your natural size is something that can gradually take care of itself after binge eating stops (see Chapter 32 for a full discussion about weight). So you have to take a leap of faith and give up the dieting behaviors—despite the negative body thoughts you have—and then once you see that eating adequately (and not binge eating) allows you to gravitate back to your healthy, natural weight, you simply won't see the point of dieting anymore, and body confidence can rapidly increase. Alternately, if you don't gravitate back toward your natural, healthy size, you'll be in a much better position to explore healthy solutions.

If everyone reading this book were satisfied with their natural weight and shape, then what's been advised thus far in this chapter would be sufficient. But some of you are undoubtedly thinking, *I don't want to be at my natural weight!* Some people desperately want to be thinner or somehow different than their body seems genetically predisposed to be. What if getting back to a normal weight for you isn't what you want? What if your body obsession feels "necessary" because you want an ideal body? Sadly, so many women and men struggle with this, and it's rare to find a woman (or man) who doesn't want to change something about her body. As addressed below, getting back to your natural weight doesn't mean giving up fitness, but it does mean you have to put aside unrealistic expectations.

If you are left with a poor body image after recovery, it doesn't make you eating-disordered, but it does make you miserable. You don't want to recover from your eating disorder and then be like the majority of women—frequently worrying about weight and wishing they were thinner. Women who haven't struggled with an eating disorder sometimes go through life as if worrying about weight and trying to lose it is the norm, without any real push to change their perspective. You have a unique advantage because now you know how much misery body obsessions cause, and you'll have the motivation to put body image issues aside, or at least not let your feelings about your body affect your actions or get in the way of achieving your goals in life.

How has binge eating affected your body and body image?

_____

_____

_____

_____

_____

_____

_____

Do you have a sense of what your natural weight or weight range might be? How do you feel about this? (It's okay if you aren't sure what your body's natural size is—you will get a better sense of it after eating adequately and not binge eating for a longer period of time.)

_____

_____

_____

_____

_____

_____

_____

Is constantly obsessing about your weight really the way you want to live? Do you want your children seeing you constantly trying to restrict your food and lose weight?

_____

_____

_____

_____

_____

What benefits can you envision if you give up your body obsession and learn to accept your natural weight/body shape?

_____

_____

_____

_____

_____

GIVING UP BODY OBSESSIONS DOESN'T MEAN GIVING UP BEING FIT

There is no denying that the obesity rate has skyrocketed in recent years, with 69 percent of Americans being overweight or obese.[134] This doesn't mean that the majority of the population's genetically determined weight suddenly shifted upward and everyone should just "accept their weight" now. Genes have been around for all of human history, and the obesity epidemic is relatively new; so our eating environment obviously comes into play in determining weight as well. In the past, only those with extremely high genetic susceptibility would become overweight or obese; but today, with ready access to a lot of highly processed foods, even people with genes that predispose them to be thin can become overweight after years of poor food choices.[135]

I'm not telling you that you have to make peace with or be proud of a body that's not functioning at its best because it's well beyond its genetic set point. When I tell you to accept your natural weight or weight range, this doesn't mean the weight you'd be if you ate excessive quantities of poor-quality food and rarely moved your body. The natural weight I'm talking about is the weight that your body is when it is treated right—when it is given decent-quality food for the most part, when portions are sensible, and when physical activity is part of your life in whatever capacity works for you in today's world. I'm not talking about some unreasonable vision of how much you'd weigh in Paleolithic times, when you wouldn't have access to modern foods or to your current cognitive and career pursuits because you'd instead spend all your time making tools, hunting, and gathering.

There is nothing wrong with wanting to make the best of your unique body in the world we live in; but if you want to pursue fitness, don't try to fight your genetics. You may not look like a bodybuilder or a marathon runner or a caveman, but your level of fitness will be sustainable and allow you to feel good performing daily activities and whatever exercise you enjoy. Don't be tempted to think that with a strict diet, you can transcend your genetics. Research shows intentional weight loss attempts predict accelerated weight gain and increase the risk of becoming overweight.[136] So remember that eating adequately is *more* conducive to fitness than restrictive dieting.

LET GO OF YOUR IDEAS ABOUT WHAT WEIGHT MEANS

If you are having a hard time accepting your natural weight and shape, consider that the problem could be stereotypes you are holding on to about what weight (wrongly) signifies about a person. In our culture, it's a common belief that over-weight people or those on the upper end of normal are lazy or lack self-control when it comes to eating. It's also commonly believed that overweight people simply aren't moving enough or are overindulging too often, that being above average weight is their fault. Those below average weight are stereotyped as well—it is assumed that thin people are obsessed with their bodies, spend too much time working out, don't eat enough, or are just plain "lucky."

The truth is that these stereotypes are not truth. Although it is of course unhealthy to be extremely underweight or extremely overweight, there is a wide, wide range of "healthy." There are some technically overweight people who are in excellent health and excellent shape—the furthest thing from lazy or over-indulgent. Conversely, there are some technically underweight people who are very healthy and eat plentifully and exercise moderately, but thinness is simply in their genes. Being "average" or somewhere in the healthy weight range does not guarantee health, and it certainly doesn't indicate anything about character traits.

We can't judge others or ourselves based on weight, and we can't force our bodies to be something they are not. Your weight doesn't mean something deep about who you are as a person.

What stereotypes do you hold about what weight means about character?

_____

_____

_____

_____

_____

_____

_____

_____

Think of people in your life who do not fit the stereotypes you hold and write about them:

_____

_____

_____

_____

_____

_____

_____

_____

_____

_____

How can you remember and remind yourself that your weight doesn't reflect who you are as a person?

_____

_____

_____

_____

_____

FOCUS ELSEWHERE

We know that when you tell yourself not to think about something—like dieting, weight, or your body—that's usually when you think about it most. Instead, just try to notice when you are thinking about these things, and then gently direct your thoughts elsewhere—to anything you choose. If negative body thoughts come up again in a few minutes, simply notice them and again gently redirect your thoughts elsewhere. Even if you are not able to redirect your thoughts every time, the more times you can, the better you will get at it.

When I was recovering, it wasn't that I never thought about my weight; it's that when those obsessive thoughts came up, I didn't assign them much significance. I tried to just get on with my life. It wasn't an immediate change, but as the weeks and months went by, my mind was much less focused on my body size. Then, when I was back down to my normal weight, approximately six months after recovery, my desire to diet was gone and my poor body image improved greatly.

I read a lot of self-help books, in particular about body image, and the message of self-acceptance helps me a lot when I feel bad about my weight. I repeat the mantra "I approve of myself" silently to myself whenever I think of it because it's almost impossible to feel bad about yourself when you repeat that. I focus on the good in my life, my husband, my job, my family, my friends, my animals, and remind myself that weight isn't that big a deal in the end.

~Lisa

It may take some practice to be able to consistently redirect your thoughts about weight and shape, because you are simply used to putting too much emphasis on your body. Any thought process that you spend a lot of time focusing on builds strong neural connections. It's not your fault you are stuck there now, but it's your responsibility going forward—for the quality of your life and those around you—that you turn your focus elsewhere and allow those neural pathways to fade. The next exercise will help you stop giving so much of your attention to dieting and body obsessions.

What habitual thoughts do you have about weight and body shape? (If you can recognize them as they arise, you'll be in a better position to remain detached from them.)

_____

_____

_____

_____

_____

_____

_____

When you have thoughts that criticize your weight or point out your body's flaws, what could you gently redirect your thoughts toward? What else can you focus on in your daily life besides your body?

_____

_____

_____

_____

_____

_____

_____

*   *   *   *   *   *   *   *   *   *   *   *   *   *   *   *   *   *   *

The last two chapters have presented a simple discussion of the behaviors and mental processes that can serve as barriers to adequate eating. For some, dieting behaviors and body obsessions are long-standing and may be difficult to put aside. If you need more help in this area, many of the resources in Appendix A can guide you further.

[23]

Draw on What You Already Know About Adequate Eating

I'd eaten in such a nonintuitive way for so long that I really had no idea what or how much of anything to put in my mouth. I looked to [others who] I considered to be mostly "normal" eaters to see how they approached food. I also realized that, even though I could look to [them] as a starting point, the true compass for my food choices had to be me. During this time, I also started studying meditation and more spiritual topics regarding consciousness and "listening to yourself," and from that and truly observing what my body was telling me (am I full, hungry, etc.), I was able to really see what I needed and how much of it I really needed. It shocked me sometimes! I never thought I'd be able to eat normal or smaller portions and be satisfied.

~Brenda

NOW THAT YOU KNOW that all you have to do is eat adequately—eat a satisfactory quantity of food and food of acceptable quality—figuring out how to eat might suddenly feel doable for you. You don't need a perfect diet; you don't need to give up a certain food group (if you don't want to); you don't have to eat *only* when you are hungry and stop at the most ideal level of fullness; you don't need to thoroughly enjoy everything you eat. You can eat in a way that you like— that feels authentic to you. Nutrition is highly individual, and it's important to stress that up front—that no two people will have the exact same diet, whether they are recovering from an eating disorder or not.

If you are reading this section, it's because you think you need advice on how to eat, but stay open to the idea that you might not need much from the pages that follow. You have the power within yourself to wake up each day and aim to eat in a way that looks and feels normal to you. Sure, eating in an adequate way might take some getting used to; after all, you've been binge eating and likely dieting as well for perhaps a very long time. Your body may need some time to adjust, but don't take that to mean you need a lot of extra help in the area of eating. Before you go any further, use the writing prompts below to help you discover what you already know about adequate eating. You may find that you haven't actually lost touch with how to eat.

Write down some of your initial thoughts on what "adequate eating" means to you:

_____

_____

_____

_____

_____

_____

_____

Think back to how you ate prior to developing an eating disorder. Are there clues there as to how you might want to go about eating adequately now?

_____

_____

_____

_____

_____

_____

_____

_____

Alternately, there has probably been at least one day in your life as a binge eater that you've eaten in a way that felt adequate. Describe what a day of adequate eating looks and feels like to you:

_____

_____

_____

_____

_____

_____

_____

_____

_____

_____

What do you already know about nutrition that could help you implement adequate eating habits?

_____

_____

_____

_____

_____

_____

_____

_____

_____

_____

_____

You've Never Eaten Adequately

If you don't think you've ever eaten in a normal way, you could think about people you've observed, like friends or family, who you feel eat in a way that seems reasonable and normal. Or you could think about your child or a child you care about and how you want them to eat, then transfer those basic principles to your own eating habits—obviously giving yourself adult-sized portions. Thinking about how you'd want a child you care about to eat is helpful for three reasons.

First, when you think about a child's eating habits, you want to make sure the child gets enough food—you don't want to risk undernourishment (satisfactory *quantity*). Second, you want to give the child nutritious, wholesome foods for the most part (acceptable *quality*). The third reason thinking about feeding a child is helpful is that you are usually willing to give a child more freedom than you give yourself. Even if you want to feed the child good-quality foods, you also want the child to be able to eat birthday cake at a friend's party or go out for ice cream and participate in life without food being an issue.

Are there any adults you've observed who eat in an adequate way? What do their portions look like? How do they balance healthy versus unhealthy foods?

_____

_____

_____

_____

_____

_____

_____

_____

_____

_____

_____

How would you want a child you care about to eat? How can you use those same ideas to introduce adequate eating into your own life?

_____

_____

_____

_____

_____

_____

_____

Your Definition of Adequate Eating

Just as you defined what binge eating means to you personally, it will be helpful here to define the term *adequate eating*, as you envision it right now, drawing on what you've learned from writing and reflecting on the prompts above. When I quit binge eating, my definition of eating normally was extremely simple: *Don't binge and don't diet restrictively.* That was all I needed to begin moving forward and trusting myself again. Your definition might be equally simple, or you may already have a more detailed description in mind. Once you pinpoint your definition, you can refer to it anytime you feel like your eating is becoming erratic or abnormal. If you still feel unsure about your interpretation of adequate eating, just skip this writing prompt for now and come back to it after you've acquired more information from later chapters.

Based on what you've learned so far, try to capture your personal definition of *adequate eating* in a few sentences:

_____

_____

_____

_____

_____

_____

_____

A Bridge to Normal

Keep in mind that if eating in an adequate way does not come easily at first, that doesn't mean you are off course. This is just a phase that some binge eaters have to go through while the body regulates itself. Going through a period of adjustment that may be confusing and even uncomfortable at times doesn't mean you are doing anything wrong; but due to physiological factors resulting from the disorder, it might take some time for adequate eating to feel right.

For example, one of these factors is stomach stretching. Studies have shown that women with active binge eating disorder and bulimia have a greater stomach capacity than women who do not binge.[137] In normal eaters, when the stomach is stretched from a meal, a network of nerve receptors in the stomach sends signals of fullness to the brain. Prolonged periods of excessively stretching the stomach through binge eating can make those nerve receptors less sensitive, so that normal quantities of food no longer trigger fullness signals. This is a problem that usually resolves itself gradually after binge eating stops, allowing you to start to feel sensations of fullness after consuming normal quantities of food.

Recovering women and men often describe what is almost like a bridge to cross between binge eating and normal eating, and during that bridge phase, there might be a little more overeating than you'd like, possibly more weight obsession than you are comfortable with, and even some digestive discomfort, especially if self-induced vomiting was involved. Giving up restrictive dieting, reconnecting with hunger and fullness, settling on a way of eating that works for you, dropping the focus on your weight, and learning how to manage cravings and overeating are often longer-term goals than stopping the binge eating itself.

Always remember that once you depart from binge eating and step onto that "bridge to normal eating," you never have to turn back. Your eating disorder itself is over, even if that bridge phase seems a little shaky. Even without perfectly stable footing, you can still put one foot in front of the other and arrive on the other side, feeling comfortable with your eating habits. Don't be surprised if you can quit binge eating in one day or one week or one month, but you still don't quite feel like you are on solid ground eating-wise.

Besides the physiological aspect, part of the reason for this is that it's easy to be hyperaware of your eating when you are coming out of an eating disorder and to therefore perceive more unsteadiness than is really there. What you consider eating "problems" may actually be issues that someone without a history of an eating disorder wouldn't even notice, or at least wouldn't worry about too much. Being aware of your hyperawareness can help you keep any problems you may have in perspective. Being overly attuned to your eating isn't necessarily a bad thing, because if you are able to recognize problems, you'll be in a better position to change them in the future.

Where do you perceive unsteadiness in your eating habits? Keep track of any improvement you notice over time:

_____

_____

_____

_____

_____

_____

_____

_____

_____

Do you feel you are hyperaware, or even hypercritical, of your eating habits? Write about any insights that help you relax a little more as you implement adequate eating:

_____

_____

_____

_____

_____

_____

_____

[24]

The Basics of Food Quantity and Food Quality

Learning about proper nutrition was the key. I need to feed my body well. I need to have enough protein. I need to eat balanced meals. Proper nutrition has helped me immensely.

~Nancy

THIS CHAPTER PRESENTS THE basics of what you need to eat adequately—in terms of quantity and quality. It is not a substitute for medical advice. Nutritionists and dieticians are great resources to help you develop a personalized plan for adequate eating, and if you feel you need professional support at any point, please don't hesitate to seek it. Again, I remind you to not increase your food intake rapidly; and if you're extremely undernourished, please seek medical help in order to safely regulate eating. For those who are not in a depleted state, this chapter gives you a foundation for charting your own path to achieving Recovery Goal 2.

THE FUNDAMENTALS OF FOOD QUANTITY

You don't have to always eat the perfect amount of food to be able to dismiss urges, but overall, you need to eat enough. I personally believe that food quantity is more important than quality in recovery, which is why it comes first in this discussion. Due to countless factors, everyone's energy requirements are different, and there is not currently an easy way to calculate a completely accurate metabolic rate for each individual. You'll always have the freedom to make adjustments to your food quantity as you see fit. When talking about the amount of food you need, it's necessary to discuss calories. Your body requires calories to function, and you obviously get those from food. But this discussion of calories does not equate to endorsing calorie counting as a long-term practice for weight control.

Shouldn't You Be Avoiding Calorie Talk?

Before getting too far into discussing energy requirements, I need to address a commonly held belief in eating disorder treatment: that people in recovery should avoid the topics of calories and calorie counting altogether because they are thought to lead to food obsessions and more disordered thinking. Calorie counting certainly has major risks if used the wrong way, and the ultimate goal will be to *not* count calories and to allow your hunger and fullness, your taste preferences, and your knowledge about food to guide your eating. But eating disorders affect your natural intuitive sense when it comes to eating, and they can render hunger and fullness signals ineffective early on in recovery. Couple the ineffectiveness of natural appetite-regulating mechanisms with the typical advice to *never* count calories, and you can see why many recovering binge eaters are baffled about how to eat in a normal way.

To reconcile this, dieticians often create meal plans for eating disorder patients that they—the dieticians—know the calorie content of, but they do not disclose that information to the eating disorder patients. This can be a helpful practice and something you may want to consider if you don't think you can manage any temporary stage of counting calories—no matter how brief—on your own. But without the guidance of a dietician, *not* knowing generally how much you are eating can possibly lead to continued food deprivation. Because of the mind-set of restrictive dieting, the patient may think that a banana for breakfast, a couple hard-boiled eggs and an apple for lunch, and a grilled chicken salad for dinner should be plenty. In reality, that amount of food wouldn't provide you with enough calories if you were lying in bed all day.

Without some form of reference, some people may not even know they are in a severe calorie deficit and then wonder why they aren't able to dismiss the binge urges. And while calculating calories in an attempt to starve yourself to lose weight is obviously dangerous, calories are, after all, just a measurement. When you put gasoline in your car, the gas gauge tells you how much you've put in, and you use that information to determine how far you can drive and to avoid running out of gas. Ideally, our bodies have an intuitive "gauge" based on hunger and fullness and taste preferences,* and if you still feel in touch with that natural gauge, then you won't need much of the rest of this discussion. But if you feel your body is lacking that intuitive sense early on in your recovery, then you have to have some sort of framework to determine adequate quantity and quality—and that's where a discussion of calories comes in.

---

*Natural mechanisms guide normal eaters for the most part. We'll discuss at length how the quality of food affects your natural gauge and how you'll always need your higher brain to some extent for making food choices in the modern food environment.

It's unfortunate that calorie counting—the same tool that can be helpful to ensure you are not depriving the body of energy—is often used for self-imposed starvation and obsessive dieting. It only makes sense that there is a strong push from traditional eating disorder therapy to get eating disorder patients to stop calorie counting. But we shouldn't throw the good out with the bad. Counting calories can be adopted in a completely different and nurturing way—akin to measuring how much water you are drinking in a day to make sure you are not dehydrated. So put aside any harmful way you've used calories in the past, and read what follows in an effort to understand how much your body needs, so that you'll soon be able to eat in a life-sustaining way without counting a single calorie.

How Much Do You Need to Eat?

Since it's now understood that discussing calories is simply a way for us all to be on the same page about how much energy your body needs, you should know that there is some controversy surrounding this—as demonstrated by the discussion in Chapter 21 about whether or not low-calorie diets may have some health benefits. On the other side of this debate are those who believe that the U.S. Food and Drug Administration's (FDA's) use of a 2,000-calorie diet as a basis for evaluating intake is insufficient—that 2,000 calories is "only enough to sustain children and post-menopausal women."[138]

In 1993, when the FDA wrote regulations for Nutrition Facts food labels, it originally intended to use 2,350 calories as the recommended daily allotment, but it was instead decided to underestimate caloric intake to 2,000 because it was an easier number to work with and because there was worry that a 2,350 standard would "encourage overeating."[139] Based on current research, it seems that even the originally proposed number was an underestimation. Using the results from the most accurate method for measuring calorie expenditure (called "doubly labeled water experiments") in hundreds of people, it has been found that, on average, adult men expend about 3,050 calories per day and adult women expend about 2,400 calories per day.[140] These results are for moderately active individuals who are neither underweight nor overweight; calorie requirements are greater for people with very high energy expenditure.[141]

Because energy expenditure increases with body weight, the more you weigh, the more calories you will require to perform daily activities—for example, a representative study found that obese individuals use an average of 3,162 calories per day.[142] There is even a note on food labels stating that people may need more or less than 2,000 calories depending on calorie needs; and yet it seems that, at least in the U.S., we have latched onto the 2,000-calorie diet as the standard of normal, so that weight loss diets typically fall below this number. If 2,000 calories is already too low, it makes restrictive dieting all the more harmful.

When it comes to those who binge, a study (utilizing the doubly labeled water method) found that total energy expenditure by female bulimic patients as compared to that by a healthy control group was the same—about 2,400 calories per day.[143] Without knowing this information at the time I recovered, this was the general range that I naturally gravitated toward when I stopped binge eating. I usually ate three flexible meals plus three or four snacks per day; and although I didn't count calories at the time, nor do I today, I knew my approximate intake because I was knowledgeable about calories—as most people with a history of eating disorders are. I was active at the time, on my feet most of the day working with kids with physical and mental disabilities, and I exercised about five times a week for 20–30 minutes.

As a side note, now, almost ten years recovered, I eat more than I did at the time I quit binge eating. I likely average about 2,600–2,900 calories a day at this point in my life, because I'm even more active taking care of my own four young children; I still exercise for about 20–30 minutes five times a week; and at the time I'm writing this, I'm still breast-feeding my youngest child, which uses a lot of extra calories. Even though my calorie intake is higher out of necessity than it used to be, it actually *looks* like I'm eating less food, from a purely visual stand-point. As most of us probably did in the 1990s and early 2000s, I used to eat lower-fat choices because I thought it was healthier; but most of us have learned in the past several years that healthy fats are absolutely vital. I now eat more calorie-dense foods—like cream, butter, healthy oils, nuts, and meat—so there are more calories packed into a smaller volume of food.

You do not need complicated formulas to calculate your energy needs; trying to get a perfect measurement promotes obsessive thinking instead of your goal of pursuing adequate nourishment. Instead, here is a simple, flexible guideline to help you eat enough: Resting metabolic rate, what your body needs to just support its basic functions, is roughly 10 times your body weight.* So if you weigh 150 pounds, you need approximately 1,500 calories per day just to lie in bed all day and do *nothing*—not walk, not talk, not brush your teeth, not go to work, not exercise. Is it any surprise that a 150-pound woman might not be able to stick to a 1,400-calorie-per-day weight loss diet? That's not even enough food to support her basic life-sustaining functions.

Most people use up *a lot* more energy during the day than their resting metab-olism requires, because much of our day is, of course, not spent resting. Even light to moderate activity during the day requires about 50 percent more calories than what the body needs just for maintenance; so the 150-pound woman in this example would need to up her intake to *at least* 2,250 calories per day, and to

---

*Resting metabolic rate can be a bit higher or lower based on factors like age, height, gender, and muscle mass.

2,850 if she were very active.[144] Often, those in recovery need even more calories, because weight restoration (in those who are underweight or below their natural weight) and physical repair of the damage caused from binge eating, purging, and restriction require energy in excess of what is required by an equivalent non-eating-disordered individual.[145] For reference, in anorexia recovery, the refeeding process generally peaks around 3,000–5,000 calories per day.[146]

I don't believe in getting overly mathematical with eating, but my job here is to convince you to feed your body well and to show you that the FDA's 2,000-calorie reference point isn't excessive *at all*. In fact, for most of you reading this book, it is *not enough* for you right now, or ever. For some people with a history of restriction, I think a daily intake of 2,000+ calories initially seems like too much simply because of a leftover belief from the now-outdated recommendation to eat low-fat foods—a fad that began in the late 1980s. It's true that 2,000 calories of low-fat foods like plain rice and salads with nonfat dressing seems like a high volume of food; but if you up your intake by adding some nourishing, calorie-dense foods like proteins and healthy fats, portion sizes won't seem excessive at all. Furthermore, many people find that healthy fats and proteins trigger satiation and satisfaction more than low-fat meals, leading to less overeating even in those without a history of binge eating.[147]

Food composition and how it affects hunger and fullness is a topic we'll return to, but for now, in summarizing the *amount* of food binge eaters need, know that—based on the studies above—2,200 to 3,000 calories per day is a good goal to work toward, although those with a higher body mass, and especially men, will need more. That's a rather wide range, but everyone is truly different in their needs, and how much you actually eat will depend on your metabolism, activity level, current weight, dieting history, and possibly a bit of experimenting. Consuming this adequate quantity of food will teach your body that you are no longer going to starve it, and it will support your efforts to dismiss binge urges, as opposed to trying to get by with only feeding your body a scanty diet of fewer than 2,000 calories in hopes of losing a few pounds.

Right now, weight loss is not a goal; dismissing urges and eating adequately are the goals, and attempting to lose weight can actually prevent you from accomplishing those goals. Some people have a mental hurdle to overcome when it comes to eating an adequate quantity of food—you may be holding on to the belief that you can somehow restrict calories *and* dismiss urges, but it should be clear by now why that is not advisable.

Based on the discussion above, do you think you are already eating an adequate quantity of food? How many non-binge calories do you estimate you consume in a day?

_____

_____

_____

_____

When and how can you add necessary calories to your diet if you haven't been eating an adequate quantity?

_____

_____

_____

_____

_____

_____

_____

How do you feel about the amount of food you need to eat? Are there any mental barriers you need to overcome?

_____

_____

_____

_____

_____

_____

_____

Clarifying What *Acceptable* Quality Means

In its most simple form, *acceptable quality* food means that you are getting enough macronutrients and micronutrients overall. Macronutrients are substances we need large amounts of for growth, metabolism, and body functions. There are three macronutrient groups: proteins, carbohydrates, and fats. Micronutrients are substances that are essential in minute amounts, such as vitamins and minerals. Consuming a sufficient amount of macro- and micronutrients ensures that you are getting the basic building blocks of life and supporting proper body system function.

The three macronutrients—proteins, carbohydrates, and fats—should be consumed in balance, but what "balance" means is open to interpretation and individualization. There is no ratio of protein to carbohydrate to fat that is best for everyone, and even what is best for you now may not be what is best for you five years from now or even next week, depending on your lifestyle and goals. Just for perspective, the National Academy of Sciences recommends acceptable macronutrient distribution ranges for adults as follows: proteins: 10–35 percent of total calories each day; fats: 20–35 percent of total calories; and carbohydrates: 45–65 percent of total calories. Some experts place more emphasis on some of these macronutrients and less on others. You can make informed decisions about what ratio is best or healthiest for you based on consultation with a nutritionist or doctor or on your own research.

You do not need to be highly specific about exact macronutrient quantities, just go about eating each day, week, and month with the overarching goal of getting good portions of each of the macronutrients. You may not always eat carbohydrates, proteins, and fats in every meal, but over the course of several days, make sure you aren't leaving out any of the groups. This applies whether you are using a structured approach to eating or an intuitive one, which we'll discuss in the next chapter. If you are using an intuitive approach, which relies more on hunger levels and taste preferences, just be aware of your food choices and notice if following your body's signals is leading to an imbalance of macronutrients. If you notice yourself gravitating toward too many carbohydrates in relation to proteins and fats, for example, try to present yourself with a wider variety of options: Buy some protein and fat sources that look appealing, keep them in the house, and prepare them in a way that's attractive to your taste so you'll be more likely to choose them when you are hungry.

As with macronutrients, you don't have to be highly precise about your intake of micronutrients either, but the common health advice to eat five to seven servings of fruits and vegetables per day is always a good guideline and will give you many vital micronutrients. Although micronutrients are only necessary in small amounts, a deficiency in one or more, such as magnesium, iron, or iodine, can lead to serious health problems. When thinking about micronutrients, it's important to consider that binge eaters, and especially those who purge, can be at higher risk for deficiencies. Although recovery doesn't require optimal nutrition, you don't want to keep your body in a depleted state, risking your health and well-being. Below, Pauline Hanuise will discuss the basics of using nutrition to support and promote physiological healing.

NUTRITION IN RECOVERY, BY PAULINE HANUISE

Most of the time, people struggling with eating issues are nutrient deficient. Everyone's nutritional needs are obviously very different, but you can experiment and become a detective of your own organism and digestion to observe what works well with you and what doesn't.

Most generally, we all need nutritious, whole foods on a regular basis to make sure we give our body what it needs to do its job. Our body is the most powerful bio-computer on earth. And to function properly, it needs many different micronutrients: amino acids, essential fatty acids, vitamins, phytonutrients, and minerals. Those will be brought to our cells via our bloodstream and are extremely important for vital functions such as cell regeneration, brain function, immune system, and heartbeat, but also for our overall health, energy, mood, and beauty (our hair, skin, eyes, nails, and much more).

To make sure your body gets what it needs to support your cells and general health, it's important to choose foods that will provide you with the best-quality micronutrients. This means choosing whole, unprocessed, and varied macronutrients, along with heaps of fresh, multicolored fruits and vegetables.

I always recommend to start taking some supplements and superfoods straightaway to help renourish the body quickly and efficiently. Spirulina, fish oil, probiotics, and a multivitamin are great to start with and can support the healing process a lot.

Digestive enzymes might be taken to help with bloating at the beginning of recovery as well. But keep in mind that extreme bloating and water retention—even though it's normal to a certain point during the first weeks of recovery—is usually a sign of digestive issues (such as food sensitivity) that need to be addressed.

Finally, as long as purging episodes are happening (be it through over-exercising, vomiting, or use of laxatives), I recommend taking some liquid minerals, such as cell food, every day. This will replenish the loss of important minerals and electrolytes incurred by purging methods. Electrolyte and mineral deficiencies can be very dangerous and eventually fatal. This is why adding electrolyte-rich foods such as coconut water, nuts and seeds, bananas, and leafy greens into your diet is also a good idea.

How will you make sure you are getting your macronutrients and micronutrients on a consistent basis?

_____

_____

_____

_____

_____

_____

_____

_____

Are there any nutritional supplements you would like to research or add to your diet to support the healing of your body?

_____

_____

_____

_____

_____

_____

_____

[25]

Set Your Sights on Authentic Eating Habits

I used to be jealous of alcoholics because they could simply quit drinking, while I had to keep eating and dealing with my food issues. My perspective changed eventually; I see food as something that can be fun and can feel good. I also think food can be used as medicine and can affect mood profoundly.

~Clare

THE NEXT CHAPTER WILL introduce four specific strategies for eating. First, however, in this chapter, there are some things to consider before choosing a strategy. You'll need to consider your eating history—notably, your history of restrictive dieting—and also set your focus on your eventual goal: authentic eating habits. The eating strategies are not cures, but launching points to settling on eating habits that fit your lifestyle and feel right for you. Before you try one of the strategies in Chapter 26, here's some key advice from Katherine Thomson, Ph.D.

Don't Mimic Previous Dieting Patterns, by Katherine Thomson

A person is going to want to think about their history of dieting, then choose or come up with a food strategy that doesn't replicate those dieting patterns. What I've noticed is that people tend to veer toward certain kinds of restriction habits when they are in their eating disorder, such as skipping meals, cutting out food groups, or becoming almost religious about certain food plans. I think a very good first step to choosing a food strategy is to take some time and honestly assess your previous dieting patterns. Ask yourself, *What is my history of restriction like? When I was dieting and cutting back on food, what form did that take?* Then use a food strategy that doesn't feel qualitatively similar.

Use the space below to write about your previous dieting patterns:

_____

_____

_____

_____

_____

_____

_____

_____

_____

_____

_____

_____

Don't Blame Binges on Your Eating Strategy

Another important thing to consider before choosing an eating strategy is that a strategy is not a cure and binges don't happen because of a faulty eating strategy. Remind yourself frequently that Recovery Goal 2 alone will not rid you of your binge urges. I remember trying different approaches for normal eating while I was bulimic, and when binge urges arose nevertheless, I'd automatically assume the eating plan was not "working" or that I was doing something wrong. It can be a dangerous setup when you think that your eating has to be just right to avoid a binge.

Unless ongoing food deprivation is involved, try not to blame your binges on how you are eating, because there will inevitably be days when you can't or don't eat perfectly and days when you are unable to follow the strategy exactly as you'd like; but a binge doesn't have to follow. If you are still undereating and that's what's prompting more binge urges, then you need to respond to those urges with an increase in your normal daily intake, not with a binge. A binge is never the solution to a problem with your eating strategy.

How have you blamed binges on imperfect eating in the past?

_____

_____

_____

_____

_____

_____

_____

Write about a day or days that you did not eat in a way you wanted to, yet you still didn't binge:

_____

_____

_____

_____

_____

_____

_____

BEYOND EATING STRATEGIES TO AUTHENTIC EATING

The strategy you choose isn't something you are stuck with for years or one you have to follow indefinitely to prevent the eating disorder from returning. The approaches are just tools to help your body regulate so that you can eventually start relying on your internal cues. To help you see what you will work toward—authentic eating habits—Katherine will end this chapter by talking about using your values and preferences to guide your eating. She'll share the experiences of some her clients who have now settled into eating habits that feel genuine to them in the hopes that these experiences can help you keep this temporary phase of structure in perspective and keep you focused on the bigger picture.

Examples of Authentic Eating Habits, by Katherine Thomson

One woman I know really loves to go on backpacking trips with her family. She loves to have big celebratory meals on family vacations, and it's rewarding for her to be able to celebrate in a festive way with food with her family. Most other times, she just eats what's easy, what's healthy, and what fuels her. What I see in this is her values coming through. She cares about her time and how she spends it, she cares about her pleasure and where it comes from, so she likes to plan on these celebratory meals with her family from time to time.

Another woman I know is vegan and gluten-free, and other people in her life eat that way as well. She likes cooking those types of foods—it's a lifestyle. She eats in a way that reflects her lifestyle, and she is very comfortable with that. The way she is eating seems aligned with her true self.

Another woman I've worked with is urban and sophisticated and likes sophisticated foods that are not so much healthy as they are "foodie" foods, like very high-quality cheeses, breads, and chocolates. For her, this is a reflection of her values, her interests—how she sees herself.

These styles of eating weren't imposed from these women's minds. These styles of eating only came about once they started to let up on the reins. Then, their natural self, their expressive self was able to come through and gravitate toward food choices aligned with their preferences. It's a beautiful thing. You can see what bubbles up—see if you like cooking, if you like eating out, if you like having lots of small meals over the day, or if you prefer two or three big meals with snacks in between. When it comes to eating, you can try to intellectually choose a style and then impose it, but it doesn't seem to work that way; rather, it seems like eating preferences just come up organically once people let go of rules. In this way, eating is kind of like art.

To gravitate toward a way of eating that works for you, you need to have patience and let go of all the shame. With binge eating and purging, there is usually so much guilt, so much self-incrimination on every level—guilt about eating too healthily, about not eating healthily enough, about eating too much, eating too little. People are embarrassed about how they eat, so there is often much hiding and isolation attached to it. Because of this, it's unrealistic to think that someone recovering from an eating disorder is suddenly going to develop real self-confidence about how they eat and embrace how they eat. There often needs to be an in-between stage where a person just doesn't judge their eating at all and just gets through the days until they feel normal again. If that means eating the same four things over and over again, then that's fine. If it means eating whatever occurs to you in the moment, and that works for you, fine. I think the fewer expectations and rules there are, the easier it will be to get away from the guilt and self-criticism.

[26]

Four Strategies for Eating Adequately

The biggest challenge was relearning how to eat: What is a normal portion?
Am I really hungry? I am still learning to listen to myself. I still do overeat
sometimes and don't always make the healthiest choices, but I am at a
normal weight and my days of feeling the incredible urge to binge feel long
behind me. I realize now that food isn't the enemy.

~Michelle

THE FOUR STRATEGIES FOR adequate eating presented below are: (1) planned eating; (2) servings-based eating; (3) calorie-minimum eating; and (4) intuition-based eating. You can pick the option that resonates most with you, you can try a combination of strategies, or you can even create your own personalized way of eating based on what you already know about Recovery Goal 2. You might discover which approach works best for you only after you try each for a few weeks, and of course you can always adjust your strategy if it doesn't feel right. These brief descriptions are only meant to be launching points to empower you to discover what works best for your body. It is important, however, to remember to avoid any strategy that mimics your previous dieting patterns.

STRATEGY 1: PLANNED EATING

Planned eating, also called "structured eating," is used in cognitive behavioral therapy (CBT) programs for eating disorders. Clinically, CBT is considered the treatment of choice for bulimia.[148] This doesn't mean CBT has extremely high success rates—the original version of the treatment resulted in only half the patients recovering,[149] and even a newer, "enhanced" version of the approach has produced only slightly better results.[150] CBT does have a lot to offer the eating component of recovery, though, because from the beginning of treatment, there is a strong focus on regulating eating, which is fundamental to the success of treatment. Usually by the third CBT session, patients are asked to eat three planned meals each day plus two or three planned snacks, with rarely more than a four-hour interval between eating times.[151] Most people find that eating about every two to three hours is a good time frame—it keeps blood sugar stable and prevents hunger from getting too strong.

Research shows that adhering to the meal schedule in CBT is associated with lower weekly binge frequency.[152] Patients in CBT can choose what they eat, with the condition that they do not purge afterward, and they are asked to confine eating to the planned meals and snacks and to avoid eating at other times. Meals and snacks should be a priority over other activities, but the plan still allows for flexibility if absolutely necessary.[153] Basically, this strategy can be boiled down to one sentence: Eat normal amounts of food at regular intervals, then don't eat again until the next eating time. This strategy involves some advanced planning, and I highly recommend getting your doctor's approval before any change in eating, especially if you have health concerns or digestive issues.

If your eating has been erratic for a long time, then when you first start using this strategy, it doesn't matter so much *what* you are eating, but that you *are* getting food in your body at regular intervals. You can start considering food quality over time—making sure you are getting adequate macro- and micro-nutrients each day. When it comes to quantity, remember you are aiming for an adequate calorie intake every day; but it's important to do this gradually if you've been through a period of restriction. If you are unsure if your plan is adequate, you can add up your intake for a few days, just to make sure you are falling in that range of 2,200 to 3,000 calories discussed earlier, but as this is not a calorie-counting approach, do this sparingly.

Planned eating is a good choice for people who currently don't have any healthy boundaries around their eating, for people who tend to skip meals throughout the day and allow themselves to get extremely hungry. On the other hand, if you were previously a restrictive dieter who ate in a highly structured way in order to enforce strict rules and if you were religious about your eating times, then this likely isn't a good choice for you. You could become overly obsessive about your meal plan, using it as a way to restrict instead of as a way to ensure proper nourishment.

Katherine's Take on Planned Eating

I tended to be the kind of restrictor who veered toward diet religiosity. I liked food plans, I liked food philosophies, I liked to micromanage what I ate. So, when I tried to use a structured meal plan in recovery, to me it felt a lot like a diet. Because of this, a structured approach didn't work for me personally, even though it has the highest success rate overall.

Do you think *planned eating* would be a good approach for you? Why or why not?

_____

_____

_____

_____

_____

_____

_____

If you'd like to try this strategy, use the chart that follows to create a planned-eating schedule for a week, copying it as needed for additional weeks.

WEEKLY PLANNED EATING LOG			
Meal	Time	Food	Place / Other Notes
DAY 1			
Breakfast			
Snack 1			
Lunch			
Snack 2			
Dinner			
Snack 3			

DAY 2			
Breakfast			
Snack 1			
Lunch			
Snack 2			
Dinner			
Snack 3			
DAY 3			
Breakfast			
Snack 1			
Lunch			
Snack 2			
Dinner			
Snack 3			
DAY 4			
Breakfast			
Snack 1			
Lunch			
Snack 2			
Dinner			
Snack 3			

DAY 5			
Breakfast			
Snack 1			
Lunch			
Snack 2			
Dinner			
Snack 3			
DAY 6			
Breakfast			
Snack 1			
Lunch			
Snack 2			
Dinner			
Snack 3			
DAY 7			
Breakfast			
Snack 1			
Lunch			
Snack 2			
Dinner			
Snack 3			

STRATEGY 2: SERVINGS-BASED EATING

The next option doesn't involve a meal plan per se and allows for more flexibility. The servings-based method is adapted from the Dietary Exchange System and is commonly used in eating disorder treatment, as well as for other conditions that require eating guidelines, primarily diabetes. This is a good method for those who have a very negative association with counting calories, because with the servings method, you can make sure you are getting an adequate quantity and quality of food without counting calories. For some, it can feel like a fresh way of looking at eating.

The servings-based method focuses on the balance of food groups and involves estimates, or "exchanges," from each of the six basic categories of food: protein (meat and meat substitutes), fats, carbohydrates (starches, grains, beans), fruit (including fruit juices), dairy (including dairy alternatives), and vegetables (non-starchy). Additionally, another category of sweets/desserts can be added or substituted in the meal plan. It is determined in advance, with the help of a nutritionist, how many servings each individual needs of each food group. An example of a balanced daily plan would be approximately eight protein servings, ten carbohydrates, four fruit, four vegetables, two dairy, eight fats, and some added sweets if desired. For reference, this sample plan would put you in approximately the middle of the 2,200–3,000 calorie range I've recommended, so you could add more or fewer servings to accommodate differing energy requirements, remembering that the main benefit of this method is not having to think about calories. You can also adjust for different macronutrient ratios if you and your dietician believe your body requires more or less of a certain category.

There are a variety of ways to get the servings of each food group. One carbohydrate serving, for example, equates to half an English muffin, a half cup of corn, or a third of a cup of cooked lentils. From the protein group, a single serving consists of one egg, one ounce of chicken, or a quarter cup of canned tuna. From the fat category: six almonds, one tablespoon of heavy cream, or a slice of bacon. Servings of fruit, vegetables, and dairy are standard portions, such as one cup of milk, one apple, or one cup of raw vegetables.*

With this approach, you do not have to plan in advance exactly what you'll eat, but it can be helpful to plan how many servings from each category you'll have in each meal. For instance, you can plan for breakfast to include two protein servings, two fruit servings, two carbohydrates, and two fats. When you wake up, you can

---

*If you want more information about food categories and servings sizes, a simple internet search for the "Dietary Exchange System" will yield many results. The University of California, San Francisco compiled easy-to-use food lists here: http://dtc.ucsf.edu/pdfs/FoodLists.pdf.

choose what foods will provide those servings based on taste preferences or what you have available.

Alternately, you may not want to do any advance planning, using the servings-based method only loosely as a way of making sure you are getting your macro-nutrients and micronutrients. You can tally up the different categories as you go about your day, noticing and correcting any areas where you might not be getting enough. An important consideration with this method is trying to avoid sticking to it like a diet: Determining your number of servings for each category is meant to help make sure you get enough nutrition; it is *not* meant to establish strict boundaries that, when exceeded, make you feel like you've failed. Having a few extra servings from one or more categories per day is better than getting rigidly locked into numbers. You don't need to precisely weigh and/or measure your foods—rough averages are fine and will help you avoid a dieting mind-set. Just keep in mind the bigger picture: that this is only a temporary strategy to help you arrive at authentic eating habits.

Katherine's Take on the Servings Method

I had more success with the servings method than structured eating because I didn't quite feel the obsession that I tended to have when I tried to do structured eating; but my personal problem with it was that I never had a plan that worked for my body. I saw three dieticians, and the information they gave me was based on averages across populations. There is very good data on what works for the average person, but very few people are the average person. In my personal instance, none of the plans the dieticians gave me had enough fat; I needed a little more fat in my diet. Also, I needed a little less starch. This I something I've learned on my own over time. It wasn't a big difference between the plan and what I needed, but enough of a difference that I didn't quite feel balanced.

Do you think *servings-based eating* would be helpful to you? Why or why not?

_____

_____

_____

_____

_____

_____

_____

STRATEGY 3: CALORIE-MINIMUM EATING

This strategy is for people who want more flexibility and freedom than the two previous strategies allow. This method consists of setting up a minimum number of calories that you need to eat in a given day, somewhere between the recommended 2,200 and 3,000 (or even higher if you are extremely active, a competitive athlete, or a person—especially a male—with larger and/or muscular body mass). With this method, you don't need to determine eating times or the number of servings of particular food groups, although you still need to keep in mind adequate macronutrients and micronutrients. Your goal is simply to consume the amount of calories you determine you need each day—let's say 2,500—not all at one time, certainly, but spread out over the day.

Calorie-minimum eating does not require you to give much forethought to meals; you just add up the calories as you eat them throughout the day. Or, if you don't like keeping track of your ongoing total all day, you can jot down approximations of what you ate, then total up your energy intake for the day that night or even the next morning. If, over the course of a few days, you notice that you are not hitting or coming close to your target number of calories, then you'll need to plan where and when you can add more food to your daily intake. Used in this way, this approach lets you *loosely* monitor your food quantity at the start of recovery to make sure it's enough.

If you are the type of person who would benefit from a lot of structure in this phase, you can use the calorie-minimum method in tandem with planned eating. To do so, you'd determine how many calories you need each day, then plan your meals accordingly to get that amount. Regardless of precisely how you apply this strategy in your life, you do not have to be exact. For example, if your set number is 2,300 calories but you actually tally 2,400 one day, 2,200 the next, and 2,500 on yet another day, that's not a problem at all—first, because there's always a little guesswork involved; and second, because, just like with the servings-based method, loose measurements are actually better, helping you avoid the trap of obsessing over calories.

How long you'll want to use this strategy as a guidepost to adequate eating is an individual decision. Some people adopt this strategy for only a week or two, some for months. What matters is your goal of getting a strong sense of what you need to eat on a daily basis to nourish your body, so that you'll eventually be able to gauge normal amounts without counting.

Katherine's Take on Calorie-Minimum Eating

This is the method that worked best for me. At the time, I was in my middle twenties and a little more active than I am now (I'm 5 feet, 6 inches), and I decided on an average of about 2300 calories. I made an informal agreement with myself that I would not binge unless I had already eaten my full day's worth of calories. What would often happen was I'd have a binge craving at let's say 2:00 p.m. and feel like I had to binge, but then I would think back and ask myself, *How much food have I eaten today?* I'd realize that I'd had quite a bit but not my full day's worth, so I'd just take a step back and say, *Well, what if I had another meal right now and then assess?* That was an extremely effective technique for me, because if I would just try to get enough food in, then I very rarely wanted to binge. Setting a minimum also prevented me from falling into the habit of restricting, which leads to bingeing. This strategy has worked for other people I have worked with as well. However, for some people who have a really strong history of calorie counting and obsession about calories, it might not be the best approach.

Do you think *calorie-minimum eating* would be a useful method for you? Why or why not?

_____

_____

_____

_____

_____

_____

To test out the calorie-minimum method for a week, you can keep track of the amount you eat each day in this chart:

CALORIE-MINIMUM EATING		
Minimum Calorie Intake per Day: _____		
Day 1	Day 2	Day 3
Day 4	Day 5	Day 6
Day 7		

STRATEGY 4: INTUITION-BASED EATING

Intuition-based eating is a strategy for those who feel relatively confident in their grasp of hunger and fullness, for those who feel they haven't lost touch with how to eat adequately, and for those who want complete freedom around food. The goal for anyone using the three previous strategies is to be able to *eventually* eat in a more natural way, without needing a plan; but here, intuition-based eating is being presented as the goal in and of itself, as a way to eat *now* and into the future if it feels helpful and authentic to you.

For some people, the three other strategies will feel too much like diets. The lower brain may react to any form of meal plan, no matter how flexible, with feelings of deprivation. When this happens, intuition-based eating is worth a try, although there are several issues to consider first. Most binge eaters trying to recover have come across the term *intuitive eating*. The term is sometimes used very loosely, but as a technique, it was first authored by Evelyn Tribole and Elyse Resch in their book *Intuitive Eating: A Revolutionary Program That Works*. The authors set up ten principles that explain how to use body signals to guide eating.[154] The basic goals of intuitive eating are to eat when you are hungry, eat what you are hungry for, stop eating when you are comfortably full, and be mindful of everything you eat.[155]

Intuition-based eating is about trusting your body's innate wisdom; this approach uses hunger and fullness—as well as the way foods make you feel—to guide what and how much you consume. In theory, your body intuitively knows what foods are best for you and how much you need to eat; so if you can just be in tune, you'll be able to effortlessly maintain good eating habits and a healthy weight. Intuition-based eating involves following your tastes and cravings, but it's not just about eating what you desire in the moment. It's also about being connected to how certain foods make you feel and making food choices based on that.

The result of intuition-based eating *should* be a good diet that fits your lifestyle and fuels your unique body in the best way possible. This does work for some people—provided the strategy is understood properly and not simply thought of as an "eat whatever you want whenever you want it for the rest of your life" approach, as it is sometimes misconstrued to be. Intuition-based eating can be a great asset for helping binge eaters give up the dieting mentality and food rules. One of the criticisms of eating based on intuition is that if we follow our appetites and cravings in our modern food environment, we will end up eating too much processed/sugary food—which applies to binge eaters and non–binge eaters alike. This does happen to some, but not everyone, so it depends on your unique body and mind.

Just being aware of this possibility can help you gauge whether intuition-based eating is right for you. You can try this strategy for a certain period of time; start with two weeks, and if, after that time, you find that you are generally eating an adequate quantity of food and adequate quality food, then this could be a great approach for you. But if you find that you are choosing too many highly pleasurable, highly processed foods, then you can either try a new strategy or adjust intuition-based eating to curb this problem. Instead of abandoning intuition, you could begin inserting more rational thought as well. You could start relying on your intuition *and* your higher brain, being a little more deliberate before following your body's innate signals and focusing more on how the food will make you feel rather than on how it tastes in the moment.

Katherine's Take on Intuition-Based Eating

When I experimented with intuitive eating, I really gave it 100 percent, just out of curiosity. I said, "I'm going to eat exactly what I'm hungry for." What I found was that after eating the food I was hungry for, over a month's time, I felt horrible. I was achy; my digestion was off; I was retaining water; I constantly felt thirsty and lacking in energy. I wasn't eating all junk, but I was eating what appealed to my mouth and my tummy at any given moment. After one day, two days, three days of eating this way, I felt fine and enjoyed the foods; but after I did that for a period of thirty days, I found that I was not craving steamed broccoli and I was not wanting sliced apples. What I found was that the more I ate salty, tasty, delicious, highly stimulating foods, the more I wanted salty, tasty, delicious, highly stimulating foods. I didn't overeat, I didn't gain weight, but it wasn't the best food for me, and I didn't feel healthy at the end of the month.

Some people who use intuitive eating eventually gravitate toward healthy foods, but that doesn't happen for everyone. For me, it was the opposite. I tend to be the kind of person that the more I eat something, the more I want that thing— and that goes for healthy foods as well as unhealthy foods. So sometimes I'll get in these patterns of eating and I'll realize that I'm stuck in a pattern, and I have to put the brakes on for a little while. For example, last spring, I got into a peanut butter cup phase. I love peanut butter cups, so I eat them, which is no big deal; however, I started to notice that I was eating them day after day and I was wanting more and more. It wasn't a problem, it wasn't hurting my life; but I realized that eating more of the peanut butter cups wasn't truly satisfying and wasn't turning off the cravings, so I took a break.

When taking a break, I didn't cut out all sugar, I didn't cut out all desserts; but I realized that, for whatever reason, there was a glitch in my system that was on repeat. Maybe it's my underlying obsessive traits, because not everyone is like this, but I've learned that I'm susceptible to keep wanting and eating the same thing. It would be really, really nice if it were true that if a person craves chocolate or salt, that's because they really need chocolate or need salt, and then the craving would be over. In many cases, that's not true.

Do you think *intuition-based eating* would be a good fit for you right now? Why or why not?

_____

_____

_____

_____

_____

_____

_____

After two weeks (or another time period of your choosing) of using an intuition-based approach, do you feel you are eating an adequate quantity of food and decent quality food? Or are your choices primarily pleasure-based?

_____

_____

_____

_____

_____

_____

_____

_____

After two weeks (or another time period of your choosing) of using intuition-based eating, how do you feel physically? How is your energy, digestion, moods, and sleep? Do you think your food choices line up with what your body needs?

_____

_____

_____

_____

_____

_____

_____

_____

The next two chapters in this section—"Hunger and Fullness" and "Where to Eat"—contain information that can help you make any eating strategy more effective and continue the process of creating your own version of adequate eating.

[27]

Hunger and Fullness

The most difficult challenge in learning how to eat a normal diet was determining the appropriate portions for someone my size. Because I went from eating very little to extraordinarily large amounts of food, I had problems deciding what would be considered a normal-sized portion. However, I eventually learned how to eat the right amount of food by listening to my body again. I was surprised how fast my body regenerated from all the damage I had done to it during my bulimia. Throughout the first week of recovery, I could not feel hunger, but I found that my body gradually regained the state it was in before I acquired my poor eating habits. This allowed me to better determine what portions provided me with satiety.

~Teresa

REGARDLESS OF WHAT, IF any, strategy is chosen to help you regulate eating, the topic of hunger and fullness is of central importance. Although it's already been touched upon, we'll now address it in more detail. Feelings of hunger and fullness are the signals that nature intended to guide eating; however, for recovering binge eaters, using these signals is often a skill that comes in time. Deliberately eating adequately, day by day, allows the natural, primary cues for eating to reemerge—sometimes quickly, sometimes gradually. Nevertheless, it makes sense to start thinking about and noticing hunger and fullness with whatever approach to eating you are taking. We'll begin with a basic explanation of how to eat based on hunger and fullness, from Cookie Rosenblum, then the chapter will continue with Katherine Thomson and me addressing some common challenges that binge eaters may face while relearning these signals.

The Basics of How to Use Hunger and Fullness, by Cookie Rosenblum

You knew hunger and fullness when you were a baby, but somewhere along the way, your signals got crossed. It might take a while to relearn those signals, especially if you've been binge eating a long time. Conversely, someone who is younger, with a shorter history of binge eating, may go back to their default factory settings more quickly. Always remember that learning hunger and fullness isn't another quick fix—it's giving a gift to yourself that will last.

Hunger and fullness are things we can quantify, but they're also very individual in that everyone has to learn what hunger and satiation uniquely feel like in their own body. That process takes practice, and it's subjective. I use a hunger scale (see Figure 1) to help the people I work with to quantify hunger. The goal when using this scale is to eat when you are a little hungry and stop when you are a little full; I suggest starting to eat when your level is –2 and stopping when your level is +2. Fullness means something different to everyone; but to me, satiation is about the lack of hunger, not a fullness where you feel stuffed or your stomach feels heavy.

The way I describe it is that when you end eating—unless it's Thanksgiving or some major occasion where everyone overeats—you should still feel light enough to be able to do something mildly physical, like yoga. Satiation does not mean you feel like you have to lie on the couch and unbutton your pants. On the flip side, it's important that you learn to feel your hunger signals as well. If you don't wait for hunger and eat before you get the signal, then it's unlikely that you are going to get a signal to stop, so working on waiting for hunger is important. For people who constantly graze, I recommend that they start to put some structure around their eating and space it out to allow hunger signals to gradually emerge.

When I am helping people train themselves to determine what the hunger and fullness signals feel like in their body, I tell them to check in with their body at regular intervals. I also recommend that when they eat, they eat slowly enough so that when the stomach starts to stretch and sends the fullness signal to the brain, they are able to notice it. In the beginning, people will often eat past the point of satiation, and they will notice what that feels like and then know they need to stop a little sooner next time. It's like an experiment. Think of it as gathering information. This process helps you learn to feed your stomach instead of feeding the pleasure centers in your brain.

FIGURE 1

Physical Hunger Scale

−10 Starved

−8 Extreme hunger

−6 Serious hunger

−4 Strong hunger

−2 Slight hunger

 0 Neutral: not full, not hungry

+2 Comfortable, satisfied

+4 Ate a little too much

+6 Uncomfortable, sluggish

+8 Stuffed, stomach may hurt

+10 In pain

*The goal is to eat at −2 and stop at +2, from a little hungry,
to comfortably satisfied.*

TRACK YOUR HUNGER LEVELS

At intervals of your choosing during the day, or whenever you are thinking about it, check in with your body and quantify your hunger using the scale above. You can also note any sensations you are feeling at that hunger level, along with the last time you ate and what you ate last, in the chart on the following page. Over time, this can help you be more aware of your body's natural signals. As you learn what different levels of hunger and fullness feel like in your unique body, you can add your own words and phrases to Figure 1 to personalize the hunger scale.

Day/Time	Hunger Level & Other Notes About Physical Sensations	Last Time/Food Eaten

EAT BEFORE YOU ARE VERY HUNGRY

The word *very* is intentionally subjective, because it includes a wide range of higher-than-usual hunger levels—basically, anywhere at or above level –4 on the hunger scale in Figure 1. It's hard to stay rational when the primal urge to eat is so strong. For normal eaters, heightened hunger can lead to mild overeating; but for binge eaters, higher levels of hunger can sometimes lead to a lapse in the ability to feel separate from the urges. If you have a history of restriction, you may have stronger hunger signals than the average person until your body gets the message that you aren't going to starve it anymore. Your body has sent hunger signals in the past that haven't worked, so hunger becomes heightened. This won't last, but during the first few weeks and months,

I try to eat foods that give me the energy I need to do well in my daily life. Sometimes I don't have enough time to eat as much as I need to throughout the day, and I'll come home and be really hungry, so I always try to pack snacks (apples, almonds, granola bars, etc.) so that I won't be ravenous. By not restricting, I have more of a social life and my quality of life has improved.

~Jackie

take extra care to avoid putting your body in that state of intense hunger, where you have less access to self-control. Sometimes this is not possible if you are leading a busy life or if you are in a situation you can't avoid; but for the most part, aim to eat regularly enough so that your hunger doesn't climb too high.

Even if you do find yourself in a situation where your hunger levels are heightened more than usual, it still doesn't have to lead to a binge. It's not an ideal state in which to dismiss binge urges, but it's still possible. When hunger is strong, remind yourself that extreme hunger is a natural state designed to motivate you to seek food and encourage you to eat a lot. All you have to do is listen to your body: Seek food and give yourself a plentiful, nourishing amount of it. It's okay and expected that you will eat more than usual when heightened hunger is present, when eating just a little snack or a normal-sized meal would be unsatisfying and thus frustrating. You of course don't want to binge, but you *do* want to give your body the signal that you are not going to starve it anymore.

Normal eaters, too, will consume more than usual or eat faster than usual when they are very hungry; however, they have a reasonable "off" switch—their satiety mechanisms work properly, so they don't just keep eating and eating. But when you are first recovering, you might not be able to fully trust your body's "off" switch, so you'll have to use your eyes and rational brain more than your body's signals of satiation in these situations. It's fine to eat abundantly, but you have to consciously decide when it is enough.

During the early stages of recovery, what changes can you make to avoid getting overly hungry (for example, pack snacks, rearrange your schedule)?

_____

_____

_____

_____

_____

_____

_____

_____

_____

_____

Write about a time when you were very hungry but still avoided letting it lead you to a binge. How did you handle the situation, and what did you learn?

TRAINING FULLNESS SIGNALS

There are ways to help your body and brain get back in touch with fullness signals. Training fullness signals is about helping yourself stop eating after consuming a reasonable amount of food (even if you don't actually feel full at that point in time). Once you do this over and over, your body will become accustomed to eating normal amounts of food and your fullness signals will start to reemerge. Here are some tactics to facilitate this process.

Decisively Pick an End to the Meal

Just decide when your meal should be over. Try not to deliberate over questions like, *If I have another serving, will that be overeating?* or *If I don't have another bite, will that be restricting?* Just sense when you've had a reasonable amount and then put away the food. If it turns out that you ate too little, try eating a little more next time. If you end up feeling like you had a few bites too many, don't worry about it—just stop a bit sooner next time.

Write about a time when you decisively chose to end a meal. Do you think you picked a reasonable stopping point, and what can you learn from that going forward?

_____

_____

_____

_____

_____

_____

_____

Wait to Eat Until Your Next Snack or Meal in a Flexible, Nonrestrictive Way

As Cookie touched on in the beginning of this chapter, it's difficult to learn appropriate levels of fullness if you are never experiencing appropriate levels of hunger. Spacing out your eating is important to regulate hunger signals, and if you are using the planned eating strategy, this is already a goal. To explain why eating at intervals is important, let's look at the example of appetite regulation in babies. There are many schools of thought about how to feed a baby, with some people believing you should nurse or bottle-feed them every time they seem to want to suck. Others say that, while babies often have a strong instinct to suck, it's not always for nourishment (breast or bottle); and by supplying them with milk too often—for example, if you let them nurse every twenty minutes—it's more difficult for their appetite to regulate.

I agree that too-frequent feeding—in babies and individuals of any age—can lead to becoming out of touch with true hunger and fullness. When my kids were infants, I tried to wait at least an hour between feedings, unless it was evident he or she was very hungry. Some caregivers take it much further than that with strict three- or four-hour infant feeding schedules. I don't think it's advisable to make a baby or make yourself wait several hours to eat if you are feeling hungry, but if you find yourself wanting food, let's say, half an hour after you last ate a normal, nourishing meal, then it's likely not real hunger—just false cravings.

If you've become accustomed to grazing, an interval of about an hour to an hour and a half between eating times is a good place to start. You don't have to be exact about this time frame; the purpose of it is simply to allow you to start noticing your own appetite. You can work toward longer intervals between meals, and then you can gradually learn to let hunger dictate when you will eat something. To help yourself wait patiently between meals and snacks, remind yourself how useful it will be to experience real hunger and then satisfy it again.

How long do you want to wait to eat between meals? Write down ideas for passing the time when you have nothing else to do:

_____

_____

_____

_____

_____

_____

_____

_____

Write about any physical sensations you experience while waiting that help you recognize and relearn your hunger:

_____

_____

_____

_____

_____

_____

_____

_____

Remember: "It's Just One Meal"

Placing a great deal of importance on each meal fuels neural pathways that keep you focused on food. When it's time to eat based on your meal plan or schedule, or when you feel hungry, pick something to eat that seems adequate, eat a reasonable amount of it, and move on. Try to be decisive about what you eat, making the best decision you can at that point in time, but also keeping in mind that it's just one meal. If you are eating three meals and three snacks a day, there will be over forty more eating times just in a week, and you don't want to be overly stressed about each of them. The decisions you make do add up over time, and you of course want to make good food choices overall; but owning your choices allows you to be in the moment and notice your hunger and fullness, rather than agonizing about what you should or shouldn't be eating.

Do you tend to be decisive or indecisive about eating? Write about times when you've been confident in your choices and if/how you've benefited from that:

_____

_____

_____

_____

_____

_____

_____

Don't Force Yourself to Leave Food Behind

Common advice for sensible eating is to leave some food behind—to not "clean your plate." Portion sizes in many restaurants, at least in the U.S., are often too big, so it makes sense to leave some food on your plate or take the remainder home as leftovers. However, when you are able to serve yourself a normal portion, give yourself permission to finish everything. Eating all of your adequately portioned plate takes all the guesswork and indecision out of it. This is especially true when you are trying to give up restriction and need to give your body the abundance signal. It can be liberating to tell yourself in advance that you *are* going to eat everything—instead of constantly worrying about when you are going to stop.

Furthermore, agonizing about the perfect stopping point can prevent you from enjoying your meal. As the portion left on your plate gets smaller and smaller, feelings of guilt can arise about how much you are eating. Some people start to criticize themselves as the amount left shrinks, which then leads to a feeling of rebellion and wanting to eat everything, and then some. Another benefit of cleaning your plate early on in recovery is that it allows you to experience slightly different levels of fullness, based on how much food was there to start the meal. Eventually, you will be able to sense when you *want* to stop, without having to force yourself.

Has trying to leave food on your plate affected you negatively in the past? Why?

_____

_____

_____

_____

_____

_____

Make yourself a normal portion of food and eat all of it. After the meal, quantify your hunger/fullness using the hunger scale in Figure 1. You can repeat this exercise daily for a couple of weeks to help you notice fullness, observing below how varying amounts of food affect your fullness differently:

_____

_____

_____

_____

_____

_____

_____

_____

End the Meal with a Positive Statement

When you've either cleaned your plate or eaten to what you believe is an appropriate level of fullness, end the meal on a positive note. It helps to actually say something positive—out loud or mentally—such as, "That was delicious" or "That's just what I needed" or "That hit the spot." Saying those things lets you focus on the enjoyment and nourishment you had and helps give your body the stop signal. Conversely, stern and negative statements—"You've had *enough*, you absolutely can't have any more"—can backfire and actually make cravings for more food even stronger. Even if you *are* having cravings after a meal, saying or thinking a positive end-of-the-meal thought will help your body associate normal levels of fullness with enjoyment and gratitude. Building positive associations with appropriate levels of fullness will make eating adequate amounts easier to repeat.

Jot down positive statements you could use to end a meal:

_____

_____

_____

_____

_____

_____

_____

Use Your Eyes to Teach Your Brain

One tool I used when it came to dealing with the uncertainty of my feelings of hunger and fullness was to rely on my eyes more than my stomach. I could *see* a normal portion based on what I already knew about proper eating, but I couldn't always *feel* it. So I used a visualization strategy of recalling the sight of normal plates of food. I ate what I visualized as normal, even though it didn't always lead to fullness at first. However, over time, my fullness signals reemerged, and I learned to link how the amount of food looked to how satisfied it made me feel.

Normal eaters naturally use their eyes to determine how a portion of food will affect their fullness. Think of a person in a restaurant, when a waiter puts a heaping plate of food in front of them: The person's eyes widen, and they say,

"Whoa, I'll never be able to eat all of that!" This is because there is a link between what they see and how they know it will make them feel. If, on the other hand, it's a tiny portion, they may say something like, "This wouldn't be enough for a mouse." The ability to visualize and connect what food looks like to how full it will make you is a wonderful skill to have.

If you are using a very structured eating approach, appropriate-sized meals are already built into your meal plan, which is a great opportunity to see what normal looks like. Take a long look at the food in front of you prior to eating it, and over time, you'll build a picture gallery of "normal." You can even visualize normal eating over the course of an entire day, learning, for example, approximately what 2,400 calories looks like. Alternately, you can get visual snapshots of normal eating by seeing what friends and family consume (the ones you consider normal eaters). Or you can take pictures of your own normal meals and snacks before you eat them. Eating based on what your eyes tell you will train your appetite-regulating mechanisms over time. An added benefit is that using your eyes to gauge eating serves as an effective bridge from calorie counting to eating without any structure.

How can you incorporate visualization into your eating?

_____

_____

_____

_____

_____

_____

Use Food Composition to Help Regulate Appetite

Different foods with the same calorie content can have a different effect on our appetite, based on food volume and composition. For example, about ten chips and sixty grapes have the same amount of calories. Does this mean you'll feel just as satisfied regardless of whether you eat ten chips or sixty grapes? Most people could easily eat more than ten chips (the highly processed kind) because of that rewarding salt/fat/carbohydrate combination that makes you want to keep reaching in the bag. However, give someone sixty grapes, and they likely won't be strongly craving the sixty-first. The grapes aren't as stimulating to the senses;

furthermore, the grapes have a greater volume and water content and therefore may trigger satiation more quickly than the more calorie-dense chips.

This is something that weight loss diets often draw upon—advising you to eat foods with high water content that have a large volume but little calories, like salads. The theory is that it can help your body achieve fullness quicker, so you eat less. Although I wouldn't advise using this strategy with a focus on weight loss, the idea that foods with high water content stretch the stomach a little and help you feel more full is something you can incorporate to regulate your appetite. Adding more fruits and vegetables—which have a higher volume and lower calorie density than other food groups—to your *already adequate* meals and snacks can help you achieve a feeling of fullness that you otherwise might not experience. Those foods can fill your stomach enough to make you feel satisfied, which can help you through the phase of residual stomach stretching from binge eating. Then, after you regulate your appetite a bit, you can gradually decrease the volume of your meals as your stomach returns to normal size—though, of course, it's always a good idea to eat lots of fruits and vegetables!

Food composition is something that you should also consider if you were a purging bulimic and fullness still triggers urges to purge. As opposed to someone who needs to stretch their stomach a little more than the average person to start learning fullness, you might be hypersensitive to any hint of fullness. In that case, you will want to focus on eating more calorie-dense, nutrient-rich, lower-volume foods, such as healthy oils, nut butters, full-fat dairy products, avocados, and seeds. This will help you get enough nourishment, but not stretch your stomach so much that it triggers urges to purge. Of course, you don't need to *act* on any urges to purge that arise, but not letting yourself get too full is a way to make the process easier on yourself. Additionally, healthy calorie-dense foods are a good source of sustained energy that helps stabilize blood sugar (a topic Katherine Thomson will discuss at the end of this chapter).

Part of training hunger and fullness based on food composition is accepting that sometimes, with a small amount of highly stimulating foods (like the ten chips in the example above), you are rarely going to feel satiation. This applies to normal eaters as well. Even though the calorie content of these pleasurable foods is relatively high, the rewarding nature of eating them combined with their low volume that doesn't stretch the stomach much all but ensures that you won't register a hint of fullness—and that's okay. You don't have to feel satiated every time you eat. You can choose to eat one cookie or a piece of candy purely for pleasure sometimes, not expecting a change in your hunger level.

How do you plan to use food composition to assist you in eating normally?

_____

_____

_____

_____

_____

_____

_____

Use Food Quality to Help Regulate Appetite

Some experts use children as examples of creatures who follow their hunger and fullness signals properly. It's true that they usually don't "binge," overeating to a large degree; however, I think children serve as a better example of the fact that appetite-regulating mechanisms don't work precisely as they should in the modern food environment, where pleasure can override those mechanisms. I've found that most babies just learning to eat solid food will gladly gobble up many vegetables, healthy starches, meats, and fruits; but once they are exposed to sugary, processed, convenience foods, they gradually lose their appetite for the healthy things. To the frustration of many parents like myself, it seems that the more processed junk they have, the more processed junk they want, eventually turning up their nose at "real" food. Young children will almost always choose a cookie over some broccoli, and they'll likely eat more cookies than their parents would like them to if given free rein.

To complicate matters, making the junk food "off-limits" and engineering kids' environments to exclude junk food can make that food even more attractive when it is available to them[156]—say, at a friend's house or at school. This does not apply to all children, of course; some kids do opt for healthier choices over junk food based on their own intuition. This

> When we eat a lot of processed or refined starches and sugar, then that will definitely make us physiologically crave more. We know that; that's proven. If your whole diet is pretty balanced and typical, and if you want a sweet, no big deal; but if that's all you eat all of the time, then you are making it harder to get in touch with what your body really needs and when and how much, because those foods do create artificial craving. You make it easier on yourself by eating foods that make it easier to stop when you've had enough.
>
> ~Cookie Rosenblum

same variability is seen in people recovering from eating disorders. You may be able to relearn hunger and fullness just fine despite our modern food environment, even feeling naturally drawn to healthy choices ... or you may need to deliberately make sure your food quality supports your efforts to get in touch with body signals.

If you are having trouble connecting with those signals, don't feel like you have to swear off all sugar and junk food. Simply make sure you are including an abundance of "real" foods in your diet as well, especially proteins and healthy fats. Unlike a child, you have reasons for wanting to override that natural instinct for pleasure in the moment; you know how too much junk food will make you feel and how it will affect your health. Ensuring that you are eating a balanced diet with some good, slow-digesting fuel incorporated into it will help you achieve mastery of your hunger and fullness more quickly. It will also help you avoid some of the blood sugar issues that Katherine Thomson will discuss next.

What changes in food quality can you make to support your efforts to relearn hunger and fullness?

_____

_____

_____

_____

_____

_____

_____

_____

BLOOD SUGAR FLUCTUATIONS AND REAL HUNGER, BY KATHERINE THOMSON

Bulimics and those with binge eating disorder often struggle with blood sugar imbalances. Part of the reason for this is the types of foods eaten during binges, which are usually high in sugar. Purging bulimics can have even worse blood sugar imbalances, because they eat tons of food and then purge all of the fiber, all of the protein, and all of the fat—but they retain all of the sugar, meaning purging bulimics basically live off of just pure sugar.

Because of this, it's important to learn to differentiate hunger from blood sugar fluctuations. It can take some time and some experimenting for people to recognize the difference. So here's a little guidance to help distinguish between the two: The kind of hunger that requires good fuel to fuel it (and by "good fuel," I'm thinking slow-digesting carbohydrates, proteins, fats, and fiber)—that kind of hunger usually feels good, provided it's not overly strong. It feels kind of pleasant, like a low-grumbling, yummy sensation that sometimes makes the mouth water. Your sense of smell becomes very refined and everything tastes very good.

In contrast, the kind of "hunger" that is actually a sign of blood sugar fluctuations usually comes with a sense of panic; it comes with the heart speeding up and constriction in the chest, with a sense of urgency, a tightness in the throat, and extreme irritability. I can look back now and see that my hunger signals were very out of balance when I was first recovering. A lot of times what I was feeling wasn't even hunger, it was blood sugar imbalances. I didn't know it was my blood sugar at the time, but I can compare how I feel now to how I felt then, and now I have about one-fifth the intensity of hunger that I used to have, or what I was calling "hunger."

In my case, the timing of my eating was appropriate; in other words, when I felt what I thought was hunger, it was usually time to eat. However, the intensity of what I was feeling as hunger was not at all proportionate to the amount of food I needed. I would have these super-intense pangs of hunger when really all I needed was just a small snack. I was actually very hard on myself for this, and I wish I hadn't been. I couldn't figure out why I wanted so much food—why my hunger was so strong. I thought everybody had hunger that strong, and it wasn't until my blood sugar rebalanced that I started to see that what I'd been experiencing was not normal hunger. For me, the rebalancing of my blood sugar was a slow process, but it's a process that could have been expedited if I'd had more guidance.

What is so upsetting to me is that for so many years, I thought those symptoms were just emotional cues. People were always telling me, "Those are signs of emotional turmoil" and "You are emotionally eating"—but that just wasn't the case. In actuality, when I was feeling strong emotions, that's when I *didn't* binge. Emotions were almost a distraction from my cravings—that's just the kind of person I am. When I look back on all those times when my therapist was saying, "Oh, this is because you must have been emotionally triggered," I now know that wasn't the problem at all. The problem was my blood sugar.

Although blood sugar imbalances can create miserable feelings, it's important to remember that those feelings won't last long once you begin to eat normally. To deal with blood sugar imbalances over the long run, what people usually need is a more consistent introduction of proteins, fats, and fiber over the course of a day.

However, until doing this balances the blood sugar, you need to take some actions to help you through uncomfortable symptoms. This advice might seem counter-productive, but I've found that a lot of people who are struggling with blood sugar imbalances do well with very diluted simple sugars. Certainly, sugar can increase and spike blood sugar variables if eaten in large quantities; but sipping a very diluted glass of juice can really help with those strong blood sugar cravings until the body balances itself.*

Keep track here of any symptoms you notice that help you distinguish real hunger from blood sugar fluctuations:

_____

_____

_____

_____

_____

_____

_____

Keep track here of any foods that help you regulate your blood sugar or affect it adversely:

_____

_____

_____

_____

_____

_____

_____

---

*Persistent and/or unmanageable blood sugar fluctuations require medical help.

Because binge eating is never a solution to blood sugar fluctuations, write about a time when you experienced abnormal blood sugar symptoms but did not let that lead to a binge. What did you learn that can help you in the future?

_____

_____

_____

_____

_____

_____

_____

_____

_____

_____

_____

[28]

Where to Eat:
A Note About Eating Environment

I notice that when I have friends over or I'm less of an introvert, it's easier for me to ignore the urges simply because of another person's presence.

~Jessie

THIS CHAPTER WILL BRIEFLY address one last consideration in creating your own version of adequate eating—and that is: where to eat. Like several other aspects of recovery, you don't need to overthink this one, because you don't want to get into the mind-set where your food environment has to be perfect to avoid a binge. Still, because we eat several times a day, it's an issue worth putting some thought into, as Katherine will discuss here.

WHERE TO EAT? BY KATHERINE THOMSON

Some people find it really helpful to have a designated eating place where they can sit down and relax. A big tenet of intuitive eating is to have such an eating place, but even if you aren't using intuitive eating, I think in the early stages of getting over an eating disorder it can be very helpful to have a spot in which to be mindful. What it's really about is relaxation, so if sitting in a particular place relaxes a person, then I say it's a good thing; but if it makes them feel more tense, more judged, and more harsh on themselves, then it's not serving its purpose.

For me personally, rules and lack of flexibility surrounding my eating weren't always helpful. I didn't want to be confined to having to eat in a particular place. I felt hindered sitting down for twenty minutes to eat—just sitting there, not doing anything else. Again, that can be a helpful stage for some people—to learn to enjoy and appreciate your food and pay more attention to hunger and fullness—but I like the flexibility of being able to stand up, and I don't want to judge myself because I'm eating standing up or doing something else at the same time.

The other day, I was waiting for my coffee to brew, and I noticed I was eating a banana standing up, and I thought, *See, this is not intuitive eating. I'm standing up, not really mindful, and I'm eating this banana. I'm kind of hungry, but this isn't necessarily what I wanted—I probably would have preferred an omelet.* And yet it was wonderful to be able to just stand in my kitchen and eat a banana.

There are times when it's important to consider your eating environment—when you are eating something that has triggered binge urges in the past or something that you frequently binged on in the past. In this case, choose a location where your heart rate can stay low, your breathing can stay slow, and you feel safe. Also, choose a place where you are not likely to have access to foods that could tempt you to act on impulses you may have. For different people, this could mean very different things. For me, this actually meant eating in restaurants—restaurants were the safest place for me to experiment with trigger foods and still stay in control. But I know another woman whose very *last* step of recovery was to be able to eat in restaurants. For me, it was one of my first steps to normalize eating, because in restaurants, I felt like I was in a container; I felt very dignified; I ate slowly with my utensils; and I didn't have quick access to cupboards and a refrigerator filled with a bunch of food. So that's where I took all my risks.

Other people take risks (i.e., eat foods that may trigger urges to binge) in their living room, on their couch, or at their table because that feels safe to them, a place they can relax. Some people prefer having others around when they're learning to regulate—maybe their spouse, friend, or child; but others would rather be alone so they don't feel watched or judged. When considering your eating environment, remember that it's going to look different from one person to another.

Based on your personal experience, what eating locations make you feel the most relaxed?

_____

_____

_____

_____

_____

_____

Write about what eating environment(s) you'd like to utilize at this time and/or why you'd rather take a completely flexible approach:

_____

_____

_____

_____

_____

_____

_____

Where would you feel most comfortable eating foods you used to binge on?

_____

_____

_____

_____

_____

_____

* * * * * * * * * * * * * * * * * * * *

You now have the basic information you need to create your own version of adequate eating—a way of eating that feels authentic to you and nourishes your body properly. If you are already on your way to eating habits you feel comfortable with, there is no need to read further into this section. The next five chapters address eating topics that recovering binge eaters often have questions about—things like what constitutes "healthy" eating, food cravings and "addiction," overeating, weight issues, and eating at night. You can come back to these chapters if you ever encounter a problem related to these topics; or—if you feel one of these issues is currently holding you back from achieving Recovery Goal 2—you can benefit from reading the chapter(s) now.

[29]

"Healthy" Eating

*I try to eat healthy, feel-good foods that will help keep my serotonin working
well, but I don't stick exclusively to it. If I try to make it into a diet or follow it
to the letter, I will rebel and immediately start sabotaging my dieting efforts.
I try to keep more of a balance—if I really want french fries, I will eat them.
I try to stay mindful while I eat them and not gobble them down. Bread and
butter is something I refuse to live without (something I never allowed myself
to eat during my disorder and fantasized about frequently). I never say any
food is completely off-limits. It actually took me years after recovery to get to
this point, but I allow myself to eat anything that I truly want.*

~Sandra

WE'VE ALREADY TALKED ABOUT choosing higher-quality foods to make appetite regulation easier. This chapter will delve a little deeper into food quality,
specifically addressing "healthy" eating and its implications for recovery. Many
binge eaters are very health conscious and want to eat well, and I've received
many questions about healthy eating in the years since publishing *Brain over Binge*.
In this chapter, I hope to assist you in finding a balance in your life that feels
healthy for you, without healthy eating becoming a "diet."

Since this isn't a nutrition book, I'm not going to tell you exactly what's healthy
and what's not—besides, there is actually not much consensus there. Nutrition
science is only in its infancy, and while there are some basic things that we know,
there is much more that we do not know. The good news is that an optimally
"healthy" diet isn't necessary to accomplish the two recovery goals of dismissing
urges and eating adequately. An optimally "healthy" diet is also no guarantee that
you can perfectly control your own behavior. Even the most well-nourished people
can have a binge eating disorder or another addiction or habit.

You may indeed benefit from some changes in food quality, but always remember that you are aiming for adequate, not perfect. This *especially* applies to those with a history of restrictive dieting, because focusing on eating only very healthy, very high-quality foods can sometimes result in accidental undereating. It's more important that you eat enough than that your food quality be pure. To begin this chapter, Cookie Rosenblum will share an overview of a helpful mind-set to have when thinking about eating healthy.

How to Think About Food Quality, by Cookie Rosenblum

Managing your body is part of managing your life. Instead of waking up and just seeing what happens to you that day, you get to choose what you want to eat and what kind of eating plan you want to give yourself—not for weight loss, just for living. This is really just part of being an adult, of being someone who is responsible for yourself and how you feel—not because you want to look a certain way or fit in a certain size of jeans, but because it is part of our job in life to take care of our bodies, to take care of our happiness, and to be responsible. I don't think that's restrictive; it's a good thing.

You are in charge; you get to decide how you want to feel today and what fuel you want to give yourself. I think it's okay to eat for pleasure, but you get to decide what percentage—not by measuring or weighing or anything like that, but just by knowing as an adult, *Hey, I feel better when I eat mostly clean, healthy foods.* Once you stop binge eating, then you get to decide what you want to do with all that available mental energy and how you would like to take care of your body. I don't honestly know anyone who is eating 80 percent donuts and chips and who feels good and is getting things done in their life. It doesn't actually feel good. If you've been a dieter, it might initially feel good to let go of restriction and eat junk, but then it just feels awful.

You Don't Have a Clean-Eating Brain and a Junk-Food Brain

It's common for binge eaters to mistakenly merge the part of themselves that wants to binge with the part of themselves that wants *any* unhealthy food. They begin to apply the lower brain/higher brain idea to the consumption of all junk food by viewing their lower brain as their "unhealthy eating" brain and their higher brain as their "healthy eating" brain. I don't think this is useful, especially when first trying to quit binge eating, because it can lead to an "all or nothing" trap. When you start trying to view all of your cravings for anything unhealthy as neurological junk, it can be overwhelming.

It can lead you to believe that if you follow a desire for a dessert or some processed or convenience food, then your lower brain has already won, so you'll be primed to believe any thoughts that say you "might as well binge." You don't actually have a good brain and a bad brain, because both the lower and the higher brain are necessary for a rich human existence. Your lower brain, with its pleasure centers, is indeed behind most of your junk-food cravings, but *everyone* has those. The lower brain also causes you to crave and take pleasure in delicious, healthy food as well, as desire for food is rarely a purely rational experience. Recovery is about trying to get rid of the "glitch" in your reward system, not banish the system altogether.

Craving french fries doesn't make you abnormal or weak, and it certainly doesn't mean your animal brain controls you. If you choose to follow those brain signals and have the fries, great—enjoy them! If you choose not to, then that's fine too—have some organic carrot sticks with almond butter instead, and enjoy those! Don't think that if you choose the french fries, you are giving in to a binge urge. Likewise, don't think that if you decide on the carrot sticks, depriving yourself of the fries will lead you to binge. It won't. There will be other opportunities for fries. The methods and advice in this book are for *quitting binge eating*, not for sticking to very strict, healthy-food-only eating plans and banishing all cravings for anything unhealthy.

Write about times when you eat junk food in moderation. (This can help you keep separate your binge eating habit and your other cravings for pleasurable food.)

_____

_____

_____

_____

_____

_____

_____

_____

KEEP NUTRITION IN PERSPECTIVE

At the time I recovered, I tried, and still try, to eat relatively healthy for the most part, although I certainly don't always do that and I definitely have all types of food in moderation. Worth noting is that when I recovered in 2005 and tried to eat "healthy," the popular definition of the word included a lot of 100 percent whole-wheat and whole-grain products and low-fat dairy. This was the generally accepted nutritional advice at the time, which has now been overturned, or at least seriously questioned.[157] Also, at the time, there wasn't such a backlash against processed food, and I thought that things like store-bought whole-grain cereal, processed lunch meat, "low-fat" (artificially) flavored yogurt, and canned vegetables were pretty good choices. Then, I'd often have desserts or sugary treats in addition to the food I thought was healthy, so that based on current knowledge, it was a far cry from an ideal diet.

Knowing that it was possible for me to recover, rather easily, on foods that are now considered to be very low quality is actually encouraging. It's an example of why quantity is more important and why quality doesn't need to be perfect. Surely, those who recover today will have a completely different definition of what is healthy, but even a new definition could one day be outdated. I sometimes feel that if you name any food, there is some expert who could label it unhealthy. We've all heard that sugar and processed foods aren't healthy; that's common knowledge by now. However, more and more foods have been blacklisted based on some scientific study or anecdotal evidence. There are nutritional experts claiming that dairy, wheat, soy, meat, eggs, starches, fruit, certain oils and fats, coffee, grains, legumes, certain nuts, eggs, and/or *anything* that isn't organic should be cut out of our diets, in the name of health. To make matters even more confusing, there are usually experts on the other side saying that we should make a point of eating plenty of those very same foods, in the name of health. If that's not bad enough, expert opinions can change over time and new research can prove previous advice wrong.

> *I would rather weigh a little extra and not stress out too much about food and what I should or shouldn't eat. That may make me less nutritionally healthy than I should be, but I prefer that to being in the psychic pain of trying to control or count every morsel I put in my mouth.*
>
> *~Shauna*

I think that, ultimately, we all have to decide what eating habits we consider healthy for our particular bodies, regardless of what the popular consensus is or what the latest nutritional research claims to prove. I think it's great to learn about nutrition, but I also think it's important to keep in mind that what might be healthy for one person might not be for another, because of food sensitivities and countless other physiological factors.

Also, nutrition is not the only factor that plays into health, and we shouldn't ignore the other factors. Stress is a huge factor that affects health, and for some, going through all the extra trouble to ensure a perfectly healthy diet can cause so much stress that it can offset any benefits of the healthy eating. For example, stress raises the hormone cortisol, which promotes storage of abdominal fat,[158] the least healthy form of body fat.[159] Stress also causes us to sleep less, which is unhealthy for a variety of reasons, but sleep deprivation has been shown to add difficulty to maintaining a healthy weight.[160] So it's possible you'd benefit more from an extra hour of sleep than from staying up late at night to prepare healthy breakfasts and lunches for you and your family.

If you feel strongly that one way of eating is the healthiest, then follow that with gusto and feel good about it; but don't let it become an obsession. Don't second-guess yourself every time you eat—eating with confidence is much less stressful than worrying about what mysterious preservatives or hydrogenated oils might be in certain food. If you are confident in what you are eating, you will be more relaxed, which is beneficial to the gastrointestinal tract and the digestive process.[161] Eating a less-than-ideal meal in a good mind-set might benefit you more than eating a "healthy" one while fretting about it.

Just do the best you can, based on what you believe is healthy for you, without letting it be a burden. As one of my wonderful friends who works in the field of nutrition said to me once, "We all have to balance nutrition with sanity." Know that it's okay to make choices for convenience sometimes or to put other priorities ahead of preparing a home-cooked meal. Eating acceptable-quality food leaves plenty of room for occasional very low-quality food. It doesn't mean you need to make it a point to eat junk food, but you may find yourself in situations where you need to just fuel yourself with any type of calories. When this happens, keep things in perspective and realize that even if a meal is of low quality, you are still getting macronutrients.

How does "healthy" eating factor into your life right now? Write down any ideas you have that will help you avoid being rigid and restrictive about healthy food:

_____

_____

_____

_____

_____

_____

_____

_____

What other areas of health could you improve to take your focus off of food?
(Examples: sleep, stress, hydration, and emotional and spiritual well-being.)

_____

_____

_____

_____

_____

STRIVE FOR ENJOYMENT

To a binge eater, the idea of *enjoying* food—both healthy and not so healthy—in normal quantities can seem foreign. When I was bulimic, I may have interpreted the advice to "enjoy your food" as justification for continued binge eating, because the binges were indeed pleasurable in the moment. But truly enjoying your food is the opposite of the empty, fruitless, fleeting pleasure of binge eating. Binge eaters experience no real enjoyment, because the act makes you feel so out of control and awful afterward—physically and emotionally.

> *The high I feel eating fresh vegetables, exercising, drinking water, and feeling my digestive system work normally is so much more fulfilling than any episode of purging. It's the difference between a quick, fly-by-night affair and finding your lifelong love.*
>
> ~Tara

You may think that once you quit, you'll have to view food as fuel only and no longer take much pleasure in eating. I believe it's quite the contrary: When you give up binge eating, you open yourself up to learning how to *truly* enjoy your food. You stop overindulging because "tomorrow starts a new diet" and learn to take genuine, satisfying pleasure in normal portions. You can stop obsessing about weight and calories, and start enjoying the taste of food without the guilt. Furthermore, you can start enjoying the way you feel after having a nourishing meal.

I would guess that, if given the resources and time to make healthy eating easy, most people would enjoy eating well more than they enjoy a diet consisting of a lot of junk food. However, it's possible that in the beginning of recovery, the signals from your body about what actually makes you feel good might not be all that clear. Residual digestive problems might prevent proper digestion and nutrient absorption, so even the healthiest of foods might leave you feeling sluggish. Still, enjoying food and how it makes you feel is something to keep in mind as the weeks and months go by and your body returns to normal.

If you don't feel at your best, don't fall into the trap of thinking you need to give up more and more foods in order to become healthier, because that can eventually backfire. You could end up unintentionally restricting calories, losing even more energy, and experiencing an increase in binge urges. If you want to make healthy changes in your eating, think primarily in terms of what healthy foods or supplements you can *add* to your life, not what "bad" foods you can strip away.

Write about the feeling of enjoyment you get from eating nourishing foods and how that differs from the temporary pleasure of a binge:

_____

_____

_____

_____

_____

_____

_____

At this point in time, are there any foods that make you feel better than others?

_____

_____

_____

_____

_____

How can you begin to strive for food enjoyment—both enjoyment of taste and enjoyment of the positive health benefits?

_____

_____

_____

_____

_____

_____

_____

_____

Considerations When Special Diets Are Necessary for Medical Reasons or Strongly Desired

While talking about health, it's important to mention that some people need to avoid certain foods due to specific disorders like diabetes or celiac disease, or because of adverse reactions to certain foods. Others may want to avoid certain foods for other reasons—such as moral or religious belief—or due to a strong desire to pursue a healthier lifestyle. If this is the case for you, it doesn't have to affect recovery, because as you know by now, the types of foods you eat do not cause binge eating. To be successful in adequate eating while on a special diet, there are some things to consider:

1. Taking Care of Yourself Is Different Than Deprivation

Since I recovered almost ten years ago, I've gone through four extended periods of time when I've had to completely eliminate certain foods, which I briefly mentioned in *Brain over Binge*. All of my children developed allergic colitis as infants while breast-feeding (a condition where the baby's immune system over-reacts to food proteins in the mother's milk and leads to irritation, inflammation, and even some bleeding in the digestive system). To treat this, I had to give up several allergenic food groups—namely, dairy, wheat, soy, eggs, and nuts. There were periods of time when I was eating nothing but potatoes, turkey, chicken, olive oil, almonds, and some mild vegetables and fruits in order to clear up my baby's digestive tract.

Restricting foods in this way while breast-feeding didn't cause any problem for me and never felt like a "diet" or like I was depriving myself. There were certainly times when I did feel a little sorry for myself as I watched the rest of my family munch down a pizza while I was eating my third meal of sweet potatoes and chicken for the day. Although it was inconvenient (and often not as tasty) to have a lack of freedom around food—and it's not something I'd want to do if I didn't have a compelling reason—it wasn't a bad experience. There was always a choice to feed my babies hypoallergenic infant formula, but that would have been costly and not as healthy for them as breast-feeding. I chose to change my diet, and I felt like that was the right thing for my babies at the time.

In the same way, people who strongly desire and choose to lead healthy life-styles and nourish their bodies well with real food don't feel "deprived" when they eliminate certain foods. The same goes for people who avoid a certain food due to a medical condition. Although they may sometimes crave the food they are eliminating, they know they are doing right for their bodies, and they feel good doing it. In all likelihood, they would actually feel "deprived" if they were forced to eat a diet consisting of foods that affected them in an adverse way. Avoiding foods in order to feel better is much different than trying to force yourself to follow a bunch of food rules just so you can lose weight. So, if you have to eat very healthy out of necessity or just because you really want to, that's okay—you don't have to force yourself to eat junk food to recover.

What are the differences in your mind between restrictive dieting and taking care of yourself by eating a certain way?

_____

_____

_____

_____

_____

_____

_____

_____

2. Ensure Nourishment (Replace Foods You Eliminate)

It's very important to make sure that you don't slip into calorie restriction and that you have *enjoyable* and nourishing replacements for the foods you are omitting. Sometimes people forget the enjoyment part, then get trapped in a mentality of deprivation. The goal should be to find foods that you *like* to eat and that make you feel good as well, which may take some experimenting. To illustrate this, I'm going to give an example from my own life of a food my family has been trying to avoid and how we've replaced it.

A few years ago, I slowly got into the habit of giving my kids processed, pre-packaged waffles—which they love—much too often. I felt like I was justified in it: I was pregnant with my fourth kid, exhausted, and couldn't find time or energy for anything better first thing in the morning that they would all eat. After the baby was born and started sleeping a little at night, I decided to learn to make healthier waffles on a waffle iron, freezing large batches of them for busy mornings. The first batch was a disaster, and the kids scoffed at the pieces I managed to scrape off the waffle maker; but after some experimenting and practice, I finally settled on a healthy recipe that tastes delicious. If you asked my kids, I'm sure they would still say they like the "waffles from the store" better, but they eat up the ones I make.

This is a simple example, but it's just a reminder that with a little effort, it's possible to find enjoyable and nourishing food to replace the foods you need or want out of your diet. It might take a little extra time, but think of all the time you dedicated to your eating disorder in the past that you'll now have at your disposal. Always keep these healthy changes to your diet separate from quitting binge eating. That way, if you choose, for example, to eat a couple processed waffles one morning, you won't pay any attention when your lower brain tells you that you've failed and you might as well eat the whole box.

Ideas for replacing foods you need or want to eliminate:

_____

_____

_____

_____

_____

_____

_____

Should You Detox?

After I wrote *Brain over Binge*, I got a few questions asking whether or not I detoxed after I quit binge eating. Since detoxing wasn't as big of a trend a decade ago as it is today, after I recovered, I didn't even consider it. During my years of binge eating, I overloaded my body with sugar, preservatives, food dyes, GMOs, nitrates ... and the list goes on and on. My non–binge eating at that time also contained a lot of gimmicky "diet" foods filled with sugar substitutes like aspartame and Splenda, and I sometimes even ate chips with the fake-fat olestra. I cringe to think of what I put into my body during that time.

Looking back and knowing more about health now, it might have been beneficial for me to give some consideration to healing my digestive system after recovery. However, if I would have quit binge eating and then immediately turned to trying to compensate for having eaten too many toxins by going on a detox diet, it likely would have kept my lower brain seeking to protect me by storing up food and fat. Furthermore, if I would have believed that being "clean" was a requirement for recovery, I might have been too intimidated to recover. Those who believe detoxes are part of recovery may be tempted to believe thoughts that tell them to have "one last binge before you detox" or thoughts saying how difficult it will be to detox, "so you shouldn't even bother trying to recover."

Maybe a year or so down the road after I recovered (when my urges to binge were long gone), healing my digestive system might have been something to consider, but the idea of being "clean," along with the idea that sugar and processed foods cause such a myriad of health problems, wasn't quite as pervasive at the time. So I simply moved on with my life and didn't experience any adverse health effects. After all, there are millions of people who eat junk food sometimes, don't detox, and yet aren't eating-disordered, and they live normal, sometimes even extremely healthy lives.

In my opinion, detoxing is not something that should be done soon after binge eating stops; and if it's done at all, I see it as a "proceed with caution" issue. Former binge eaters should avoid fasting and low-calorie detoxes simply because they create an unnecessary risk. Starvation isn't actually necessary for a detox to be effective. I believe that eating a robust and healthy diet, drinking lots of water and natural juices, possibly taking some supplements, trying to eliminate stress for a short time, and getting a lot of sleep is a much better approach to

I haven't dieted specifically for weight loss in years. However, I recognize that my "detox" diets can trick my brain into feeling it is being starved. Of course, when the brain feels it is being starved, it will rebel.

~Debbie

cleansing and healing. But even this robust and healthy detox could have the effect of making you feel like you are on a diet, creating unwanted stress and obsessions that you'd be better off without. So, like many questions that come up after recovery, there is no one right answer for everyone.

[30]

Food Cravings and Food "Addiction"

I've learned a lot over the past few years about the food industry and the use of high-fructose corn syrup, MSG, and sodium to keep people addicted to manmade foods. It's in everything. There is a lot of truth to the "simple carbohydrate addiction" topic, and I hope it becomes more widespread. Does it cause us to binge? It's possible. I know when I have a carb-laden food, I want more carb-laden foods shortly afterwards. When I eat vegetables, I don't feel that way.

~Gwen

EATING IS SO INTERTWINED with our existence that we can't expect our strong desire for food to go away after binge eating stops. That's like thinking that a person who is cured of insomnia will never want to stay up late again or that someone who stops a pornography addiction will never find another human being attractive. Once your body regulates itself, there will still be food cravings. There will be times when you want a donut, when the only thing you are hungry for is fast food, when you feel like licking the cake batter off the spoon or eating the ice cream straight from the carton. Sometimes you might choose to do those things, other times you might choose not to; but always remember that cravings are an expected part of life.

For some of you, though, your cravings—while not binge urges—might feel above and beyond what you would consider normal, and you may believe you have a food *addiction*—a term discussed later in this chapter. In Recovery Goal 1, you learned to put other food issues aside while you practiced dismissing binge urges, so this section is primarily for those who are ready to move on to improving other areas of their eating. However, there are some people who have trouble separating problematic cravings from binge urges—especially when binges are small. If this is the case for you, it's okay to work on problematic cravings alongside binge eating. The advice in this chapter assumes you have some flexibility in your approach to eating or that you've moved beyond using any of the eating strategies. If you still feel you need a structured approach right now, you may not apply what follows in this chapter until later.

FOUR TYPES OF CRAVINGS

Food cravings can be of four basic types, the last two of which can (sometimes) be problematic.

1. **Hungry cravings for quality food.** This is when you are feeling sensations of true hunger and you feel driven toward something that will satisfy that hunger in a nourishing way—you are craving a decent meal or snack. This is a healthy desire from your body and brain, and you can simply follow this type of craving.

2. **Nonhungry cravings for quality food.** This is when you don't truly feel a sense of hunger, but you are craving something that's (mostly) healthy. For example, out of the blue, you want a big, juicy apple. These cravings are rarely problematic and usually indicate that the body is in need of a nutrient that the food contains, so it makes sense to follow these cravings in a way that feels good to you. I have a daughter who absolutely loves baked kale chips, and she will eat a whole batch of them even if she is not hungry. I would never stop her from doing that.

3. **Hungry cravings for unhealthy food.** This is when you feel true sensations of hunger, but what seems most appetizing is the box of cookies in the pantry—not the leftover chicken, vegetables, and rice in the refrigerator. When you have these cravings, you have a choice: You can follow your cravings as they are, or you can steer yourself in a more nourishing direction. Having cookies for lunch one day is not a big deal, but over time, it can obviously become problematic.

4. **Nonhungry cravings for unhealthy food.** This is the type of craving most likely to be problematic and the one that recovering or recovered binge eaters often become most concerned about. Wanting something that isn't good for you when you aren't even hungry can cause anxiety in some people, and if followed, these cravings can lead to thoughts like, *I've blown it, I might as well binge.* Indeed, these cravings are the most similar to binge urges, and just like with binge urges, you can choose not to act on them. However, acting on these types of cravings now and then doesn't make you abnormal.

WHAT TO DO ABOUT PROBLEMATIC CRAVINGS

If you are bothered by what you think are too-frequent problematic cravings, there are four things you can do:

1. Make Sure You Are Eating Enough

I keep coming back to this point in the book, because so many of what seem to be eating "problems" are just the results of restrictive dieting. When you are in a self-imposed calorie deficit, lower brain regions implicated in the reward value of food are unusually activated, making food more tempting—particularly energy-dense, palatable food—and the brain also prompts you to pay more attention to food. The longer the calorie deprivation, the more the brain regions are activated and the more enticing food seems to the dieter.[162]

There is also a cascade of biological processes that make your cravings heightened. It has been shown that when a weight loss diet decreases body fat, there is an increase in the levels of hormones that produce hunger—namely, ghrelin, gastric inhibitory polypeptide, and pancreatic polypeptide. Meanwhile, the hormones that trigger fullness—peptide YY, cholecystokinin, and leptin—decrease, and these changes can still be present even *a year after dieting stops*.[163] So, even if you aren't currently dieting, consider that the cravings you are experiencing are residual effects of dieting before you assume something is wrong with you.

It seems counterintuitive, but to overcome these cravings, you don't need more willpower, you need to say yes to food more. Trying to fight off a craving for, say, a cookie after a meal might prolong your problem. Instead, if you just *have* the cookie—giving your body the signal that you aren't depriving it anymore—treats like this will eventually become less and less appealing. However, some people worry that following those types of cravings will become habitual as well, and it certainly can, so it is a balancing act. If you find that, after eating adequately and following these types of cravings in a sensible way for a few months, they aren't decreasing (or if you are very health conscious and don't like the idea of giving in to too many unhealthy food cravings), then you can use the additional strategies below.

Do you think that current or former calorie restriction is behind your problematic cravings?

_____

_____

_____

2. Choose Healthier Foods to Satisfy Cravings

If you've never been a restrictive dieter, consider that your amplified cravings could be from binge eating such large quantities of sugar and carbohydrates, which can create a sort of dependence on those types of foods. Even though you might not be binge eating anymore, you may find yourself wanting and possibly eating more sugar and carbohydrates than you would if you'd never had an eating disorder. This, too, can resolve over time, but to get you through this time of heightened cravings, it can help to try to satisfy those cravings in a healthier way. This could mean eating fruit when you are craving sugar or making your own simple, healthier desserts—replacing sugar in recipes with healthier sweeteners like pure maple syrup or honey. By doing this, you'll feel better about what you are eating and you'll also be gradually working toward reducing your body's dependence on large amounts of sugar.

Ideas for healthy replacements for foods you are craving too often:

_____

_____

_____

_____

_____

_____

3. Use Detachment

If you feel your body has gotten the message that you aren't going to starve it anymore but your cravings still don't eventually lessen after several months of being binge-free, then you can address these cravings as minor forms of conditioned, brain-based habitual urges. You've likely conditioned your brain to crave junk food in certain situations, and now you know you are perfectly capable of breaking those patterns—with detachment.

People who have a healthy relationship with food detach from problematic cravings naturally. Without even realizing it most of the time, they sense when they shouldn't follow a craving. This isn't something they force upon themselves, it's just a simple thought like, *That's probably not a good idea* or *I've already had enough*, and they (usually effortlessly) put the fork down or don't pick it up in the first place. In my experience of recovery, doing this feels like a recognition of false wanting and making a choice to honor your body. The false wanting usually goes away in seconds to minutes—without a struggle.

To use detachment effectively with cravings you feel are problematic, you'll need to decide which eating habits you are okay with keeping (at least for now) and which ones are so harmful that you want to give them up right away. The set of questions below will help you get a better idea of which cravings you consider problematic—because they will help you see which cravings are far out of line with what you truly want. You don't have to be highly specific with these answers, but exploring your concept of what's reasonable will help you begin to place healthy but flexible limits around your eating.

How much sugary food do you think is okay for you to eat in a day? (Don't write your "ideal" amount here, which may be none; be realistic based on your current situation.) **How much above and beyond that do you crave?**

How many "desserts" per week do you feel is appropriate? How much above and beyond that do you crave?

When and how often do you think it makes sense to have highly processed foods? How much do you crave above and beyond that?

Based on the questions above, list the cravings you feel are most problematic right now—the ones you can try to detach from:

_____

_____

_____

_____

_____

_____

_____

_____

_____

4. Explore Physiological Causes and Solutions

Besides the consequences of dieting and binge eating, along with the effect of habit, there are countless other physiological reasons for cravings. If you know you are eating enough, if you've given your body time to regulate, and if detachment isn't effective, then it makes sense to explore the physiological basis of the cravings and work toward solutions (I recommend with a doctor or nutritionist). Addressing all the possible causes of cravings would take up the rest of this book; but know that the following health issues can be at least partially to blame:

- Hormone imbalances
- Vitamin/mineral deficiencies
- Insulin resistance
- Food allergies
- Candida
- Hypoglycemia
- Diabetes
- Adrenal insufficiencies
- PMS
- Thirst
- Stress
- Depression
- Substance use
- Sleep deprivation

Getting some baseline blood work is helpful in determining if you are deficient in any vitamins and/or minerals that can sometimes lead to food cravings. For example, sugar cravings, specifically chocolate, can signal low magnesium and chromium levels. The blood work might also pick up on thyroid or insulin resistance problems, which can cause some weight gain.

~Stacey Cohen,
Integrative Nutritionist

Whatever issues you may be dealing with, one thing is certain: Binge eating is *never* the cure or an appropriate response to *any* physiological problem causing abnormal food cravings. Some people are tempted to blame their binge behavior on one of the problems above—that's the opposite of the intent of this section. The appetite for binges is much more habitual and brain-based than the physiological imbalances that cause problematic cravings. A benefit of keeping the two issues as separate as possible is that, even if the methods you use to try to reduce problematic cravings don't work, you'll know that a binge does *not* need to result.

The brain and body, especially the digestive system, are intimately connected; and as mentioned in the beginning of the book, binge urges do not operate exclusively in the brain. But the difference between a conditioned habit and abnormal physiology creating problematic cravings is a distinction worth making. For some people, this distinction can be subtle, and the two can certainly be related—because problematic cravings can lead to binge urges. Whereas it would be easy to separate a habitual urge to smoke, for example, from problematic food cravings caused from, say, a vitamin deficiency, it's less clear when both the habit and the problematic craving call for *food*. Nevertheless, in both cases, the habitual urges (for smoking or binge eating) need to be ignored, and the cravings due to the vitamin deficiency should not be ignored, but should instead be addressed from a body-centered perspective more than a brain-centered perspective.

To illustrate this, I'll explain how I've dealt with a mild physiological problem that has caused abnormal cravings, both while I was bulimic and after recovery—and even today, but to a much lesser extent. I have dealt with what I believe is a form of sluggish function of my adrenal glands (glands that produce stress-regulating hormones), which some doctors with a background in natural medicine term "adrenal fatigue."[164] Adrenal fatigue is basically a physiological reaction to prolonged high stress levels and sleep deprivation, which leads to the body being less able to regulate stress and energy levels. Part of this disregulation can lead to cravings for "pick-me-up" foods like sugar and caffeine.

In my case, I believe this physiological issue is at least partially responsible for what I've experienced as strong fruit and fruit juice cravings over the years, both while I was bulimic and after recovery. I never wanted to *binge* on fruit; but I used to crave juice, raisins, pineapples, apples, and oranges with what often felt like an urgent thirst (even when I clearly wasn't thirsty). After learning about adrenal fatigue, I realized that satisfying the cravings by eating the fruit or drinking the juice actually isn't the best idea—it perpetuates the problem by revving up the adrenal glands, leading to a temporary energy fix but more fatigue in the long term.

When I was a binge eater, the fruit cravings could certainly lead to binge urges. If I strongly craved a large portion of fruit and I followed that craving, I would sometimes have thoughts like, *I've already given in, so I might as well keep eating and start over tomorrow.* Following the physiologically based cravings set in motion the habitual thought patterns that led to binges; this is a common experience. However, once my binge eating ended and the urges were deconditioned, having and even following these same cravings didn't lead to the same brain reaction, and I stopped experiencing any desire to binge along with the fruit cravings. Nevertheless, feeding or not feeding my physiologically based cravings was still a balancing act that required me to rely on my higher brain a little more than my appetite.

Regardless of what's going on in the body, the prefrontal cortex still gives us the ability to choose how we respond. In my case, the best response was to follow recommendations for gradually eliminating the fruit cravings. Those were to sip lightly salted water throughout the day, to eat snacks and meals that balanced my blood sugar, and to reduce my consumption of fruit. I often heeded this advice, but sometimes I didn't and I just ate the fruit. That still holds true today even though the issue seems to be mostly resolved. I think that just taking minor actions to change my responses to the fruit cravings—even though I didn't do them all the time—was enough to alleviate whatever abnormality was there.

I handled cravings during pregnancy in a similar way. Like most women, I often had strange cravings for unhealthy food that I knew likely had a physiological basis in my pregnancy hormones. Sometimes I followed those cravings in a reasonable way and enjoyed the food, and sometimes I didn't—instead deciding to eat or drink something that I believed would be better for the baby or that would stabilize my body chemistry to eliminate the abnormal cravings. Cravings are, after all, just your body's *suggestions* for what you should eat—and knowing this can help get you through times in your life when cravings are irregular for one reason or another.

A word of caution when addressing cravings from a physiological perspective: Even if you treat the causes of physiologically based cravings, you will still crave the pleasure of the desired foods. Using myself as an example, even if I could completely get rid of the adrenal fatigue or whatever underlying biochemistry causes my fruit cravings, I still really *like* fruit and doubt I'll ever stop wanting it just for the pleasure of it.

Another example: One cause of cravings is nutrient deficiency—so craving chocolate, for instance, which is high in magnesium, might be a sign of a magnesium deficiency. In theory, then, if you take magnesium supplements, it should make your craving for chocolate go away.[165] Although this nutritional deficiency theory is valuable, it fails to address the brain's reward center. Magnesium in supplement form doesn't taste as good as chocolate; it doesn't provide whatever pleasurable benefits you receive from chewing and swallowing chocolate; and it doesn't lead to the same "feel-good" brain chemistry as actually eating chocolate. So, even if a magnesium deficiency or another biochemical imbalance is the reason someone started eating chocolate too often in the first place, correcting it doesn't guarantee the cravings will stop. The primitive brain might still seek the reward value, and for this reason, a combination of the strategies of detachment and working on physiological causes is warranted.

Possible physiological conditions or causes of your cravings that you want to explore:

_____

_____

_____

_____

_____

_____

Solutions to the above problems that you've discovered on your own or with your doctor/nutritionist:

_____

_____

_____

_____

_____

_____

FOOD "ADDICTION"

Sugar, carbohydrates, and unhealthy fats affect everyone in different ways, and even most normal eaters in today's sugar-and-processed-food-laden environment have more cravings than they probably "should" in an ideal world. However, some people experience much more frequent, intense, and difficult-to-resist cravings. I'm not talking about a mild craving for a latte or a pastry (or both) in the afternoon;

I'm talking about feeling like you are going to die if you don't get those things ... and then feeling the same way a couple hours later about ice cream ... and then a couple hours later about pizza.

Having a pastry, ice cream, and/or pizza during the day—if you aren't bothered by it and it doesn't affect your mood or mind-set or energy level or health in a negative way (and it's not *every* day)—can be completely fine. But if you feel *obsessively* driven toward it, like you can't live without your fixes, then it's a problem, one that you might call an "addiction." Addiction is characterized by repeatedly and compulsively seeking or using a substance or activity despite the negative psychological, social, and/or physical consequences. It is often (but not always) accompanied by physical dependence, withdrawal syndrome, and tolerance.

By this definition, binge eating certainly has addictive qualities (on both behavioral and neurobiological levels), and since food is the substance involved, it's fair to say it's a type of food addiction. There has yet to be a large body of research about the relationship between "food addictions" and bulimia/BED, but recent studies show that an "addictive-type response to highly palatable food may be contributing to eating-related problems, including obesity and eating disorders."[166] Food addiction doesn't always involve *binge* eating, and even normal eaters can feel certain foods are "like a drug" to them. The truth is that eating does activate the same reward center as drugs,[167] and eating something extremely pleasurable can be like a hit—for some people more than others.

The way I see it, the information that sugar and carbohydrates are "addictive" should be no surprise—it's a simple survival mechanism. Drugs aren't necessary for survival, and sugar is (well, glucose, anyway). Tellingly, in an animal study of food and drug addiction, rats—even those addicted to cocaine—chose to ingest a sweet substance over the cocaine.[168] If eating weren't highly pleasurable and potentially addicting, we might not be motivated to keep doing it day after day. Of course, there is a difference between healthy desires and addictions. Craving food and finding it pleasurable is healthy; but just as healthy desires for intimate relationships can get warped into pornography addictions or affairs, healthy desires for food can become potentially compulsive and destructive.

Before my eating disorder, I'd spent my young life eating moderate amounts of sweets and desserts without it ever being a problem. During my binge eating, however, I indeed felt like sugary food was an addiction; and I believe this was the result of the temporary glitch in my reward system—brought on by dieting and the binge eating habit itself. Ingesting and digesting large amounts of sugar and carbohydrates does change biochemical pathways in the brain, leading to abnormally strong cravings.[169] I didn't have a brain "disease"—my brain simply adapted to my repeated actions, becoming temporarily "addicted."

Once I quit binge eating, this feeling of being hooked on certain foods went away, and I got back to eating sugar and refined carbohydrates in a sensible way. It wasn't immediate, but as I ate those foods in moderation over the course of a few months, it became second nature. My experience of food addiction being a temporary state that improves with recovery has been demonstrated in current research. A 2014 study of bulimia and food addiction[170] found that all participants with current bulimia received a food addiction diagnosis, whereas only 30 percent of women with remittent bulimia did.[*]

For some people, even a long time after recovery, it still feels like certain foods have too much of a hold on them. Additionally, some people might feel that they've always had a form of food addiction—even before bulimia or binge eating disorder started—and that eating highly pleasurable foods in moderation has never been normal for them. If this is the case for you, an uneasy feeling about eating habits may understandably persist after binge eating stops. You may worry that what you perceive to be a food addiction will send you right back into binge eating, or there may be a blurred line between overindulgence in certain foods and binge eating.

Do you feel like you are addicted to certain foods? Which ones?

_____

_____

_____

_____

_____

_____

Did your food addictions arise after your binge eating started, or did they predate the eating disorder?

_____

_____

_____

_____

---

[*]A food addiction diagnosis was made using the Yale Food Addiction Scale (YFAS), which was developed according to the diagnostic criteria for substance use disorders in the DSM-4 (*Diagnostic and Statistical Manual of Mental Disorders*, Fourth Edition).

Currently, what is the relationship between your food addiction and binge eating?

_____

_____

_____

_____

_____

_____

_____

Brain Research on Addiction Doesn't Rule Out Choice

Binge eaters sometimes find comfort in studies that confirm their suspicions that sugar and carbohydrates are addictive. I know when I was a binge eater, I certainly found it oddly encouraging that I was like a drug addict. It made my problem more legitimate in my mind. It seemed all too weird, disgusting, and embarrassing to be hooked on enormous amounts of *food*; but if binge eating was akin to shooting heroin, then it felt completely understandable why I did what I did. Thankfully, when it came to recovery, the idea of being addicted didn't seem like a barrier, because I'd learned from the Rational Recovery® approach that addiction is a voluntary behavior.[171] Even studies that show how addictions operate in the brain don't rule out free choice.

In neuroscience research, food addiction has been found to be a combination of intense wanting (overactivity in the lower brain areas responsible for craving) and disinhibition (less brain activity in the higher brain areas responsible for self-control).[172] Individuals *without* subjective symptoms of food addiction have, comparatively, less of a response in these same brain regions. Similar differences are seen in those who are addicted to drugs and those who are not.[173] However, the fact that we can now see what "intense wanting" and "disinhibition" look like on a brain scan doesn't mean we are at the mercy of our brains.

An important thing to understand is that this type of addiction research shows us *neural correlates* of addiction[174]—meaning, a glimpse of the brain states that correlate with the subjective sensations of addiction (i.e., the feeling of craving and a lessening of self-control). But just because we know more about what the brain is doing when you want, let's say, sugar, that doesn't mean choice does not exist in the process. Sure, when craving is present, the brain is *priming* you to act in a certain way, but even drug addicts have been shown to make a different choice when an enticing reward—such as money—is offered for doing so.[175]

Binge eaters show their capability of choice when they confine their behavior to times and places that they are not likely to be seen. The rational brain perceives the consequences of being seen by someone else to be too great, so it overrides the urges from the lower brain. Although it's likely you've done some shameful things that seem to point to you having no control, "you"—your higher brain—is just not being used at the time you are acting on your addiction. Not operating rationally is not the same as physically losing all control of your actions. There have been times when you've delayed eating the foods you believe you are addicted to, times when you've eaten a sensible amount of them, and times when you've said no altogether—maybe not as often as you'd like, but the point here is that you retain the capacity to say no.

Based on a representative survey by the Partnership for Drug Free Kids and the New York State Office of Alcoholism and Substance Abuse Services, it is estimated that one in ten adults in the U.S. have overcome problematic use of and possibly addiction to drugs or alcohol.[176] People choose to stop using drugs, stop drinking alcohol, stop smoking, and stop performing other poor habits; no one recovers in exactly the same way, but the point is that they do recover, and they have done so prior to science discovering the neural correlates of their behavior. If the signs of addiction in the brain represented an unavoidable force, no one could have achieved recovery without a specific brain treatment for the abnormalities seen on the brain scan.

Anyone who has put aside an addiction in the past has changed their brain without even knowing it, just like someone who learns any new skill—calculus or the guitar, for example—changes their brain without knowing exactly how and where those changes occur. Even a child who has a thumb-sucking habit, I'm sure, has some abnormalities in the areas of craving and disinhibition, which resolve with the cessation of the habit. The fact that we can now *see* the signs of addictions on brain scans shouldn't intimidate you or make you think you are somehow diseased.

I think we have to be careful as a society not to give too many negative behaviors "addiction status" and not let differences in brain scans excuse too many actions. We could run into major problems if we eventually say that "intense wanting" coupled with "disinhibition" renders people helpless to control themselves, because this combination is present in so many wrong actions. Think of criminal offenses as extreme examples—theft and rape—and moral dilemmas such as affairs. Research shows that not only food, but problematic gambling,[177] Internet overuse,[178] pornography,[179] and compulsive shopping[180] reveal similar brain activity to that of alcoholics and drug addicts.

Part of the human condition is wanting what's not good for us—everyone has a susceptibility to different "vices" based on genetics, environmental factors, and experiences; and every culture and time period has offered explanations for why harmful desires occur. Currently, it's popular to explain this universal human condition with brain scans, but we must always remember that we are *human* and thus have the ability and the higher brain power to avoid automatic actions.

Keep track of times when you experience addictive symptoms yet are able to control your behavior. What do you learn from these situations?

_____

_____

_____

_____

_____

_____

_____

_____

Insights you have about how choice operates in addiction:

_____

_____

_____

_____

_____

_____

_____

_____

Responding to Addictive Symptoms

Now that you know you have a choice when you experience addictive symptoms, know also that you don't have to fix things by sheer will or "white-knuckling." If your food addiction symptoms don't self-resolve gradually after binge eating stops, you can use the same strategies you would for any form of problematic craving—the same ones suggested earlier in the chapter to deal with intense food cravings: (1) make sure you are eating enough; (2) choose healthier replacements; (3) use detachment; and (4) explore physiological causes and solutions. There is not just one single physiological cause of food addictions,[181] but many possible avenues to developing those feelings of "intense wanting" and "disinhibition" around certain foods.

A common course of action to address the physiological cause is to give up the "addicting" foods, just as a drug addict needs to stop using the drug. This is the approach typically employed by groups like Food Addicts Anonymous and Overeaters Anonymous, which use the addiction model. The reason for abstinence from the problematic foods is the belief that even after one bite, the food addict is not able to control him- or herself (although, as we've discussed, evidence points toward a *reduction* in control, not a total loss—even in drug addicts).[182] Using this philosophy, some see giving up the addictive foods— which usually include all sugar, all flour, and even certain fats—as a requirement for binge eating recovery.[183]

I think my neural pathways are wired so hard that I almost have to look at certain foods like an alcoholic would look at booze. Some foods just trigger me so much that moderation really isn't the answer for me on certain foods right now. For me, it's the processed foods. Anything with high-fructose corn syrup just sends me off in the wrong direction. I can now keep from going into a binge after eating those foods, but it's hard, and I think it's just from all the years of having the habit. I'm now enjoying getting away from the processed foods and eating a more natural diet.

~Jeremy

Whether abstaining from "addictive" foods is helpful, harmful, or neutral to *binge eaters* is a subject of debate. If "addictive" foods are what primarily trigger binge urges and you eliminate those foods, then in theory, yes, you should have fewer urges and therefore fewer binges. However, for some—especially those with a history of restrictive dieting—giving up those foods can lead to feelings of deprivation and, actually, *more* urges. The brain and the body are so multi-faceted, and each person is so unique, that abstinence from certain foods can have unpredictable and unintended effects, or simply not "work" to reduce binge urges.

There is no doubt that the abstinence approach has helped people; there are many personal testimonies on the Internet, in books, and in articles by people who have overcome eating problems and experienced other life-enhancing benefits from giving up certain foods. These testimonies are inspiring, and there are of course health benefits to eating less sugar, flour, unhealthy fats, and processed foods in general; however, for binge eaters and former binge eaters, the abstinence approach is something to carefully consider before jumping into it, because despite the personal success stories, this approach is difficult and doesn't have a high success rate overall.

One independent study of over 8,000 former patients of a psychiatric hospital's food addiction program found that for patients using an "addictive model" program, only about one-third were able to maintain abstinence from problematic foods for a year, some of whom abstained for up to five years, which was the end of the study.[184] The author of the study concluded that food addicts could be treated *at least as effectively* using the addiction model as alcoholics and drug addicts who are treated in residential chemical dependency programs.[185] Considering the statistics from chemical dependency programs, the success rates of which aren't very high, this actually isn't too encouraging. There is a dropout rate of about 62 percent for drug addicts and 43 percent for alcoholics,[186] with a 40–60 percent relapse rate for those who do complete treatment.[187]

So it isn't that the addiction model is completely ineffective, it's just that it's not for everyone. There are three primary reasons why I believe trying to cure food addiction and/or binge eating with abstinence can miss the mark:

1. **The psychological aspect of banning foods may trump the physical benefits.** In research, banning foods causes study participants to think about those foods more often,[188] and believing that one bite will spiral into out-of-control eating can be self-fulfilling. Furthermore, it can be stressful to maintain a diet that bans so many food choices—and stress leads to lower prefrontal cortex function and therefore lower self-control.

2. **Binge eaters can binge on anything.** Although science finds certain foods most "addictive"—sugar, fat, flour, wheat, salt, artificial sweeteners, and caffeine—it has been shown that binge eaters can also have what's called "volume addiction," which means habitually eating large amounts of *all* types of foods.[189]

3. **Eliminating foods does not address the habitual nature of urges.** If you eliminate all addictive foods, you are not deconditioning associations between those foods and binge eating. Learning to eat the foods in moderation makes it so that those foods no longer produce habitual urges to binge or other forms of problematic craving. Eliminating the foods means that if you *do* eat them in the future, urges may arise. For example,

when people eliminate certain carbohydrates, many have immediate trouble maintaining moderate portions when they reintroduce them.[190]

Because of these reasons, I believe that in most cases, it's helpful to learn to eat former binge foods in moderation—to decondition the habit; *but* if you are dealing with distressing symptoms of food addiction, this may prove to be too challenging. If you've read and understood all of the information in this book so far but you are still struggling with what feels like too-powerful cravings (or binge urges), there is nothing wrong with exploring new ways of eating in hopes of reducing those addictive-like symptoms. You have the final choice of how you eat, which means you can include any nutritional strategy you think will assist you,* provided that you ensure you are well nourished.

Have you ever tried eliminating addictive foods? Was your experience positive or negative and why?

_____

_____

_____

_____

_____

_____

What has been your experience with eating addicting foods in moderation?

_____

_____

_____

_____

_____

_____

*Please consult your health provider before making any drastic dietary changes.

Based on your answers to the two questions above, as well as your takeaway from this section, what are some ways you can begin dealing with food addiction?

_____

_____

_____

_____

_____

_____

_____

_____

_____

[31]

Overeating

Sometimes I overeat (eat another slice or finish the chocolate block), but I recognize this now as a "normal" behavior, in that everyone overeats from time to time and I'm not strange or alone in doing that.

~Kate

IN *BRAIN OVER BINGE*, I shared that even after recovery, I still overate from time to time, and that still holds true today. I consider all of my eating to be normal, even if I sometimes eat past a perfect point of satiety. This type of "overeating" is fully chosen, in balance, and infrequent. It is not something I feel driven to do or feel guilty about doing. I haven't been uncomfortably full in over ten years, nor would I have any desire to be. But have I been more full than usual after a nice dinner at a restaurant? Absolutely. Have I eaten a dessert even after I was satisfied from my meal, simply because it was delicious? Yes. Have I been physically satisfied yet still chosen to have a few more bites of a favorite dish? Of course. Have I been offered a snack when not physically hungry and ate it anyway, just to be social or because it looked yummy? Certainly.

On the flip side, have I not eaten enough in a day because I was so busy or hadn't gone to the grocery store or didn't have much of an appetite? Yes. I'd venture to guess that I probably eat a bit more than I think my body needs about 2–3 percent of the time, and the same probably goes for eating less. I am just talking about *amount* of food here—I'm not saying I eat healthy food 94–96 percent of the time. I say "think my body needs" because of course there is no perfect blueprint on what amount is exactly right, and overeating, like binge eating, is a subjective experience.

The topic of overeating has considerable overlap with the previous chapter, because you'll most likely be able to link many overeating episodes to problematic cravings, and people tend to overeat the same highly stimulating, highly processed foods that are involved in food "addiction." You can address overeating using the same four strategies described in the last chapter. Overeating, however, is more about the *amount* of food than the type. Problematic cravings and/or food addictions can exist without actually overeating the foods you crave; additionally, overeating can exist without any of those "addicting" foods being involved at all. In this chapter, I'll give you some additional things to think about if you feel you are overdoing food quantity.

Overeating is, of course, one of those issues that you should put aside until after binge eating stops and one that can resolve itself gradually with the resolution of binge eating and restrictive dieting—due to the resolution of stomach stretching, a decrease in your dependency on large amounts of sugar and carbohydrates, and taming of the survival instincts. However, just like the distinction between problematic cravings and binge urges, sometimes there can be an unclear line between overeating and binge eating—especially when binges are small and overeating has a compulsive quality—which can lead to difficulty accomplishing Recovery Goal 2.

What does overeating look like in your life right now?

_____

_____

_____

_____

_____

_____

_____

_____

IS YOUR OVEREATING PERCEIVED OR REAL?

If you have a history of calorie restriction, you'll want to focus more on releasing the food deprivation before considering any overeating issues. Giving the body the signal of food abundance is more important for former dieters than stopping eating at an ideal point of satiation each time. Even those who have not dieted need to make sure not to drop their calories too low, so it's important to carefully consider if what you think is overeating is truly that.

Take some time to consider how you define *overeating*, because many people think that they are eating too much when they are in fact eating normally—just not dieting anymore. Individuals who have a history of starving themselves might view what are actually normal portions as excessive; and since people with eating disorders tend to be perfectionists, there can be an element of "being too hard on yourself" involved in what you perceive to be overeating. For example, if a dieter is trying to restrict calories to 1,500 per day and "overeats" one day to reach 2,200 calories, they haven't truly overeaten at all, just eaten more in line with their calorie needs.

Breaking unrealistic resolutions or being unable to stick to overly restrictive eating regimens is *not* overeating. This type of perceived overeating, however, often spirals into true overeating or an out-of-control binge. This is because when a binge eater or recovering binge eater breaks a diet, the lower brain is likely to send faulty messages saying, *You've already failed* or *You have no self-control*—in other words, *You might as well binge.*

If you determine that your overeating is real overeating—not just you being too hard on yourself—your ultimate goal is still not to banish it altogether. Even once you've settled on authentic eating habits, eating past a perfect point of satiety is going to happen from time to time. It would not necessarily be healthy to have complete heroic control of everything you put in your mouth. Recent research shows that in many areas of our lives, too much self-control is not good for us. The following excerpt, from Kelly McGonigal's *The Willpower Instinct*, explains why this is so:

> Just like some stress is necessary for a happy and productive life, some self-control is needed. But just like living under chronic stress is unhealthy, trying to control every aspect of your thoughts, emotions, and behavior is a toxic strategy. It's too big a burden for your biology. Self-control, like the stress response, evolved as a nifty strategy for responding to specific challenges. But just as with stress, we run into trouble when self-control becomes chronic and unrelenting. ... You will have to choose your willpower battles wisely.[191]

With this in mind, be discriminate about what overeating habits you want to work on. This also applies if you are still using a structured approach to eating right now. Remember that the approach is there for guidance—not to make you feel guilty if you eat a little more than you planned. If overeating happens even on an eating plan, use the opportunity to practice not letting it lead you to a binge. Early in recovery, it's common for binge urges to arise after overeating, due to conditioning, but you can detach from the urges, reminding yourself that binge eating is never a rational solution to overeating. It's only the neurological junk from the lower brain that will tell you a binge "makes sense" now because you've already overeaten.

Do you think you are being too hard on yourself in how you define overeating? Is it possible some of your overeating is just perceived—a result of a focus on dieting?

_____

_____

_____

_____

_____

What overeating habits do you think are relatively normal—those that you can stop worrying about—so as to not impose too much self-control?

_____

_____

_____

_____

_____

_____

What overeating habits are most distressing for you—those to which you want to apply your self-control resources now—or, if you have yet to stop binge eating, as soon as you are confident in being binge-free?

_____

_____

_____

_____

_____

_____

Don't Let Overeating Derail You

In the beginning of recovery, how you handle situations where you overeat in a minor way can be the difference in who goes on to a full recovery and who gets set back. If you have an episode where you eat, say, two full-sized cupcakes after you already had dinner, remind yourself of stomach stretching and the fact that you've been eating huge quantities of sweets for a long time, so your body has some adjusting to do. Also, remind yourself that some overeating is normal. No, it wouldn't be normal to eat two cupcakes every day after dinner, and no, it's not something you'll feel proud of, but it's important to realize that even normal eaters have moments where they eat more than they would have liked. Don't focus on your guilt about the cupcakes, get excited about the fact that you won't be following the overeating episode with a binge.

It's also vital that you don't purge after minor overeating, as this can set the restriction/binge cycle right back in motion. Remember that the ramifications of something like two cupcakes as they relate to weight and/or health are very insignificant. Just mark the behavior down as one of those less-than-ideal eating episodes you'd like to improve on in the future, consider it no big deal, and move on. The next time you are hungry, or when it would be an appropriate time to eat, nourish yourself well—don't be tempted to skip the next meal to compensate. If months go by and situations like this are still happening too often, then you can use the following three strategies.

1. Focus on How Overeating Makes You Feel

You can use situations where you eat more than you would have liked to teach yourself about how you *want* to eat going forward. Practice noticing how overeating makes you feel afterward. For example, after eating two cupcakes following an already filling dinner, you probably won't feel very good, mentally or physically. You might get sleepy afterward, have low energy, or feel bloated or extra thirsty. If you keep track of those symptoms and remember them, then next time you are in a situation that encourages overeating you can make a genuine choice to say no. Your "no" will not be because you are on a diet, but simply because you've learned that eating that way doesn't help you live life to the fullest.

Teaching myself that my brain was saying "continue" [while] my body was saying "I am full" was very difficult at first. My biggest challenge was learning to listen to my body after so many years of ignoring it. Honestly, I think time helped the most. Each time I listened to my body, it felt good, I didn't feel stuffed. Each time I didn't listen to my body, it felt bad, I felt too full. I didn't like that feeling.

~Ana

Write about specific overeating episodes you have and how they make you feel physically and mentally:

_____

_____

_____

_____

_____

_____

_____

_____

Write about opportunities you have to overeat, but you choose not to. How do you feel afterward? Note the positive effects of not being overly full.

_____

_____

_____

_____

_____

_____

_____

_____

2. Practice Limits in Tempting Situations

This strategy is similar to how you can use detachment for problematic cravings, by first deciding what eating habits you are okay with and then dismissing the urges for the eating habits you truly don't want. But, with overeating, again, it's more about the amount than the type of food. First determine situations where you are most likely to overeat, then create your own stopping point using your higher brain. This simply means deciding on what you are going to eat before you eat it, sticking with it, and putting the fork down after you've reached the limit you set. For example, let's say you ordered a pizza: Decide in advance how much would be appropriate (possibly one to three slices, depending on the size of the slices and your hunger level), then, even if you find yourself craving another piece, honor your higher brain's previous choice and treat the craving for more as neurological junk.

The idea of having a limit on the food you are going to eat can make some people feel uncomfortable at first—because, ultimately, we do want freedom and flexibility. Know that using limits, like meal plans, is only a temporary tool until you feel you have gained control. You can set limits for problematic foods or situations at any time before eating—days or hours in advance, while waiting for your food at a restaurant, while cooking your food, or even in the moment before you take the first bite.

Just because I can have a piece of cake and not binge afterward doesn't mean it's healthy to eat a piece of cake every night after dinner. You have to find that balance of not restricting, but also taking care of your body.

~Zoey

Make sure you decide on a nourishing portion, and don't shortchange yourself in the name of weight loss. You can also use limits after you've already eaten something. There may be times when you didn't set a limit in advance, yet you find yourself having desires to eat some more after you've had a meal or snack. In this case, you can decide on a limit in the moment when you are wanting more. For example, if you are eating chips and think you've likely had enough but you keep wanting to reach in the bag for more, pause and decide how much more your higher brain self is okay with eating. Ask yourself what amount is going to allow you to still feel pretty good afterward. It may be another two chips, seven chips, ten chips; and in some cases, it might be none. It's subjective and based on what you feel is right for your own body.

One thing to keep in mind is that the lower brain can adopt the message that it's okay to overeat sometimes (which is true), then use it to encourage problematic overeating. If you experience this, my suggestion is: As soon as you hear that voice saying *It's okay to overeat*, take a step back and visualize what amount would feel reasonable, enjoyable, and still allow you to feel good afterward. Then confidently enjoy your food until you've reached the limit, relishing not feeling too stuffed afterward. Try not to second-guess yourself when you do this. The line between how much you truly want and how much is just false wanting is never completely clear, but that doesn't prevent you from doing the best you can to make sensible estimates. Surely, picking any reasonable limit is better than allowing your every desire to overtake you.

The temporary tool of limit setting is an excellent practice in self-control, because—while it certainly would be fine in most cases to have a little more even after you've finished your set limit—sticking to the amount you decided on in advance proves to yourself that you can control your actions regardless of your desires. You are building stronger connections in the prefrontal cortex when you practice saying no, as well as deconditioning the desires to overeat. Once you feel you've reined in most of your problematic overeating and you feel accustomed to eating normal amounts, you can let up on the limit setting.

In what specific situations do you tend to overeat, where you may need to set limits in advance?

_____

_____

_____

_____

_____

_____

Use this space to brainstorm about how much you think is okay to eat in these challenging situations. (The actual amounts you decide on when facing these situations may vary depending on your hunger level, when you've last eaten, when you'll be able to eat again, etc.)

_____

_____

_____

_____

_____

_____

_____

3. Practice Gratitude

The last strategy is a change in mind-set when addressing overeating. I first wrote about the concept of using gratitude to curb overeating in my blog in November 2013. At the time, I was writing a series on overeating; I had completed two posts and was planning to get started on a third when a terrible typhoon hit the Philippines, leaving thousands of people without food and water. Right after this tragedy, it simply felt wrong for me to write about conquering *over*eating when so many victims of the storm were starving as they waited for aid. With a heavy heart, I put blogging on hold for a few days.

Seeing the news coverage of so many in dire need affected not only my blog plans, it deeply affected my own attitude about food. During the months leading up to that day, I'd gotten into a bit of a funk in regard to feeding my kids—worrying about many of the ingredients in the foods we were buying and feeling like a terrible mother because I couldn't manage home-cooked, natural foods for every meal and snack. Not being able to keep my family's diet more "clean" had begun to get me down, so much so that I'd started to approach most meals with a sense of guilt and worry. But a few days after the typhoon, I took a trip to the grocery store—my four young kids in tow—and filled up my cart with a renewed sense of thankfulness for all the available food. I looked at the imperfect items that we could afford in my shopping cart with nothing but appreciation.

It immediately occurred to me that cultivating a sense of thankfulness could be useful for those struggling with overeating as well, so that's what I ended up focusing on in the next installment of my blog series. Trying to be more thankful doesn't mean you should feel guilty about having plentiful food when others have little. I'm simply recommending that when you begin to worry about eating too much of this or that, or when you feel a little too full after a meal, try to gently remind yourself how fortunate you are to be able to nourish your body and feel satisfied, even if you don't always do it perfectly.

Most people with eating disorders have developed an antagonistic relationship with food over time, so this mind-set may take some getting used to. If you are able to cultivate a deep sense of gratitude for food in the present, while also being thankful for food that will be there for you in the future, it can help curb the desire to each too much *right now*. If you fully appreciate that you'll have food next time you are hungry, you will be more likely to stop eating before you are overly full.

Keep track of insights that help you cultivate an attitude of thankfulness for nourishment:

_____

_____

_____

_____

_____

_____

_____

_____

_____

_____

_____

_____

[32]

Weight

You have to get the habit under control before you even think about losing the weight. From my own experience, if I restricted myself, even just a little bit, I would get so angry and rebel against myself. It was almost a year and a half after I stopped binge eating before I started making some changes to my diet.

~Chris

EVEN IF I NEVER lost a single pound after recovery, recovery still would have been 100 percent worth it. Binge eating brought so much misery to my life, and the weight gain was only a small portion of that misery. Sure, it was good to get back to my regular size after recovery, but that was certainly far from being the greatest benefit. Stopping binge eating doesn't guarantee you'll be happy with your weight, and recovery doesn't require you to lose weight. However, there is no doubt that binge eating affects your weight, so you may have questions or concerns about it as it relates to recovery and remaining binge-free.

WAIT FOR WEIGHT LOSS

First and foremost, it's not advisable to actively *try* to lose the weight you've gained from binge eating right away. There are three primary reasons for this:

1. Weight Loss Attempts Ignite Survival Instincts and Food Cravings

A weight loss attempt is likely the reason you started binge eating, so it just doesn't make sense to try to do that again now. Even if a weight loss attempt didn't precede the onset of your binge eating, we've discussed extensively how restrictive dieting leads to heightened cravings, elicits a primal desire to eat, and can prevent binge urges from fading. We'll talk later about options for losing weight in a healthy, non-calorie-restrictive way, but even this should be put on hold for a long time. It is simply too risky to shift your focus to weight loss soon after binge eating stops. I would recommend waiting six months to a year before you address weight in a nonrestrictive way.

2. Weight Will Likely Take Care of Itself After Binge Eating Stops

If you are currently over your natural weight, the idea of waiting six months to a year after binge eating stops to try to lose weight in a healthy way may seem discouraging. But waiting to address your weight issues doesn't mean you won't lose weight after recovery sooner than that. Most people don't need to "try" to lose binge weight—it just comes off as metabolism is normalized and the extreme surplus of calories ceases. No, the weight won't come off in a week; but it's healthier in the long run to lose it very gradually and naturally. Although some patience may be needed, by stopping binge eating alone, you are giving your body the chance to gravitate back to its natural size, because the larger size can only be maintained with an overabundance of calories.

If you are a bulimic who self-induces vomiting, this idea may be hard for you to accept at face value because you may think purging helps you mitigate weight gain. You may think that without the bulimia, you'd surely gain a substantial amount of weight. This is untrue. It is estimated that the body still absorbs up to 75 percent of the calories from a binge, even if purging occurs right after.[192] It's also possible that the body adapts to self-induced vomiting by absorbing calories much earlier in the digestive process, slowing down metabolism, and becoming more efficient at storing calories.[193] New research shows that the majority of bulimics reach their highest *ever* weight while in active bulimia.[194] This is true even if a substantial amount of weight was lost in the process of developing the eating disorder, lending more support to the idea that bulimia can lead to significant weight *gain* over the long term.[195] In fact, the higher frequency of purging actually predicts more weight loss once the behavior is stopped.[196]

3. Healthy Solutions for Weight Loss Are Best Found as a Non–Binge Eater

If stopping binge eating doesn't gradually lead to weight loss, you shouldn't just abandon recovery and go back to binge eating. Binge eating only brings you farther away from real solutions to reaching a healthy weight for your particular body. The biology behind weight can be complex—the number you see on the scale reflects a multitude of different metabolic processes, including brain systems that regulate appetite and enzymes that determine how efficiently calories from food are converted to energy. Additionally, the multitude of processes that influence weight are affected by environmental factors, such as the foods you eat and your lifestyle. You can see why it wouldn't make sense to deal with the complex issue of weight while binge eating—it just throws a wrench in the whole process.

Once eating habits are normalized and the urges to binge are long gone, it will be possible to explore non-diet solutions and discover any physiological issues that could be causing your body to be above your natural weight range. I'll address this later in the chapter, but first, I'm going to talk about making peace with the extra weight you may be temporarily carrying now.

How to Deal with Extra Weight Before You Lose It

Binge eating brought me significantly over my natural weight, and during that time, I felt like I was in someone else's body. When I stopped binge eating and began eating adequately, I was *still* well over my natural weight and I *still* felt like I was in someone else's body. There were about six months between stopping binge eating and reaching my normal weight that I simply had to deal with the extra pounds and have patience. Prior to quitting binge eating, I'll admit, I hadn't dealt with the extra weight very well. I wore only loose-fitting clothes for most of my college years, and I avoided places where I would have to wear a bathing suit.

My shame wasn't about just my appearance, but what my appearance represented to me. Prior to the weight gain from binge eating, I was a good athlete, and that's how I had defined myself since I was a child. I had received a college scholarship for cross-country and track, and instead of succeeding as a runner, I ended up gaining a lot of weight and quitting the team. My weight signaled to me that I had failed—that I had lost the competitive, talented part of myself. There are, of course, athletes of all different sizes, but my weight while binge eating was not *my* natural weight, and I no longer felt athletic at all. In my mind, the weight gain took away part of my identity.

As I walked around campus, I dreaded seeing any of my former teammates who were all super fit. When I did see them, I imagined that they were saying terrible things behind my back. I knew my thoughts about my weight weren't fully rational; I mean, if any of my friends or teammates would have gained weight, I wouldn't have thought any less of them. I also knew that if any of my friends or teammates truly had any of the cruel thoughts that I envisioned them having, then they weren't worth my time anyway. Nevertheless, I couldn't feel good about myself or my body or be confident in my relationships when I felt so out of control.

If my heaviest weight while bulimic was in fact my natural weight and the point at which my body functioned best, then that would have been absolutely fine. But I felt such shame at how I had gotten to that point. Once I stopped binge eating, I was pleasantly surprised that most of the shame about my weight went away *before* I actually lost the weight, which showed me that it was more about what I was doing to be that weight than the weight itself. I still didn't look forward to seeing people who knew me when I was very fit, but it didn't bother me nearly as much once I knew I was recovered. During the six months it took my body to gravitate back to normal, I tried not to put much emphasis on my weight. I was just glad to have my freedom and my life back, and I knew that my body would eventually settle in a good place for me.

From my experience and talking to others who have stopped binge eating, I've learned that focusing on the other benefits of being binge-free is a defense against impatience about weight coming off. Instead of focusing on whether or not you are losing weight, focus on what you are gaining in your life. Remind yourself that if the extra weight doesn't come off after a long time, you can deal with that—in the healthiest way possible—later. Remind yourself that being happy with your body is not a requirement for recovery and that this won't be the only time in your life when you aren't happy with your body.

The fact that you walk out of your door every day and face the world carrying your binge weight is building character in ways that you'll recognize only later. It will teach you the meaning of true friendships, because the people you really want in your life are those who do not care how much you weigh. Keep your head up and smile as much as you can, knowing that this is temporary and that you'll one day feel like yourself again. I know right now it might be hard to think of your weight in a positive way, but try not to be so anxious about it. Try to be open and allow it to be a humbling, not a humiliating, experience. Be gentle with yourself and realize that you've been incredibly successful already, whether you've lost a pound or not.

Also keep in mind that your lower brain might use your weight as fuel for the binge urges. If you don't see your weight dropping (Katherine Thomson will discuss whether or not to use a scale next), you may hear thoughts like, *You are not losing weight, so you might as well give up on recovery.* Rationally, you know how ridiculous that sounds, but in the moment of an urge, that message from your lower brain can seem convincing. Always remember that your weight never determines your ability to dismiss binge urges—or your worth as a person.

What benefits do you notice of being binge-free that have nothing to do with weight?

_____

_____

_____

_____

_____

_____

_____

_____

_____

_____

What life lessons have you learned or can you learn from carrying extra weight?

_____

_____

_____

_____

_____

_____

_____

Insights that help you put your weight in perspective and stay patient about losing it:

_____

_____

_____

_____

_____

_____

_____

_____

_____

THE SCALE, BY KATHERINE THOMSON

Some eating disorder books say to throw out the scale, and if you want to, that's fine. It all goes back to trusting that you can decide what is best for you. Provided that you don't need to be medically monitored, you don't have to track your weight. Scales are such crude tools, and frankly, I'm surprised our modern society lacks better, accessible methods of gauging body composition and overall size.

People react differently to the scale. If your reaction is that you get frustrated and annoyed and it ruins your day, then pitch it. If your reaction is to get very anxious not knowing your weight, then monitor it every now and then to see trends. It's about doing whatever doesn't produce too much tension. If you do choose to track your weight, it's important to keep focused on the big picture, not on minor, everyday fluctuations.

My view on the scale is that it's helpful as long as people can really grasp the concept of muscle, water, and food weight. One thing I notice with clients is that many tend to gain muscle in the early stages of recovery, and I think it's because active bulimics are essentially living off sugar. As soon as all the "good" food gets incorporated and digested, the muscles happily take as much protein as they can get. So the scale might reflect a higher weight, but this doesn't mean your body is any larger in size; it only means the composition has changed.

Furthermore, purging artificially reflects a lower weight than the body really is, because it eliminates fluids. A bulimic often stops binge eating and purging but has digestive problems and fluid difficulties because of the disorder, and so that person will see that they've gained five or six pounds, which is not truly accurate. They just have extra water and food in their system. This is why I recommend that if a person has been purging and then stops purging, especially with self-induced vomiting, then it's a good idea to not weigh oneself for at least two weeks.

I'm always surprised when I hear people say they've gained or lost a pound, because numbers like that are so within the range of daily fluctuations. My own weight fluctuates about four pounds at any given moment. I typically weigh myself several times a month, although in the past year, I've gone several months without weighing myself. It's important to understand that within a five-pound range, it's really hard to tell whether you are gaining or losing because of natural weight fluctuation. If you find yourself 10 pounds up or down, then that might indicate an actual change in whether your body has more muscle and fat or not.

For me, the scale was helpful in the beginning because it helped prevent the habits of both under- and overeating. However, some people I've talked to have found that the scale is not something good for them because it makes them more obsessed with weight and makes them feel worse about themselves. I know some people who've been able to find nutritionists who will weigh them and keep track of their weight for them, without having to see the numbers themselves. This can be really helpful because it allows them to stop worrying about weight loss or gain. But when I tried that, I hated it, because to me, it felt disempowering to have someone knowing about my weight and my body when I didn't.

If you are unsure how to use the scale, start with weighing yourself about once or twice a month. You'll need to find a way of doing it that doesn't feel obsessive and focuses on the overall picture rather than the fluctuations. When deciding when to weigh yourself, if you are a woman, consider your menstrual cycle and don't weigh yourself during the two weeks before a period. I see people slip in terms of binge eating when the scale goes up, sometimes just because they are premenstrual. To avoid this when tracking your weight, weigh yourself during week one and week two of your cycle, then don't weigh yourself again for a month.

How do you plan to use the scale, if at all?

_____

_____

_____

_____

_____

_____

_____

_____

ADDRESSING WEIGHT ISSUES AS A FORMER BINGE EATER

Research suggests that the treatment of binge eating needs to include helping patients establish a healthier approach to achieving long-term weight stability.[197] This means that treatment professionals and self-help methods shouldn't ignore the weight concerns of binge eaters, telling them to just "accept their bodies." Without providing alternative solutions for weight regulation, binge eaters can be tempted to go on extreme diets, which may exacerbate their weight problems. This book doesn't contain magic solutions when it comes to weight, but I'll give you five suggestions to think about and try for yourself if weight continues to be a concern for you long after binge eating stops:

1. Focus on Health

In any weight loss attempt, weight loss shouldn't actually be your number one goal. Research indicates that not only individuals, but the health care community as a whole should shift the focus from "weight-management to health-improvement strategies," because focusing on weight is ineffective and harmful for most people and costly to society.[198] Indeed, people who focus on what they *can* do to improve their health, rather than forbidding foods in the name of weight loss, have exhibited *better* weight loss outcomes.[199] If you go from binge eating to eating adequately and yet you don't eventually lose weight, then a gradual shift to focusing on health—without reducing calories at all—may be all you need.

> *I didn't focus on my weight at all, I just focused on health. I knew that if my body is healthy, then it will lose or gain how many kilos it had to. Of course there were times when I looked at myself and wondered when I would be able to lose weight, but I just gave myself time. If it takes two years to start losing weight, so be it.*
>
> *~Eve*

Making some changes to the composition of your diet, without letting it become an obsession and still allowing for flexibility, is a much better approach than banning food groups and slashing calories. We've talked about the myth that a 3,500-calorie deficit leads to one pound of fat loss, and part of the reason for this is that food quality factors into how different foods are processed by the body and also affects satiety mechanisms.

To allow for natural, healthy weight loss, don't focus on eating less, focus on eating better. What "better" means for each individual is open to interpretation and personalization. It has been shown that eating more refined or processed foods and sugar-sweetened drinks is associated with weight gain, whereas eating more unprocessed foods, such as fruits, nuts, and vegetables, is associated with weight loss.[200] This information seems like common sense by now; but it serves as a reminder that just making whatever simple changes you can will help you toward reaching your personal health goals.

Some people might find that changing diet composition to make it more plant-based helps them feel better and lose extra weight, while others find that eating more animal protein and healthy fats helps them achieve the same results. It's about finding what works for your unique body while accepting imperfection, so it doesn't feel like a diet and you can maintain the changes over the long term. Focusing on health can also mean incorporating vitamins, minerals, and even certain foods that are thought to help metabolism function properly. I would never recommend artificial diet pills or weight loss "tricks," but there are certain natural foods—for example, green and white tea,[201] apple cider vinegar,[202] coconut oil,[203] dark chocolate,[204] and some natural supplements (such as probiotics[205] and zinc[206])—that may support the body in losing unhealthy weight.*

Keep track of ways you can focus on health instead of weight loss:

_____

_____

_____

_____

_____

_____

_____

2. Exercise

Using exercise to maintain a healthy weight is another common-sense tip, but I'm going to address exercise as it relates specifically to former binge eaters. I am an advocate of exercise as a way to support a healthy weight, although I think it should be done with a greater focus on health than on weight loss. Exercise, like eating habits, has to fit your lifestyle and goals and what you truly want—not what some fitness guru says you should want, like six-pack abs. It's not only about the results, however; a focus on *enjoyment* during exercise helps keep you interested and motivated. Finding forms of exercise that make you feel good, then focusing on those good feelings, will help make exercise a beneficial habit in your life.

A very important consideration is fueling any activity you choose. Always make sure you are eating enough to support your activities, and of course make sure you are healthy enough to start any new fitness routines. If you don't properly fuel your exercise routines by adding more food to your diet, you will be left feeling increased hunger, which can be distressing to some people. This type of hunger is not a problematic craving, and satisfying it is not overeating—it's your body's natural signal that you need more food to support your activity level.

It should be noted that the types of exercise that were promoted for weight loss not too long ago, like cardio—often for up to an hour at a stretch—have been replaced in the past few years by promises that shorter-duration, higher-intensity workouts will give you better results.[207] For example, the CrossFit program (which consists of constantly varied functional movements at high intensity) has become

---

*As with any nutritional advice, it's easy to find contrary opinions. These are only suggestions to research and/or discuss with your doctor.

popular for those trying to lose weight and get in shape. I am of the opinion that different exercises will work for different people for different reasons, and again, there is no one right way. Sometimes it's really hard to get motivated to do a high-intensity workout, even if it lasts only fifteen minutes. It may actually be easier to motivate yourself to go for a walk or ride an exercise bike at the gym at a moderate speed while reading an enjoyable book—something that doesn't seem so daunting if you are already tired from a busy day.

Exercise shouldn't be something you endure for a little while and then quit once you've achieved results; it has to be something you always want in your life, and your routines will inevitably evolve over time based on your interests and other plans. If you ever find that your exercise routine is leading to added stress or weight obsessions, it is time to change course—take a break or try something different. It is not healthy or enjoyable to feel trapped into completing daily exercise routines or to feel like you have to log a certain number of miles of running per week. But if you listen to your unique body, exercise can be a source of stress reduction and assist you in maintaining a healthy weight.

What exercises do you enjoy? How do these exercises support your lifestyle and goals?

_____

_____

_____

_____

_____

_____

How do you plan to incorporate enjoyable exercise into your life?

_____

_____

_____

_____

_____

3. Determine What Is Preventing Weight Loss

If you do everything that's recommended—stop binge eating, give your body time to regulate, focus on changing diet composition to make it healthier, and add healthy, enjoyable exercise—and you still don't lose extra weight, the next step is to look into physiological reasons for that. There are a myriad of problems that can contribute to not losing weight, and science currently has an incomplete understanding of why some people can lose weight easily while others struggle. Here's a list of possible issues that can make weight loss less likely, many of which are similar to the physiological issues that can cause abnormal cravings:

- Hormonal imbalances
- Insulin and/or leptin resistance
- Poor digestion and absorption of nutrients
- Sluggish liver function
- Thyroid problems
- Infections
- Damage to the organs involved in metabolic control
- Chronic dehydration
- Sleep deprivation
- Anxiety

It's common for hormonal profiles of overweight or obese individuals to differ from those of people of normal weight, and this difference may encourage an abnormal metabolism and promote the accumulation of body fat.[208] For example, if you have low thyroid function and low thyroid hormones, it could mean you have a low resting metabolic rate, which, in theory, makes weight loss more difficult.[209] However, because of the multitude of factors involved in regulation of body weight, the relationship of any one hormone to body weight is usually not so predictable. Your physician can help you determine if there are any obvious factors preventing weight loss, but since there is only so much that basic blood work will show, more extensive testing might be called for with a specialist such as an endocrinologist or naturopathic doctor.

4. Accept Your Natural Weight

The last of the healthy solutions for weight loss doesn't actually involve the loss of any weight. If you've gone through the recommendations above and ruled out any physiological imbalances, your body is likely at its natural weight—the weight it's programmed to be at this point in time. If you are outside of this range, multiple systems in your body will make changes to push you back toward your natural weight, which goes for people who are biologically predisposed to be on the heavier side or the thinner side.[210]

An important study compared the weights of over 500 adopted children to the weight of their biological parents and their adoptive parents. Researchers found that the children's weights did not correlate with their adoptive parents, but correlated strongly with the weight of their biological parents.[211] This lends strong support to the idea that genetics heavily influence our weight and that learned eating habits and environment play less of a role than most people would hope.

I exercise daily and I focus on healthy eating and balanced meals. I lost a lot of bloat, but I have not lost much weight. However, I believe that my body is normalized now. I am a normal size 8. I would love to be a 4; however, my true health and taking care of my body is the most important thing.

~Isabella

The bottom line is that we come in all different shapes and sizes, and what's a healthy weight for one person of a certain height might not be a healthy weight for another person of that same height; furthermore, what is healthy for you now might not be what was healthy for you ten years ago or what will be healthy for you ten years from now. Some weight loss authors say that everyone has the potential to be thin, or at least "lean,"[212] but I do not agree. The unique makeup of some individuals doesn't allow for that, and I believe it's possible to be fit and healthy even if you're technically overweight.

To finish this topic, I'll leave you with the helpful words of Traci Mann, Ph.D., from her book *Secrets from the Eating Lab: The Science of Weight Loss, the Myth of Willpower, and Why You Should Never Diet Again*:

> Unless you want to battle evolution, biology, and psychology and be hungry every single day for the rest of your life, I wouldn't suggest trying to live below your set weight range. I understand that for many people, the goal is simply to be thin, but you also want to enjoy your life. Losing some weight but staying within your set range is a healthy goal; getting so thin that you are below this range is a very difficult and self-defeating one.[213]

Insights for being at peace with your own body:

_____

_____

_____

_____

_____

FOR THOSE WHO NEED TO GAIN

Not everyone who binges needs or wants to lose weight. While purging is not an effective means of weight control, those who do it sometimes lose weight in the short term and may need to gain weight after recovery. At the beginning of this book, I warned that being underweight is an issue that warrants medical monitoring; the advice here is for those who are *still within a healthy weight range* but think they may be lower than their own personal natural weight. After all, we don't all intrinsically know our natural weight—it's something we arrive at after a period of normal eating habits.

The first thing to do if you think you need to gain weight is the same as if you need to lose weight: simply give your body some time to adjust after you stop bingeing/purging and restrictive dieting. After a few months of eating adequately go by, if you have not gradually gained weight, then you can follow advice similar to that already given for those who need to lose. You can shift your focus toward health over weight, ensure that you are getting robust nutrition, possibly add some natural vitamins and supplements to your diet, and follow a moderate and enjoyable exercise regimen. If the scale does not gradually gravitate back upward, you'll need to look into physiological causes for this, such as an underlying hormonal problem that is preventing weight gain.

If you do all of this, find that you are healthy, but don't gain as much weight as you want or think you should, then you, too, need to learn to be at peace with your own body. You of course don't want to be malnourished, but you don't need to reach a certain weight to be recovered. Eating disorder websites and recovery advocates often praise curvier, fuller bodies and women who look "real"—which usually means women who are *not* skinny.

When I was in therapy, I definitely had the idea that a recovered woman couldn't be skinny. This was confusing to me at the time, as I knew some normal, healthy, hearty-eating women who were indeed very thin, and I knew that my own natural weight was thin. As already discussed, there can be some stereotypes of skinny individuals, with the underlying assumption that they must be chronic dieters and/or spend too much time exercising or obsessing over their bodies.

With all we've learned so far about how dieting actually leads to more weight gain, you can see how unfounded this common misconception is. Thin people are more likely to remain thin because they *don't* diet, not because they do. The only time I was ever not thin in my life was a direct result of dieting.

I think that praising "real" bodies is definitely a good thing, but we must always remember that "real" also includes thin bodies. I personally would love to have a more shapely figure, but the "real" Kathryn unfortunately has scrawny arms and legs (and a susceptibility to gain weight only in my midsection)—genetically, I have my dad's side of the family to thank for that. Being on the low end of normal isn't a problem—provided you are eating abundantly, not overdoing the exercise, and there are no underlying health problems. You can't force your body to be something it's not, and purposefully overeating or eating too much junk food to try to change your natural weight will only lead to adverse health consequences.

[33]

Night Eating

I always got urges at night, after dinner, when watching TV, and sometimes around afternoon tea on a Sunday. They came when I'd done everything I was supposed to do in a day, then got the chance to unwind and relax.

~Leah

A LOT OF BINGE eaters binge more at night, and even after binge eating stops, you may still find yourself having more food cravings late in the day. Most people don't get up in the morning craving a piece of cake, but after the work of the day is done, the piece of cake may seem much more appealing. If we look at night eating in terms of the brain, it makes sense that night is a common time for binge eating or overeating. Our primitive brains are wired to be more interested in food at night, especially high-energy foods. One study found that appetite and interest in sweet, salty, and starchy foods, meats, and fruits peaks around 8:00 p.m. as part of our natural circadian rhythm.[214]

There are many theories as to why this is so, one being that the evening peak in appetite could simply be to promote larger, higher-calorie meals before the fasting period necessitated by sleep. There is also a convincing evolutionary perspective on this: During the day, we are in "hunt" mode—working, moving, and doing (and, in the ancient past, hunting); but once we slow down at night, our survival mechanisms recognize this and turn our focus toward food, in order to replenish the energy stores we lost during the day and store up more for tomorrow.[215]

Another reason for cravings at night, especially for sweets, is for energy fixes in moments of exhaustion. At night, we are tired and energy depleted, so if we choose to stay awake, our brains will naturally view sugary food as more attractive and rewarding because it's a source of quick energy.[216] Compounding all of this is the fact that our self-control functions in the prefrontal cortex are at their weakest late in the day when we are exhausted, rendering everyone more likely to follow these natural cravings, and binge eaters more likely to act on binge urges that occur at night.

Conditioning is another reason why binge urges and cravings in general often occur more at night. During the day, there are typically other people around or responsibilities to be fulfilled, so it's not possible to binge, or even to sit down to enjoy some dessert or another food you like. Splurging a little (or much too much in the case of binge eaters) at the end of a long, busy day can easily become a conditioned habit. Additionally, if restrictive dieting precedes the development of binge eating, the dieter is often able to impose tight control of eating during the day, but due to the heightened natural drive to eat more at night, binge eating can result—and soon become an automatic late-night activity. Even without binge eating, individuals can develop what's called "night eating syndrome," which is characterized by eating at least 25 percent of one's daily calories *after* supper and/or waking up to eat late at night at least three times per week.[217]

When I was a binge eater, I learned that night eating in general and night bingeing in particular were supposedly signals of an emotional void left unfulfilled by my life or by that day. Alternately, I was told, night bingeing signaled that I hadn't eaten the right foods for breakfast, lunch, and dinner. However, even when I had deeply satisfying days on which I ate well, I was still often overcome with cravings and binge urges at night. I made too much of this natural, brain-based, extremely common tendency to want to eat at night—it had simply become amplified into a terrible habit.

DEALING WITH NIGHT EATING

Common advice for night eaters includes: keep healthy food options in the house, do some light exercise at night, stay hydrated, keep yourself occupied, make plans for when cravings hit, and/or just go to bed earlier. These suggestions are useful, especially the last one, because our reserves of willpower need to be replenished at the end of the day by sleep, so going to bed earlier is the most common-sense solution. However, an early bedtime is not always possible or desired, and it can be difficult to go to sleep if you are experiencing cravings; so having some alternate strategies makes sense. Below, I'm going to give you a few more things to think about when night cravings arise.

Stop Telling Yourself You "Shouldn't" Eat at Night

Instead of working harder to dismiss the cravings you have, try doing the opposite. Give yourself permission to eat, adequately, at night. Although it's of course not okay to binge or overeat frequently at night, it's perfectly fine to have a snack late in the evening, even right before bed. If you are using a structured approach to eating right now, try planning a generous late-night snack as part of your daily intake, then sit down to enjoy it.

When I worked with a nutritionist during my bulimia, she created a meal plan that spread out my calories evenly throughout the day. However, I didn't find myself wanting a big breakfast or lunch, so I basically forced them in. Come the end of the day, when I did have an appetite, dinner and my bedtime snack didn't feel like they were nearly enough. I was frustrated that all of that daytime eating hadn't seemed to change my heightened attraction to food at night. Usually, I'd decide to have something extra at night, feeling guilty about that and not truly enjoying it. This negative mind-set often led directly to that oft-repeated thought pattern by now: *I've already blown it, so I might as well binge.* So I'd proceed to eat several thousand more calories after the snack I initially felt guilty about. Now I can see that I simply needed more calories at night than during the day, and that's how I tend to eat now. Reorganizing my meal plan wouldn't have taken away my binge urges completely, but it would have helped with overall satisfaction with my eating and prevented so much unnecessary guilt for eating at night.

If you aren't planning meals right now, then you can eat at night in a more flexible, intuition-based way, using your higher brain to help guide your choices. By giving yourself permission to eat late at night, you'll most likely end up eating *less* than if you tried, in vain, not to eat at night. You will prevent your body and brain from feeling deprived, because you will be going with the flow of their natural tendencies while still not giving in to binge urges. I'm not suggesting that everyone do this across the board—just those individuals who feel the common, heightened interest in food at night. Furthermore, eating your biggest meal at the end of the day when it's time to relax *is* more practical than eating your largest meal at breakfast or lunch and then possibly feeling tired and lethargic when you really need to be productive. High blood glucose levels like those after eating a big meal can switch off the brain cells that normally keep us awake and alert.[218]

Some people worry about allowing night eating because somewhere along the way, they've heard that night eating is more likely to lead to weight gain than calories consumed during the day. There is evidence suggesting that this is a myth, or at least that night eating and weight gain don't have a causal relationship,[219] and some research actually pointing to night eating as being *better* for weight loss. A 2011 study from the *Obesity Journal* found that a group of dieters that ate most of their carbs at dinner experienced greater weight loss and sharper reductions in abdominal circumference and body fat than dieters whose carbs were spread more conventionally throughout the day.[220] Of course, you won't be dieting like the study participants, but this just goes to show that you need to question the weight-loss advice you hear and avoid making rigid, unrealistic rules for yourself.

Night Waking

Allowing night eating also applies to middle-of-the-night eating—when you wake up out of sleep and want to eat. However, this area can be a little trickier because you are operating in an only partially awake, not fully rational state. Some people wake up and go directly to the refrigerator, feeling in a daze, and commence eating (and if you are still binge eating, then bingeing) without much fore-thought at all; and some even have a hard time remembering the episode in the morning. It's as if the lower brain takes advantage of the weakened, sleepy state of the higher brain. But once you begin viewing urges as neurological junk, you can learn to dismiss them even when you're not 100 percent coherent.

My best explanation for how I was able to do this relates to the earlier discussion about whether or not to drink alcohol when recovering. Even in the less rational state of intoxication, it's still possible to exert choice and avoid wrong actions; in the middle of the night, the same theory applies. People are able to muster up necessary brainpower in the middle of the night for a variety of reasons. Think about parents who need to rouse themselves in the middle of the night to feed their babies or tend to the various needs of small children or even pets. They may be dazed and exhausted, but they can still do what is necessary. Imagine you were to wake up in the middle of the night and have a sudden urge to walk out of the house on a freezing night. I'd bet you would just roll over and go back to sleep, because even though you are groggy, you know that nonsensical desire is not worth considering.

Begin to think of both middle-of-the-night binge urges and excessive, problematic food cravings as a false alarm. You programmed this "alarm" in the past on the basis of your actions, and now it is set to automatically go off; but you don't have to respond to its call—at least not in the way it wants you to. There is nothing wrong with eating a *reasonable* snack in the middle of the night, provided it doesn't become too frequent of an occurrence that disrupts your sleep. Some people feel not just craving or false wanting, but true hunger in the middle of the night. It might feel like hunger wakes you up, or alternately, hunger may arise after long stretches of being awake.

Keep in mind that the reason most people don't eat at night isn't because they have more willpower than you; it's because they either don't have a tendency to get hungry at night or they are *sleeping*. If you aren't sleeping—because of insomnia, because you have to be awake for one reason or another, or because hunger wakes you up—then you should satisfy that hunger regardless of the time on the clock. I've gone through phases of my life where I've struggled with the inability to sleep, and during those times, I'd eat something about every two and a half to three hours at night, just like I would during the day. I didn't plan my night eating; that's just when my body naturally signaled hunger. Also, during the many months that I was awake at night with my newborns, I would get hungry and have snacks.

If you tend to feel hunger at night, having a prepared snack waiting for you can help ward off overeating. You'll be more likely to eat the prepared snack and, while you are eating it, wake up enough to dismiss any desires to continue eating. Even though this is fine, most people want to eventually sleep through the night—you don't want to be waking up every night to eat. To address this, you'll need to figure out why you are waking up. A sleep study can help identify conditions such as sleep apnea, snoring, or restless leg syndrome that may be causing you to wake up and then subsequently feel your hunger. Or, if the hunger itself is waking you up, it could be that you are having drops in blood sugar that you can discuss with your doctor. Some people find it helpful to eat something to balance blood sugar right before bed, such as some protein, healthy fat, or possibly some high-quality carbohydrates.

PART III:

FINAL THOUGHTS

[34]

Applying These Ideas to Other Problems

by Amy Johnson, Ph.D.

UNDERSTANDING THAT URGES FOR many addictive or habitual behaviors are coming from the loud but powerless lower brain, and that the only way those urges continue is if you choose to act on them, has value far beyond recovery from binge eating. The same insights and steps you used to stop binge eating can be applied to a variety of issues you might experience. In the same way that you've come to insightfully see your urges so that you can calmly ignore them, you can detach from and wait out *any* unwanted thought or emotion. Any thought that is stressful, painful, or leads you away from what your "true self" wants is essentially neurological junk.

THE NATURE OF THOUGHT

Our thinking creates our experience of life. Everything we experience comes to us via thought—it can't be any other way. It appears as if other people, the circumstances of our lives, and things that happen out in the world directly affect us. When you fight with your partner, a friend says something hurtful, or you don't perform up to expectations at work, it certainly feels as if those things cause you to feel bad.

Likewise, when you become engaged to be married, have a wonderful conversation with a close friend, or receive accolades at work, it seems like those external events create your positive feelings. Although it will always appear as if things outside of ourselves directly impact how we feel, they never do. How we feel—in fact, our entire experience of life—is created internally, by our own thinking about those things.

You have no doubt noticed how several people in the exact same situation can come to wildly different interpretations of it. A divorce might be the worst thing that ever happened to one person and the best thing that happened to another. A cross-country move can be unbelievably stressful for one person and easy or fun for another. It is never what actually happens that determines our experience, it's our own personal and unique thoughts.

Given the extreme importance of the role of thought in our lives, it is not surprising that most people misunderstand the nature of thought. We tend to take our thinking as truth. In a society that lauds reasoning, intellect, and logic—the higher brain, essentially—we assume that the thoughts that run through our minds all day every day are valid, true, and inherently meaningful. When you think, *I am kind* or *I am moody* or *I like sushi*, you naturally assume those thoughts reflect some objective reality that exists outside of your thinking. Even when we think things that we sense are not hard facts, such as *I am smarter than my colleague* or *I'm not as attractive as my neighbor*, most of us still relate to those thoughts as if they are somewhat factual and based in objective reality.

The truth, however, is that the thinking that passes through your mind all day every day is not objectively true. Thought is highly subjective and biased. Personal thinking is extremely unique in that no two people have the exact same thoughts; even when they have conceptually similar thoughts, those thoughts might feel very different and have a distinct impact on the thinker. If you have ever said in disbelief, "I can't believe she said that!" or "I would never do such a thing!" you have seen that we each live in our own version of reality.

In addition to being subjective and unique, thought is also not innately meaningful—that is, our thinking in and of itself is neutral and meaningless until we (using more subjective thought) add interpretation, story, and meaning to it. The thought *I am all alone* is neutral and meaningless in and of itself. It may be a statement of fact, but that fact isn't inherently good or bad—it is simply fact. It is only when our busy thinking minds add a layer of subjective storytelling to that thought that it takes on some personal meaning and evaluation. *I am all alone* can be a sad, lonely, or scary thought for a young adult living away from home for the first time or for someone going through a breakup. Or, in the case of many introverts or mothers of toddlers, it can impart a feeling of bliss and joy. Without a personal, subjective story, the thought *I am all alone* is a meaningless statement of fact.

THOUGHT AS NEUROLOGICAL JUNK

Because thought is subjective, biased, unique to each person on Earth, and innately meaningless, all meaning-infused harmful thoughts are essentially neurological junk. Anytime you are led astray by your own thinking—when it is full of worry or fear, full of assumptions or predictions about the future, or full of old programming that says you don't measure up in some way—you are, very innocently of course, falling for it. In the same way that you may have once believed that urges to binge eat were meaningful or based in some valid need, you may be taking your random thinking as meaningful and valid when it is not.

In the same way that an urge to binge is neurological junk, an old fear or a destructive or painful thought is neurological junk. And in the same way that you can label urges to binge eat as neurological junk and simply wait for them to fade, you can do that with any thought that does not feel consistent with your own inner peace.

APPLYING THESE INSIGHTS TO OTHER HABITUAL THOUGHT

What follows are two case studies that demonstrate how you can use the ideas in this book—detaching from thought, viewing thought as neurological junk, and waiting for thought to pass without acting on it—to deal with nearly any mental or behavioral habit.

GINA

Gina was burdened by thoughts of not measuring up. According to Gina, she wasn't thin enough, smart enough, successful enough, popular enough in her neighborhood, or respected enough by her family. Since middle school, Gina had felt like she was struggling to be part of what she called the "inner circle," but she always fell short.

Gina was perplexed in the same way many binge eaters are. On the one hand, she intellectually knew that she wasn't a complete failure. She had a loving family and a few close friends, and she could easily recall compliments from others and times she received external validation that ran counter to her insecurities. In her stronger moments, she had some ability to see herself in a way that was much kinder and more compassionate, and part of her believed *that* view was more based in reality than the negative view that often took over.

On the other hand, that intellectual knowing did not necessarily feel genuine or translate into any real confidence. Similar to how a binge eater might intellectually understand that her urges will fade but give in to them nonetheless, Gina usually reasoned that she probably was quite successful and appreciated, but she never truly felt it. She felt hijacked by insecure thinking, and most of the time, that insecure thinking determined Gina's emotions and behaviors.

When Gina learned that her insecure thoughts were not necessarily based in any reality—that they were habitual thoughts that were automatic and deeply wired in her brain but that they did not protect her or point her toward any valid truth—she felt some relief. Gina had a small insight: Maybe the part of her that said she was not as bad as she believed *was* in fact the wiser part, and the part that insisted she didn't measure up was the less wise, but highly conditioned, lower brain.

With this insight, Gina naturally began to view her incessant insecure thinking in a new way. She realized that each time she fought against or gave a lot of energy and attention to her insecure thoughts, she strengthened them in her brain. When she learned that her insecure thinking was reflexive and automatic but due only to strong, faulty wiring—it was neurological junk, basically—she simply saw it differently.

When Gina began to recognize her insecure thoughts as neurological junk rather than truth, their emotional impact changed. While those thoughts once had the power to instantly ruin her day and set off a cycle of self-doubt, they now were "just those junky thoughts again." Gina was less impacted by them, and with less attention placed on them, they began to fade.

Gina still has those old thoughts from time to time, but they simply don't pack the emotional punch they once did. Before she knows it, those thoughts are replaced with new thoughts. Gina's emotional life is much less roller coaster–like than it had been. Her insecure thinking is a fraction as frequent as it once was, and she spends much more time in a calmer place of confidence and self-acceptance.

JOHN

John had been afraid of speaking in front of groups for as long as he could remember. His fear held him back to some extent in high school and college, but it wasn't until he began his corporate human relations job that it became a real hindrance. In his work life, John was often expected to lead trainings and give presentations to groups of five to fifty people. John loved HR but was very distressed about this aspect of it, so much so that he often considered choosing a new line of work.

John learned that his persistent fear of public speaking was nothing more real than lower brain fear responses (not much different than urges to binge). Although they felt extremely compelling in the moment, as if they signaled a legitimate danger, and although they were met with sometimes intense physical reactions such as difficulty breathing, dizziness, and mental fog, those fears were simply faulty wiring in his brain. Each time he focused on those fears, they were reinforced.

This understanding changed things for John. The next time he was tasked with leading a group training, he felt the familiar fear rise to the surface, but his inner dialogue about it was different. He realized there was nothing he had to do about that fear. John felt the familiar desire to run from the room; he felt the familiar shakiness and mental fog; and he waited. To his surprise, he was able to wait out those symptoms quite calmly when his mind wasn't so busy interpreting his reactions and crafting stories about his eventual failure.

When John waited out his fear response, he was shocked at how quickly it began to fade. John was able to sit with his initial panic and carry on with his presentation such that no one in the audience had any clue what he was feeling.

Each of John's presentations became easier—the fearful thoughts appeared less real and the physical symptoms became less strong—until public speaking was no longer an issue for him. Two years later, John even volunteers to lead group trainings now, something he never would have predicted previously. As soon as John learned that his fear of public speaking was only the lower brain's conditioned response and nothing he ever had to *do* anything about, things completely turned around for him.

IF THOUGHT IS NEUROLOGICAL JUNK, WHAT CAN YOU BELIEVE?

At this point, you might be wondering what *is* real. If your personal thinking is inherently meaningless, somewhat random, and highly subjective—essentially neurological junk, in many cases—is *anything* that floats through your mind trustworthy?

You have probably noticed that thought takes on many different qualities. Sometimes your thoughts are racing and very emotional and dramatic. Other times your thoughts are slower and calmer. Sometimes thought feels mentally taxing—if you could turn your mind off, you would. Other times thought feels easy and unburdening, even enjoyable. There is a spectrum along which thought falls, from highly personal, chatty, and mentally taxing to less personal, less verbal, and less mentally tiring. If you pay attention, you tend to get a feeling for where your thought falls along that spectrum.

In general, personal thinking—the kind that is most biased and random—tends to be very verbal. It comes quickly and is often laced with emotion. Personal thinking is opinionated and not always kind. Personal thinking is what tells you that because you followed that last urge, you're clearly never going to stop binge eating. Personal thinking is what warns you that everyone is going to notice that you've gained a couple pounds, or that you aren't as smart as your colleagues, or that if you don't finish your project this week, you might as well not finish it at all. If your thoughts are pressure-filled or using scare tactics to "motivate" you into action, or if your thoughts are unkind or all-or-nothing, you are experiencing the very biased, personal thinking that falls at one far end of the spectrum. This type of thinking is most obviously neurological junk.

At the other end of the spectrum is thinking that is less personal—something more akin to what you might refer to as inner wisdom, insight, or inner guidance. Inner wisdom is thought, but it doesn't always feel or sound like the very verbal kind of mental dialogue that is personal thinking. Inner wisdom sometimes comes more in the form of common sense or a simple "knowing" than any verbal directive. Inner wisdom is patient; it's not in a hurry. Inner wisdom is kind; it will never shame or scare you into action.

Inner wisdom might say, *You don't really want to eat that* or *Call the doctor* or *Don't go to that party*. It doesn't always communicate in what feels like words; many times you simply have a feeling or a hunch and you find yourself acting on it without a lot of conscious thought. Inner wisdom doesn't always tell you what you want to hear, but it communicates with kindness, patience, and certainty. Personal thinking, on the other hand, might say, *You're going to get fat if you eat that and then you'll never find a date*, or *There is probably something wrong with you—get in to see the doctor immediately*, or *If you go to that party, you'll have a terrible time*.

Try not to analyze the qualities of your thoughts or where they fall on the spectrum too much. Instead, feel the difference. Some thoughts feel clear and certain, and those are likely closer to inner wisdom. Others feel heavier, more verbal, and less clear or kind. Those are likely closer to neurological junk. You don't need to determine where each and every thought you have falls along the spectrum, simply follow your feelings. If a thought seemingly goes against what your "true self" wants, if it is unkind or critical in any way or creates pain or stress, treat it as if it is neurological junk.

[35]

Be Your Own Recovery Guide

I now have a new perspective on life. I listen to my inner voice guiding me. I look around and see that no one is perfect and everyone has some kind of issue they are struggling with. I feel empowered knowing so much about the brain. I will never doubt myself again.

~Ariana

HOPEFULLY, YOU'VE BEEN ABLE to use some or all of the information in this book to stop binge eating, maybe even improve other problems or habits in your life. Anytime your recovery starts to seem complex or overwhelming, remind yourself that you are trying to do only two things: (1) dismiss binge urges and (2) eat adequately. Bringing your focus back to your two recovery goals keeps you out of the labyrinth that some envision recovery to be.

You've now learned the basics of dismissing urges and eating adequately, but you know yourself best and can become your own recovery guide. Empower yourself to adapt and modify the ideas you acquire from this book, or elsewhere, to keep moving toward your authentic recovery. Making personalized decisions about your own recovery includes determining when and if more help or professional guidance is warranted.

If you've reached the conclusion of this book and you have not stopped binge eating, don't be discouraged. You may simply need more time to allow insight to occur and for new ideas to translate into new actions. If, however, weeks and months go by and you are not improving at all, don't allow your approach to recovery to become habitual as well. Change things up, seek additional advice, and try new ways to put a stop to the binge eating. Take what has helped you from this book, then keep looking for resources that will keep you on a path to an eating-disorder-free life.

In Appendix A, I've listed some recommended resources—books, coaches, websites, and other options for support—that are somewhat aligned with the ideas in this book, but that also contain original and intelligent interpretations and advice. It's truly amazing how we are all so different, how no one relates to ideas in the same way, so that sometimes just a slight change in perspective can make all the difference.

Regardless of where you go next after closing this book, don't ever give up—there is always hope; there is always another piece of information that could help; there is always another form of support; there is always another personal insight forming under the surface. Recovery will come—regardless of what form it takes. Become a force to guide the change you want in yourself, but also be patient about when and how it comes. You likely won't know it at the time, but one day you will have a last binge, and although that won't magically bring you peace and joy, you'll be free to create your own authentic life.

Appendix A: Helpful Resources

The recommended resources listed below have been divided into two categories, based on which recovery goal the resource primarily addresses. Although there is some overlap between the two categories, this presentation will hopefully target the areas in which you're looking for some extra help.

RECOVERY GOAL 1: DISMISSING URGES

Books

Rational Recovery: The New Cure for Substance Addiction by Jack Trimpey. This 1996 book on substance addiction helped me take full responsibility for my own recovery from bulimia and quit.

The Little Book of Big Change: The No-Willpower Approach to Breaking Any Habit by Amy Johnson, Ph.D. This book combines spiritual wisdom with modern neuroscience to help you see your habit in a new way and turn attention away from the urges to perform it.

Being Human: Essays on Thoughtmares, Bouncing Back, and Your True Nature, also by Amy Johnson. This collection of essays can help you overcome harmful thoughts and rediscover your own natural state of well-being.

The Willpower Instinct: How Self-Control Works, Why It Matters, and What You Can Do to Get More of It by Kelly McGonigal. This is a practical book on using self-control to end habits that don't serve you well. It explains the science behind willpower and helps you put your brain to work for you.

The Mind and the Brain: Neuroplasticity and the Power of Mental Force by Jeffrey Schwartz, M.D., and Sharon Begley. This book explains the science behind neuroplasticity—the brain's ability to change based on our actions.

You Are Not Your Brain: The 4-Step Solution for Changing Bad Habits, Ending Unhealthy Thinking, and Taking Control of Your Life by Jeffrey Schwartz, M.D., and Rebecca Gladding, M.D. This is a self-help guide to using neuroplasticity to overcome bad habits and other challenges.

Willpower: Rediscovering the Greatest Human Strength by Roy Baumeister and John Tierney. This book can help you better understand, harness, and utilize your self-control resources.

Before I Eat: A Moment in the Zone Guidebook: Real-Time Tools to Manage Eating Urges and Food Cravings by Alen Standish. This book is written by a former binge eater to help you through the moments when urges are present. I also recommend the Before I Eat app (available for iOS or Android smartphone or tablet), which is full of practical tools you can use to track your progress and move toward recovery.

Coaches

Amy Johnson, Ph.D. (dramyjohnson.com). Amy, who is the main contributor to this book, is a psychologist, master certified coach, and binge eating recovery coach. She uses innovative coaching tools to help her clients see the truth about their urges to binge and stop acting on them.

RECOVERY GOAL 2: EATING ADEQUATELY

Books

The Bulimia Help Method: A Revolutionary New Approach That Works by Ali Kerr and Richard Kerr. This book is written by the founders of Bulimia Help (bulimiahelp. org), a comprehensive web-based home treatment program and support network for recovering binge eaters. While *The Bulimia Help Method* also offers assistance with overcoming urges, it has a strong focus on reestablishing normal eating—guiding you from a structured approach to an intuitive one.

Ditching Diets: How to Lose Weight in a Way You Can Maintain by Gillian Riley. This is a practical, easy-to-read book for anyone who wants to eat in a healthy way—without dieting, obsessing over food, or overeating. Gillian also has a helpful website, eatingless.com, where she offers private consultations and seminars.

Clearing Your Path to Permanent Weight Loss: The Truth About Why You've Failed in the Past, and What You Must Know to Succeed Now by Cookie Rosenblum. Cookie is a weight loss coach who understands binge eating, the importance of avoiding starvation diets, and how lasting weight loss can be achieved.

Secrets from the Eating Lab: The Science of Weight Loss, the Myth of Willpower, and Why You Should Never Diet Again by Traci Mann. This is a great resource if you are having trouble giving up dieting, because it explains the research behind why diets don't work.

Coaches

Katherine Thomson, Ph.D. (katherinethomsonphd.com). Katherine is a professor and medical sociologist who mentors individuals as they change beliefs and behaviors, especially concerning food. She draws from social psychology and mindfulness, and meets with clients in person as well as online.

Cookie Rosenblum, M.A. (realweightlossrealwomen.com). Cookie is a master certified coach and weight loss expert who can assist you if you are struggling with weight issues while recovering or after recovering from binge eating. Cookie has personal and professional experience with binge eating.

Pauline Hanuise (paulinehanuise.com). Pauline is a holistic health and bulimia recovery coach who offers private coaching as well as her Make Peace with Food online program for bulimics and binge eaters. Make Peace with Food presents a practical step-by-step process that has received great results. Pauline also gives a free introductory two-week coaching series on her website.

Stacey Cohen (bingefreeme.com). Stacey is a holistic health and lifestyle coach who recovered from binge eating using neuroplasticity and now helps others do the same. She has extensive training in nutrition, which is a great asset to those who want more guidance in healthy eating.

MORE COACHING OPTIONS

Polly Mertons (getbusythriving.com). Polly is a recovered bulimic who offers private coaching and other useful information for bulimics on her website.

Wendy Hendry (healthcanbeyours.com). Wendy is a personal health coach who recovered from thirty-five years of binge eating. She understands how to guide binge eaters toward healthier lifestyles.

Lydia Wente (lydiawente.com). Lydia is a lifestyle coach and recovered binge eater who can help you further understand and utilize the *Brain over Binge* principles and improve your eating habits.

Tania Veronese (seedoffreedom.com). Tania is a spiritual transformation coach and emotional eating specialist who can guide you toward a healthy relationship with food.

Appendix B: My Story

FOR THOSE WHO HAVE not read *Brain over Binge*, I'm including a brief version of my own story here.

In 1997, at the age of 15, I gradually took up "dieting"—cutting back on calories and increasing exercise in an effort to control my weight. The more I cut back on my food intake, the more I wanted to eat—which of course is the natural, biological response to food deprivation—and my binge eating began in March 1999, less than two years after I started restricting my food. My binge eating (and purging, in the form of excessive exercise and increased food restriction following binges) increased gradually until it became a life-consuming habit.

Despite much therapy, nutritional counseling, and medication, my binge eating continued for six years. In therapy, I learned the common theme of most conventional eating disorder treatment: Eating disorders are not about food. I learned that my bulimia was a symptom of psychological problems like depression, anxiety, low self-esteem, and family conflicts. I learned that my destructive eating behavior signaled an inner emotional crisis. My therapists said I used my bulimia as a coping mechanism to deal with issues and feelings I couldn't face. They said my binge eating filled an important need or void in my life—a need that was much more than physical.

I learned I didn't have much control over my own behavior; that is, until I addressed the underlying emotional issues that supposedly drove the binge eating. I tried to address those issues for years. I set out on a path of self-discovery, hoping to find some answers to why I binged, hoping that if I made some changes in my life, healed past hurts, or built new relationships, the incredible urges to binge would go away. I learned ways to deal with depression, reduce anxiety, and build healthy self-esteem. I battled my perfectionism and learned to cope with the events and feelings that supposedly triggered my binge eating episodes. I tried to figure out what purpose the bulimia served in my life. But all the while, I continued to binge and purge.

I don't blame my therapists because, after all, they were only trying to help me—using the widely accepted advice of the time, and they were always sensitive and supportive. Therapy didn't work for me because it did not target my problem directly; instead, I tried to address all sorts of issues that didn't have much to do with my real problem: binge eating. Furthermore, the view of my bulimia as a complicated problem that helped me fill some sort of emotional need gave me countless excuses to indulge my habit and countless reasons to avoid responsibility for my own actions. When I believed I was binge eating to deal with depression, cope with anxiety, avoid feelings and problems, ease pain from the past, or because I had a disease, it gave me all the more reason to go ahead and binge.

I was able to recover only after I learned to view my eating disorder differently: by dismissing the belief that I binged for deeper, more profound reasons and completely changing how I approached my problem. I recovered rather abruptly in May 2005. My recovery did not involve meal plans, emotional self-discovery, or spiritual enlightenment. It did not result from a decrease in anxiety, an increase in happiness, an improvement in self-esteem, a new medication, or any major life change. It was simply me, armed with a bit of knowledge, finally taking control of my own actions. This knowledge came primarily from reading *Rational Recovery: The New Cure for Substance Addiction* by Jack Trimpey, as well as from having my own insights into the true nature of my problem.

The most important thing I learned from *Rational Recovery* and afterward was that there was nothing wrong with me. I was not diseased or psychologically or emotionally unwell. I'd simply become a temporary victim of my own healthy brain—a brain that was only doing its job through all the years I was bulimic. I decided to stop viewing my binge eating as a symptom of underlying emotional issues and psychological problems, and start seeing it as a symptom of something very real and concrete going on in my very healthy brain. I decided to dismiss the belief that I binged to cope with problems and emotions, and instead learn how my brain worked to drive my destructive behavior.

My brain drove my binge eating by sending out strong urges to binge—which included all the thoughts, feelings, sensations, and cravings that led me to the refrigerator, pantry, or the nearest fast-food restaurant. These urges to binge were the one and only cause of each and every binge, from my first binge to my last. If I'd never had urges to binge, I never would have binged. It was that simple. My urges to binge were not symptoms of anything; they were the problem, the only reason I was bulimic.

Rational Recovery taught me a simple thinking skill called Addictive Voice Recognition Technique (AVRT®), which allowed me to start viewing the urges as not truly coming from "me," but from a much more primitive part of my brain (the lower brain) that is responsible for survival and automatic behavior. The urges first appeared when I was dieting because of survival instincts, and the urges continued because my repeated binge eating conditioned a habit into my brain. But the urges no longer had to control me. I learned that regardless of the messages from the lower brain, my true self—residing in my higher brain—could veto the urges and choose to avoid acting on them. I only had to stop giving the urges attention, significance, and power. I started viewing them as meaningless, and my experience of urges changed almost instantly.

I was able to avoid acting on the urges day after day, and even though I felt tempted at times, as long as I stayed detached from my urges—remembering that they were separate from my true self and not laden with deep emotional meaning—I was able to simply move on with my day and with my life as a whole. My urges to binge began to fade quickly after I stopped acting on them, and they were completely gone after about nine months of dismissing them. I was blown away by this, and at times, I was concerned that my problem would come roaring back; but the change felt so real and permanent, and I couldn't fathom ever turning back to binge eating. I was overjoyed to have my freedom back, and although I was not the perfect, successful, confident, shining example of what I once thought a recovered bulimic should be, I suddenly had the opportunity to live a real life without bulimia consuming me.

I still had many of the same faults, problems, and weaknesses that my therapists had once suggested contributed to my bulimia, and although I was happy about my recovery, I felt frustration that I had spent a long time trying to cure my bulimia by addressing these separate issues. I felt sorrow about the wasted years of my life, and most of all, I felt a strong desire to help others avoid wasting valuable time. Even years before my recovery, I had promised myself if I ever found a way to quit binge eating, I'd write a book to help others struggling with the same problem. Then, after I recovered in such a simple, nontraditional way, this goal was renewed. I was convinced I had a powerful story to tell that could shed new light on eating disorders and provide a different path to recovery.

I started writing notes and rudimentary chapters in early 2006, slowly documenting my experience and piecing together the insights and information that allowed me to put bulimia behind me. I came across telling information on the connection between dieting and binge eating, which helped me understand how I succumbed to binge eating in the first place; and I came across fascinating information on neuroplasticity, which explained to me how my habit was created and how I was able to extinguish it. I was able to put into words exactly how I stopped acting on binge urges, which became the Five Steps in my first book and the Five Components in this book. I will summarize the components here as I applied them in my own life, which will also serve as a review for those who have completed this book:

1. **I viewed my urges to binge as neurological junk.** I quit believing the urges signaled a real need—physical or emotional—and stopped assigning the urges any value whatsoever. I viewed them as automatic brain messages generated in my lower brain that had absolutely no significance.

2. **I separated my higher brain from my urges.** I realized the urges weren't really me, but instead were generated in brain regions inferior to my true

self. My true self resided in my prefrontal cortex—my higher brain—and it gave me the ability to say "no" to binge eating. I realized that my urges were powerless to make me binge and that my true self had ultimate control over my voluntary actions.

3. **I stopped reacting to my urges.** I stopped letting my urges to binge affect me emotionally. I simply let them come and go without getting wrapped up in them. This made the urges tolerable and not difficult to dismiss.

4. **I stopped acting on my urges.** This was the cure for my bulimia, made possible by the three preceding components. I didn't have to substitute any other behavior or emotionally satisfying activity for binge eating. I only had to refrain from following the urges.

5. **I got excited.** This was a natural product of not acting on the urges. By rejoicing in my success, I sped along the brain changes that erased my bulimia.

Together, these components are what I came to refer to as my "brain over binge" philosophy, and thus was born the title of my books. This concept is definitely an offshoot of "mind over matter," because it was my mind—my true self, my prefrontal cortex, my higher brain—that had the capacity to override the harmful matter (my urges to binge) coming from my primitive, lower brain. The prefrontal cortex—the seat of the true self—lies structurally above and forward of (over) the lower brain; therefore, my recovery was not only mind over matter, it was, quite literally, brain over binge.

It has now been over a decade since my recovery, and I simply live a normal life. I am a stay-at-home mother of four young children, so my days are filled with nonstop demands and challenges—big and small—but also joy and love. As far as eating goes, my story since writing *Brain over Binge* has been one of improvement, but certainly not perfection. Although I thought I was eating pretty well when I recovered, nutritional advice has changed a lot in ten years, and today I believe I eat much more nourishing foods for the most part. I think of food as fuel, but as pleasure too. I enjoy eating and exercising. I wish I could say I feel optimally healthy and energetic, but that's not the case. Although I'm sure I could make improvements in what I eat, I mostly blame fatigue on being chronically sleep-deprived since the birth of my first child over nine years ago, along with the stress of parenting.

Even though I'm eating healthier now than after I recovered, I now believe even more strongly that having an attitude of restriction and deprivation—even in the name of health—isn't healthy. I strongly feel that it's healthier to allow all foods (provided there is no allergy), even if most of the time you make a genuine *choice* not to eat certain foods. Eating better has to come from a place of truly wanting to eat better because it makes you feel better. I don't impose any food rules on myself, and I definitely have my share of processed foods and sugar—primarily in the name of convenience. Now that junk food isn't off-limits, I actually don't want it all that much. Sure, sugar and processed foods can taste delicious and I crave certain desserts or treats sometimes, but most of the time when I eat junk, it's not because I'm strongly desiring it—it's because I'm strapped for time or money or not well enough organized to have home-cooked meals or healthy snack options available.

Regardless of variations in my eating habits over the years, once my urges to binge went away ten years ago, they never came back—not even for a moment. It's hard to believe that I once thought bulimia was something I'd always deal with at some level, and now it's something I can no longer vividly remember. I did not accomplish this because there is something different or special about me. During my bulimia, I could have pointed out all of my flaws that I thought made me incapable of recovery. I can still point out all of my flaws, but that only means I'm human—I'm simply a normal person who learned to control and overcome an abnormal habit. I fully believe that if recovery was possible for me, it's possible for anyone.

Notes

Important Considerations and Disclaimers

[1] Mehanna et al., "Refeeding Syndrome."

[2] Mehanna et al., "Refeeding Syndrome."

[3] Casey and Galvan, "The Adolescent Brain."

Introduction

[4] American Psychiatric Association, DSM-5, 345.

[5] American Psychiatric Association, DSM-5, 345.

[6] National Eating Disorders Association, "Bulimia Nervosa."

[7] Mirasol, "Eating Disorder Statistics."

[8] American Psychiatric Association, DSM-5, 345.

[9] National Association of Anorexia and Associated Disorders, "Bulimia Nervosa."

[10] Binge Eating Disorder Association, "What Is BED?"

[11] American Psychiatric Association, DSM-5, 350.

Chapter 1

[12] National Eating Disorders Association, "Factors That May Contribute to Eating Disorders."

[13] Schmidt and Campbell, "Treatment of Eating Disorders Can Not Remain 'Brainless.' "

[14] Rikani et al., "A Critique of the Literature on Etiology of Eating Disorders."

[15] Schmidt and Campbell, "Treatment of Eating Disorders Can Not Remain 'Brainless.' "

[16] Friederich et al., "Neurocircuit Function in Eating Disorders."

[17] Kaye et al., "Neurocircuitry of Eating Disorders."

[18] WebMD, "Who We Are."

[19] WebMD, "Binge Eating Disorder Health Center."

[20] For a full discussion of survival instincts, see Hansen, *Brain over Binge*, 113–136.

[21] For a full discussion of habit, see Hansen, *Brain over Binge*, 137–149.

[22] Mathes et al., "The Biology of Binge Eating."

[23] Riley, *Ditching Diets*, 10–11.

[24] Akkermann et al., "Food Restriction Leads to Binge Eating."

[25] Mathes et al., "The Biology of Binge Eating."

[26] Umberg et al., "From Disordered Eating to Addiction."

[27] Mathes et al., "The Biology of Binge Eating."

[28] Mathes et al., "The Biology of Binge Eating."

[29] Manwaring et al., "Risk Factors and Patterns of Onset in Binge Eating Disorder."

[30] Mathes et al., "The Biology of Binge Eating."

[31] Mathes et al., "The Biology of Binge Eating."

[32] Mathes et al., "The Biology of Binge Eating."

[33] Pike et al., "Antecedent Life Events of Binge-Eating Disorder."

Chapter 2

[34] University of Cambridge, "Hormone Regulates Fondness for Food."

[35] Frank et al., "Altered Temporal Difference Learning in Bulimia Nervosa"; and Wierenga et al., "Are Extremes of Consumption in Eating Disorders Related to an Altered Balance Between Reward and Inhibition?"

[36] Swenson, "Limbic System."

[37] National Institute on Drug Abuse, "Drugs, Brains, and Behavior."

[38] Mathes et al., "The Biology of Binge Eating."

[39] Avena and Bocarsly, "Dysregulation of Brain Reward Systems in Eating Disorders."

[40] Friederich et al., "Neurocircuit Function in Eating Disorders."

[41] Friederich et al., "Neurocircuit Function in Eating Disorders."

[42] Mathes et al., "The Biology of Binge Eating."

[43] Friederich et al., "Neurocircuit Function in Eating Disorders."

[44] Pool et al., "Stress Increases Cue-Triggered 'Wanting' for Sweet Reward in Humans."

[45] McGonigal, *The Willpower Instinct*, 113.

[46] Salamone and Correa, "The Mysterious Functions of Mesolimbic Dopamine."

[47] Buckley, "UConn Researcher: Dopamine Not About Pleasure (Anymore)."

[48] McGonigal, *The Willpower Instinct*, 112.

[49] McGonigal, *The Willpower Instinct*, 125.

[50] Umberg et al., "From Disordered Eating to Addiction."

[51] Wang et al., "Enhanced Striatal Dopamine Release During Food Stimulation in Binge Eating Disorder."

[52] Umberg et al., "From Disordered Eating to Addiction."

[53] Wang et al., "Enhanced Striatal Dopamine Release During Food Stimulation in Binge Eating Disorder."

[54] Berridge, Robinson, and Aldridge, "Dissecting Components of Reward."

[55] Berridge, Robinson, and Aldridge, "Dissecting Components of Reward."

[56] Berridge, Robinson, and Aldridge, "Dissecting Components of Reward."

[57] McGonigal, *The Willpower Instinct*, 112.

[58] Mathes et al., "The Biology of Binge Eating."

[59] Umberg et al., "From Disordered Eating to Addiction."

[60] Bello and Hajnal, "Dopamine and Binge Eating Behaviors."

[61] Umberg et al., "From Disordered Eating to Addiction."

[62] Umberg et al., "From Disordered Eating to Addiction."

[63] Mathes et al., "The Biology of Binge Eating."

[64] Mathes et al., "The Biology of Binge Eating."

[65] Avena and Bocarsly, "Dysregulation of Brain Reward Systems in Eating Disorders."

[66] McElroy et al., "Pharmacological Management of Binge Eating Disorder."

[67] FDA, "FDA Expands Uses of Vyvanse."

[68] Shire, "About Vyvanse for Adults."

[69] Salamone and Correa, "The Mysterious Motivational Functions of Mesolimbic Dopamine."

[70] Mental Health Daily, "Vyvanse Approved for Binge Eating Disorder."

[71] Schwartz and Begley, *The Mind and the Brain*.

[72] Schwartz and Gladding, *You Are Not Your Brain*, 21–22.

Chapter 3

[73] Schwartz and Gladding, *You Are Not Your Brain*, 21.

[74] Schwartz and Begley, *The Mind and the Brain*, 366.

[75] Goldberg, *The Executive Brain*, 209.

[76] Friederich et al., "Neurocircuit Function in Eating Disorders."

[77] Friederich et al., "Neurocircuit Function in Eating Disorders."

[78] Friederich et al., "Neurocircuit Function in Eating Disorders."

[79] Friederich et al., "Neurocircuit Function in Eating Disorders."

[80] McGonigal, *The Willpower Instinct*, 64–65.

[81] McClelland et al., "A Systematic Review of the Effects of Neuromodulation on Eating and Body Weight."

[82] Poulsen et al., "A Randomized Controlled Trial of Psychoanalytic Psychotherapy or Cognitive-Behavioral Therapy for Bulimia Nervosa."

[83] Poulsen et al., "A Randomized Controlled Trial of Psychoanalytic Psychotherapy or Cognitive-Behavioral Therapy for Bulimia Nervosa."

[84] Schwartz and Gladding, *You Are Not Your Brain*, xiv.

[85] Hedges, *The Power of Presence*, 145.

[86] Hedges, *The Power of Presence*, 145.

Chapter 5

[87] Trimpey, *Rational Recovery*, 113.

[88] Trimpey, *Rational Recovery*, 120.

[89] Glass, *The Animal Within Us*, 84.

Chapter 8

[90] Friederich et al., "Neurocircuit Function in Eating Disorders."

[91] Pool et al., "Stress Increases Cue-Triggered 'Wanting' for Sweet Reward in Humans."

[92] Pool et al., "Stress Increases Cue-Triggered 'Wanting' for Sweet Reward in Humans."

[93] McGonigal, *The Willpower Instinct*, 51–54.

[94] Riley, *Ditching Diets*, 78.

[95] Riley, *Ditching Diets*, 78.

[96] Parker, Parker, and Brotchie, "Mood States Effects of Chocolate."

Chapter 12

[97] Hedges, *The Power of Presence*, 147, 151.

[98] Hedges, *The Power of Presence*, 153.

[99] Hedges, *The Power of Presence*, 153.

[100] Histed, Pasupathy, and Miller, "Learning Substrates in the Primate Prefrontal Cortex and Striatum."

Chapter 13

[101] Czerner, *What Makes You Tick*, 144–145.

[102] Schwartz and Begley, *The Mind and the Brain*, 333–334.

Chapter 15

[103] Hedges, *The Power of Presence*, 145–146.

[104] Trimpey, *Rational Recovery*, 140.

[105] Trimpey, *Rational Recovery*, 122–123.

Chapter 16

[106] Trimpey, *Rational Recovery*, 59.

Chapter 19

[107] McGonigal, *The Willpower Instinct*, 24–25.

[108] McGonigal, *The Willpower Instinct*, 24.

[109] McGonigal, *The Willpower Instinct*, 25.

[110] McGonigal, *The Willpower Instinct*, 26.

[111] McGonigal, *The Willpower Instinct*, 55–65.

Recovery Goal 2

[112] Oxford Dictionaries Online, def. 1 of *adequate*.

Chapter 21

[113] For a full explanation of why urges continue in the absence of dieting, see Hansen, *Brain over Binge*, 129–136.

[114] Lowe, Witt, and Grossman, "Dieting in Bulimia Nervosa Is Associated with Increased Food Restriction and Psychopathology but Decreased Binge Eating."

[115] Jaminet and Jaminet, *The Perfect Health Diet*, 261.

[116] Gailliot, "Hunger and Reduced Self-Control."

[117] Redman and Ravussin, "Caloric Restriction in Humans."

[118] Teff et al., "Dietary Fructose Reduces Circulating Insulin and Leptin."

[119] Paddon-Jones et al., "Protein, Weight Management, and Satiety."

[120] Redman et al., "Metabolic and Behavioral Compensations in Response to Caloric Restriction."

[121] Hill, "Does Dieting Make You Fat?"

[122] Martin et al., "Effect of Calorie Restriction on Resting Metabolic Rate and Spontaneous Physical Activity."

[123] Martin et al., "Effect of Calorie Restriction on Resting Metabolic Rate and Spontaneous Physical Activity."

[124] Klesges, Isbell, and Klesges, "Relationship Between Dietary Restraint, Energy Intake, Physical Activity, and Body Weight."

[125] Hill, "Does Dieting Make You Fat?"

[126] Pankevich et al., "Caloric Restriction Experience Reprograms Stress and Orexegenic Pathways and Promotes Binge-Eating."

[127] Heilbronn et al., "Effect of 6-mo. Calorie Restriction on Biomarkers of Longevity."

[128] Mattson, "Dietary Factors, Hormesis and Health."

[129] Mann et al., "Medicare's Search for Effective Obesity Treatments."

[130] Mattison et al., "Impact of Caloric Restriction on Health and Survival in Rhesus Monkeys."

Chapter 22

[131] Harris, "Role of Set-Point Theory in Regulation of Body Weight."

[132] Leibel, Rosenbaum, and Hirsch, "Changes in Energy Expenditure Resulting from Altered Body Weight."

[133] Kolata, "Genes Take Charge, and Diets Fall by the Wayside."

[134] Centers for Disease Control and Prevention, "Obesity and Overweight."

[135] Renki, "Are You Destined to Inherit Your Mother's Body Shape?"

[136] Pietiläinen et al., "Does Dieting Make You Fat?"

Chapter 23

[137] Geliebter, Yahav, and Hashim, "Gastric Capacity, Test Meal Intake, and Appetitive Hormones in Binge Eating Disorder."

Chapter 24

[138] Nestle, "Why Does the FDA Recommend 2,000 Calories Per Day?"

[139] Nestle and Nesheim, *Why Calories Count*, 84

[140] Nestle and Nesheim, *Why Calories Count*, 80–81.

[141] Vinken et al., "Equations for Predicting the Energy Requirements of Healthy Adults."

[142] Leibel et al., "Changes in Energy Expenditure."

[143] Kotler et al., "Total Energy Expenditure as Measured by Doubly-Labeled Water in Outpatients with Bulimia Nervosa."

[144] This estimated intake was arrived at using the Harris Benedict Equation, which multiplies resting metabolic rate by an appropriate "activity factor" to determine total daily energy expenditure. Explanations of the activity factor can be found at: http://www.bmi-calculator.net/bmr-calculator/harris-benedict-equation/.

[145] YourEatiopia.com, "I Need How Many Calories?"

[146] Mehler et al., "Nutritional Rehabilitation."

[147] Suchy, "Why Protein Makes You Feel Full Faster"; and ABC News, "13 Things Diet Experts Won't Tell You About Weight Loss."

Chapter 26

[148] Murphy et al., "Cognitive Behavioral Therapy for Eating Disorders."

[149] Wilson, Grilo, and Vitousek, "Psychological Treatment of Eating Disorders."

150 Fairburn et al., "Transdiagnostic Cognitive-Behavioral Therapy for Patients with Eating Disorders."

151 Murphy et al., "Cognitive Behavioral Therapy for Eating Disorders."

152 Zendequi, West, and Zandberg, "Binge Eating Frequency and Regular Eating Adherence."

153 Murphy et al., "Cognitive Behavioral Therapy for Eating Disorders."

154 The ten principles can be found on the Original Intuitive Eating Pros® page: https:// www. intuitiveeating.com/content/10-principles-intuitive-eating.

155 Tribole and Resch, *Intuitive Eating*.

Chapter 27
156 Rollins et al., "Affects of Restriction on Children's Intake Differ."

Chapter 29
157 Examples of books that suggest wheat (and low-fat dairy) are harmful: Jaminet and Jaminet, *The Perfect Health Diet*; Davis, *Wheat Belly*; and Wolf, *The Paleo Solution*.

158 Mann, *Secrets from the Eating Lab*, 27.

159 Abrams, "Study: Belly Fat Officially the Worst."

160 Mann, *Secrets from the Eating Lab*, 27.

161 Konturek, Brzozowski, and Konturek, "Stress and the Gut"

Chapter 30
162 Stice, Burger, and Yokum, "Caloric Deprivation Increases Responsivity."

163 Sumithran et al., "Long-Term Persistence of Hormonal Adaptations to Weight Loss."

164 Wilson, *Adrenal Fatigue*, 7–11.

165 Wilson, *Adrenal Fatigue*, 157–158.

166 Gearhardt, Boswell, and White, "The Association of 'Food Addiction' with Disordered Eating."

167 Gearhardt et al., "The Neural Correlates of 'Food Addiction.'"

168 Cantin et al., "Cocaine Is Low on the Value Ladder of Rats."

169 Cheren et al., "Physical Craving and Food Addiction."

170 Meule, von Rezori, and Blechert, "Food Addiction and Bulimia Nervosa."

171 Trimpey, "Orientation to AVRT-Based, Family-Centered, Addiction Recovery."

172 Gearhardt et al., "The Neural Correlates of 'Food Addiction.'"

173 Gearhardt et al., "The Neural Correlates of 'Food Addiction.'"

174 Gearhardt et al., "The Neural Correlates of 'Food Addiction.'"

175 Wesley et al., "Choosing Money over Drugs."

176 Feliz, "Survey: Ten Percent of American Adults Report Being in Recovery."

177 Mitka, "Research Suggests Pathological Gambling Is an Addiction Issue."

178 Jaslow, "Internet Addiction Changes Brain Similar to Cocaine."

179 Withnall, "Pornography Addiction Leads to Same Brain Activity as Alcoholism or Drug Use."

180 PsychGuides.com, "Shopping Addiction Symptoms, Causes, and Effects."

181 Cheren et al., "Physical Craving and Food Addiction."

182 Slate, "Do Drug Addicts Lose Control of Their Drug Use?"

[183] Werdell, "Science of Food Addiction."

[184] Carroll, "The Eating Disorder Inventory."

[185] Cheren et al., "Physical Craving and Food Addiction."

[186] Braune et al., "Determinants of Unplanned Discharge from In-Patient Drug and Alcohol Detoxification."

[187] National Institute on Drug Abuse, "Drugs, Brains, and Behavior."

[188] Mann, *Secrets from the Eating Lab*, 26.

[189] Cheren et al., "Physical Craving and Food Addiction."

[190] Cheren et al., "Physical Craving and Food Addiction."

Chapter 31

[191] McGonigal, *The Willpower Instinct*, 49.

Chapter 32

[192] Liberty, "Does Bulimia Help You Lose Weight?"

[193] Liberty, "How Bulimia Leads to Weight Gain."

[194] Shaw et al., "Elevated Pre-morbid Weights in Bulimic Individuals."

[195] Shaw et al., "Elevated Pre-morbid Weights in Bulimic Individuals."

[196] Umberg et al., "From Disordered Eating to Addiction."

[197] Lowe, Witt, and Grossman, "Dieting in Bulimia Nervosa Is Associated with Increased Food Restriction."

[198] Bacon and Aphramor, "Weight Science."

[199] McGonigal, *The Willpower Instinct*, 227–228.

[200] Mozaffarian et al., "Changes in Diet and Lifestyle and Long-Term Weight Gain."

[201] Goldman, "The Drink That Can Help You Lose More Weight."

[202] Taylor, "How to Drink Apple Cider Vinegar for Weight Loss."

[203] Assuncão et al., "Effects of Dietary Coconut Oil."

[204] Crain, "Can Eating Chocolate Melt Belly Bulge?"

[205] Sanchez et al., "Effect of Lactobaccillus Rhamnosus CGMCC1.3724 Supplementation on Weight Loss and Maintenance."

[206] Coleman, "Weight Loss & Zinc."

[207] Kiefer, "Women: Running into Trouble."

[208] Better Health Channel, "Obesity and Hormones."

[209] American Thyroid Association, "Thyroid and Weight."

[210] Mann, *Secrets from the Eating Lab*, 24.

[211] Mann, *Secrets from the Eating Lab*, 19.

[212] Example of the philosophy that everyone has the potential to be thin/lean: Spinardi, *How to Have Your Cake and Your Skinny Jeans Too*.

[213] Mann, *Secrets from the Eating Lab*, 31.

Chapter 33

[214] Scheer, Morris, and Shea, "The Internal Circadian Clock Increases Hunger and Appetite in the Evening."

[215] Nate, "Four Reasons to Eat More Calories (and Carbs) at Night."

[216] Yoo, "Why You Crave Junk Food When You're Sleepy."

[217] Leman, "Night Eating Syndrome."

[218] New Scientist, "Why We Need a Siesta After Dinner."

[219] Berkhan, "Is Late Night Eating Better for Fat Loss and Health?"

[220] Sofer et al., "Greater Weight Loss and Hormonal Changes After Six Months Diet with Carbohydrates Eaten Mostly at Dinner."

Bibliography

ABC News. "13 Things Diet Experts Won't Tell You About Weight Loss" (March 20, 2012). http://abcnews.go.com/Health/diet-secrets-13-things-experts-weight-loss-good/story?id=15954615.

Abrams, Lindsay. "Study: Belly Fat Officially the Worst." *Atlantic* (August 28, 2012). http://www.theatlantic.com/health/archive/2012/08/study-belly-fat-officially-the-worst/261630/.

Akkermann, K., Hiio, K., Villa, I., and J. Harro. "Food Restriction Leads to Binge Eating Dependent upon the Effect of the Brain-Derived Neurotrophic Factor Val66Met Polymorphism." *Psychiatry Research* 185, nos. 1–2 (2011): 39–43. doi: 10.1016/j.psychres.2010.04.024.

American Psychiatric Association. *Diagnostic and Statistical Manual of Mental Disorders*, Fifth Edition (DSM-5). Washington, DC: American Psychiatric Association, 2013.

American Thyroid Association. "Thyroid and Weight" (June 4, 2012). http://www.thyroid.org/thyroid-and-weight/.

Assuncão, M. L., H. S. Ferreira, A. F. dos Santos, C. R. Cabral, Jr., and T. M. Florencio. "Effects of Dietary Coconut Oil on the Biochemical and Anthropometric Profiles of Women Presenting Abdominal Obesity." *Lipids* 44, no. 7 (2009): 593–601.

Avena, N. M., and M. E. Bocarsly. "Dysregulation of Brain Reward Systems in Eating Disorders: Neurochemical Information from Animal Models of Binge Eating, Bulimia Nervosa, and Anorexia Nervosa." *Neuropharmacology* 63, no. 1 (2012): 87–96. doi: 10.1016/j.neuropharm.2011.11.010.

Bacon, L., and L. Aphramor. "Weight Science: Evaluating the Evidence for a Paradigm Shift." *Nutrition Journal* 10 (2011): 9. doi: 10.1186/1475-2891-10-9.

Baumeister, Roy, and John Tierney. *Willpower: Rediscovering the Greatest Human Strength*. New York: Penguin, 2011.

Bello, Nicholas T., and Andras Hajnal. "Dopamine and Binge Eating Behaviors." *Pharmacology Biochemistry and Behavior* 97, no. 1 (2010): 25–33. doi: 10.1016/j.pbb.2010.04.016.

Berkhan, Martin. "Is Late Night Eating Better for Fat Loss and Health?" Leangains.com (June 16 2011). http://www.leangains.com/2011/06/is-late-night-eating-better-for-fat.html.

Berridge, Kent C., Terry E. Robinson, and J. Wayne Aldridge. "Dissecting Components of Reward: 'Liking,' 'Wanting,' and Learning." *Current Opinion in Pharmacology* 9, no. 1 (2009): 65–73. doi: 10.1016/j.coph.2008.12.014.

Better Health Channel. "Obesity and Hormones." https://www.betterhealth.vic.gov.au/health/healthyliving/obesity-and-hormones (accessed August 4, 2015).

Binge Eating Disorder Association. "What Is BED?" http://bedaonline.com/understanding-binge-eating-disorder/what-is-bed/#.VPvIc-w5DIU (accessed April 22, 2015).

Braune, N. J., J. Schroder, P. Gruschka, K. Daecke, and J. Pantel. "Determinants of Unplanned Discharge from In-Patient Drug and Alcohol Detoxification: A Retrospective Analysis of 239 Admissions." *Fortschritte der Neurologie Psychiatrie* 76, no. 1 (2008): 217–224. doi: 10.1055/s-2008-1038116.

Buckley, Christine. "UConn Researcher: Dopamine Not About Pleasure (Anymore)." *UConn Today.* http://today.uconn.edu/2012/11/uconn-researcher-dopamine-not-about-pleasure-anymore/# (accessed July 16, 2015).

Cantin, L., M. Lenoir, E. Augier, N. Vanhille, S. Dubreucq, F. Serre, C. Vouillac, and S. H. Ahmed. "Cocaine Is Low on the Value Ladder of Rats: Possible Evidence for Resilience to Addiction." *PLOS ONE* 5, no. 7 (2010): e11592. doi: 10.1371/journal.pone.0011592.

Carroll, M. T. "The Eating Disorder Inventory and Other Predictors of Successful Symptom Management of Bulimic and Obese Women Following an Inpatient Treatment Program Employing an Addictions Paradigm." Tampa, FL: Department of Psychological and Social Foundations, University of South Florida, 1993.

Casey, B. J., S. Getz, and A. Galvan. "The Adolescent Brain." *Developmental Review* 28, no. 1 (2008): 62–77. doi: 10.1016/j.dr.2007.08.003.

Centers for Disease Control and Prevention. "Obesity and Overweight." http://www.cdc.gov/nchs/fastats/obesity-overweight.htm (accessed May 8, 2015).

Cheren, M., M. Foushi, E. H. Gudmundsdotter, C. Hillock, M. Lerner, M. Prager, M. Rice, L. Walsh, and P. Werdell. "Physical Craving and Food Addiction: A Scientific Review Paper." Sarasota, FL: Food Addiction Institute, 2009. http://foodaddictioninstitute.org/FAI-DOCS/Physical-Craving-and-Food-Addiction.pdf.

Coleman, Erin, R.D., L.D. "Weight Loss & Zinc." LiveStrong.com (June 23, 2015). http://www.livestrong.com/article/216201-weight-loss-zinc/.

Crain, Esther. "Can Eating Chocolate Melt Belly Bulge?" *Women's Health* (November 12, 2013). http://www.womenshealthmag.com/weight-loss/dark-chocolate-benefits.

Czerner, Thomas B. *What Makes You Tick? The Brain in Plain English.* New York: Wiley, 2001.

Davis, William. *Wheat Belly: Lose the Wheat, Lose the Weight, and Find Your Path Back to Health.* New York: Rodale, 2011.

Fairburn, C. G., Z. Cooper, H. A. Doll, M. E. O'Connor, K. Bohn, D. M. Hawker, J. A. Wales, and R. L. Palmer. "Transdiagnostic Cognitive-Behavioral Therapy for Patients with Eating Disorders: A Two-Site Trial with 60-Week Follow-Up." *American Journal of Psychiatry* 166, no. 3 (2009): 311–319. doi: 10.1176/appi.ajp.2008.08040608.

Feliz, Josie. "Survey: Ten Percent of American Adults Report Being in Recovery from Substance Abuse or Addiction." Partnership for Drug-Free Kids (March 6, 2012). http://www.drugfree.org/newsroom/survey-ten-percent-of-american-adults-report-being-in-recovery-from-substance-abuse-or-addiction/.

Frank, G. K., J. R. Reynolds, M. E. Shott, and R. C. O'Reilly. "Altered Temporal Difference Learning in Bulimia Nervosa." *Biological Psychiatry* 70, no. 8 (2011): 728–735. doi: 10.1016/j.biopsych.2011.05.011.

Friederich, H. C., M. Wu, J. J. Simon, and W. Herzog. "Neurocircuit Function in Eating Disorders." *International Journal of Eating Disorders* 46, no. 5 (2013): 425–432. doi: 10.1002/eat.22099.

Gailliot, Matthew. "Hunger and Reduced Self-Control in the Laboratory and Across the World: Reducing Hunger as a Self-Control Panacea." *Psychology* 4 (2013): 59–66. doi: 10.4236/psych.2013.41008.

Gearhardt, A. N., R. G. Boswell, and M. A. White. "The Association of 'Food Addiction' with Disordered Eating and Body Mass Index." *Eating Behaviors* 15, no. 3 (2014): 427–433. doi: 10.1016/j.eatbeh.2014.05.001.

Gearhardt, A. N., S. Yokum, P. T. Orr, E. Stice, W. R. Corbin, and K. D. Brownell. "The Neural Correlates of 'Food Addiction.' " *Archives of General Psychiatry* 68, no. 8, (2011): 808–816. doi: 10.1001/archgenpsychiatry.2011.32.

Geliebter, A., E. K. Yahav, and S. A. Hashim. "Gastric Capacity, Test Meal Intake, and Appetitive Hormones in Binge Eating Disorder." *Physiology & Behavior* 81, no. 5 (2004): 735–740.

Glass, Jay D., Ph.D. *The Animal Within Us: Lessons About Life from Our Animal Ancestors.* Corona Del Mar, CA: Donington Press, 1998.

Goldberg, Elkhonon. *The Executive Brain: Frontal Lobes and the Civilized Mind.* New York: Oxford University Press, 2001.

Goldman, Alison. "The Drink That Can Help You Lose More Weight." *Women's Health* (November 8, 2013). http://www.womenshealthmag.com/weight-loss/weight-loss-drinks.

Hansen, Kathryn. *Brain over Binge: Why I Was Bulimic, Why Conventional Therapy Didn't Work, and How I Recovered for Good.* Phoenix, AZ: Camellia Publishing, 2011.

Harris, R. B. "Role of Set-Point Theory in Regulation of Body Weight." *FASEB Journal* 4, no. 15 (1990): 3310–3318. http://www.fasebj.org/content/4/15/3310.long.

Hedges, Kristi. *The Power of Presence: Unlock Your Potential to Influence and Engage Others.* New York: American Management Association, 2012.

Heilbronn, L. K., L. de Jonge, M. I. Frisard, J. P. DeLany, D. E. L. Meyer, J. Rood, T. Nguyen, C. K. Martin, J. Volaufova, M. M. Most, F. L. Greenway, S. R. Smith, D. A. Williamson, W. A. Deutsch, and E. Ravussin. "Effect of 6-mo. Calorie Restriction on Biomarkers of Longevity, Metabolic Adaptation, and Oxidative Stress in Overweight Subjects." *JAMA* 295, no. 13 (2006): 1539–1548. doi: 10.1001/jama.295.13.1539.

Hill, A. J. "Does Dieting Make You Fat?" *British Journal of Nutrition* 92, no. 1 (2004): S15–18. doi: 10.1079/BJN20041135.

Histed, M. H., A. Pasupathy, and E. K. Miller. "Learning Substrates in the Primate Prefrontal Cortex and Striatum: Sustained Activity Related to Successful Actions." *Neuron* 63, no. 2 (2009): 244–253. doi: 10.1016/j.neuron.2009.06.019.

Jaminet, Paul, and Shou-Ching Jaminet. *The Perfect Health Diet: Four Steps to Renewed Health, Youthful Vitality, and Long Life.* Cambridge, MA: YinYang Press, 2010.

Jaslow, Ryan. "Internet Addiction Changes Brain Similar to Cocaine: Study." *CBS News* (January 12, 2012). http://www.cbsnews.com/news/internet-addiction-changes-brain-similar-to-cocaine-study/.

Johnson, Amy, Ph.D. *Being Human: Essays on Thoughtmares, Bouncing Back, and Your True Nature.* Inner Wellness Publishing, 2013.

Johnson, Amy, Ph.D. *The Little Book of Big Change: The No-Willpower Approach to Breaking Any Habit.* Oakland, CA: New Harbinger Publications, 2016.

Kaye, W. H., A. Wagner, J. L. Fudge, and M. Paulus. "Neurocircuitry of Eating Disorders." *Behavioral Neurobiology of Eating Disorders, Current Topics in Behavioral Neurosciences* 6 (2010): 37–57. doi: 10.1007/7854_2010_85.

Kerr, Ali, and Richard Kerr. *The Bulimia Help Method: A Revolutionary New Approach That Works.* Glasgow: Bulimia Help, 2014.

Keifer, John. "Women: Running into Trouble." *Elitefts.com* (November 7, 2001). http://www.elitefts.com/education/training/women-running-into trouble/.

Klesges, R. C., T. R. Isbell, and L. M. Klesges. "Relationship Between Dietary Restraint, Energy Intake, Physical Activity, and Body Weight: A Prospective Analysis." *Journal of Abnormal Psychology* 101, no. 4 (1992): 668–674.

Kolata, Gina. "Genes Take Charge, and Diets Fall by the Wayside." *New York Times Online* (May 8, 2007). http://www.nytimes.com/2007/05/08/health/08fat.html?pagewanted=all&_r=1&.

Konturek, P. C., T. Brzozowski, and S. J. Konturek. "Stress and the Gut: Pathophysiology, Clinical Consequences, Diagnostic Approach, and Treatment Options." *Journal of Physiology and Pharmacology* 62, no. 6: 591–599.

Kotler, L. A., M. J. Devlin, D. E. Matthews, and B. T. Walsh. "Total Energy Expenditure as Measured by Doubly-Labeled Water in Outpatients with Bulimia Nervosa." *International Journal of Eating Disorders* 29, no. 4 (2001): 470–476.

Leibel, R. L., M. Rosenbaum, and J. Hirsch. "Changes in Energy Expenditure Resulting from Altered Body Weight." *New England Journal of Medicine* 332 (1995): 621–628. doi: 10.1056/NEJM 199503093321001.

Leman, Cathy. "Night Eating Syndrome." *Today's Dietician* 12, no. 1 (2010): 8. http://www.todays dietitian.com/newarchives/011110p8.shtml.

Liberty, Catherine. "Does Bulimia Help You Lose Weight?" *Bulimia Help* (June 28, 2011). http://www.bulimiahelp.org/articles/bulimia-lose-weight.

Liberty, Catherine. "How Bulimia Leads to Weight Gain." *Bulimia Help* (June 27, 2011). http://www.bulimiahelp.org/articles/how-bulimia-leads-weight-gain.

Lowe, M. R., A. A. Witt, and S. L. Grossman. "Dieting in Bulimia Nervosa Is Associated with Increased Food Restriction and Psychopathology but Decreased Binge Eating." *Eating Behaviors* 14, no. 3 (2013): 342–347. doi: 10.1016/j.eatbeh.2013.06.011.

Mann, Traci, Ph.D. *Secrets from the Eating Lab: The Science of Weight Loss, the Myth of Willpower, and Why You Should Never Diet Again.* New York: HarperCollins, 2015.

Mann, T., A. J. Tomiyama, E. Westling, A. M. Lew, B. Samuels, and J. Chatman. "Medicare's Search for Effective Obesity Treatments: Diets Are Not the Answer." *American Psychologist* 62, no. 3 (2007): 220–233. doi: http://dx.doi.org/10.1037/0003-066X.62.3.220.

Manwaring, J. L., A. Hilbert, D. E. Wilfley, K. M. Pike, C. G. Fairburn, F. A. Dohm, and R. H Striegel-Moore. "Risk Factors and Patterns of Onset in Binge Eating Disorder." *International Journal of Eating Disorders* 39, no. 2 (2006): 101–107. doi: 10.1002/eat.20208.

Martin, C. K, L. K. Heilbronn, L. de Jonge, J. P. DeLany, J. Volaufova, S. D. Anton, L. M. Redman, S. R. Smith, and E. Ravussin. "Effect of Calorie Restriction on Resting Metabolic Rate and Spontaneous Physical Activity." *Obesity* 15, no. 12: 2964–2973. doi: 10.1038/oby.2007.354.

Mathes, W. F., K. A. Brownley, X. Mo, and C. M. Bulik. "The Biology of Binge Eating." *Appetite* 52, no. 3 (2009): 545–553. doi: 10.1016/j.appet.2009.03.005.

Mattison, J. A., G. S. Roth, T. M. Beasley, E. M. Tilmont, A. H. Handy, R. L. Herbert, D. L. Longo, D. B. Allison, J. E. Young, M. Bryant, D. Barnard, W. F. Ward, W. Qi, D. K. Ingram, and R. de Cabo. "Impact of Caloric Restriction on Health and Survival in Rhesus Monkeys: The NIA Study." *Nature* 489 (2012): 318–321. doi: 10.1038/nature11432.

Mattson, M. P. "Dietary Factors, Hormesis, and Health." *Ageing Research Reviews* 7, no. 1 (2008): 43–48. doi: 10.1016/j.arr.2007.08.004.

McClelland, J., N. Bozhilova, I. Campbell, and U. Schmidt. "A Systematic Review of the Effects of Neuromodulation on Eating and Body Weight: Evidence from Human and Animal Studies." *European Eating Disorders Review* 21, no. 6 (2013): 436–455. doi: 10.1002/erv.2256.

McElroy, S. L., A. I. Guerdjikova, N. Mori, and A. M. O'Melia. "Pharmacological Management of Binge Eating Disorder: Current and Emerging Treatment Options." *Therapeutics and Clinical Risk Management* 8 (2012): 219–241. doi: 10.2147/TCRM.S25574.

McGonigal, Kelly. *The Willpower Instinct: How Self-Control Works, Why It Matters, and What You Can Do to Get More of It.* New York: Penguin, 2012.

Mehanna, H., P. C. Nankivell, J. Moledina, and J. Travis. "Refeeding Syndrome: Awareness, Prevention, and Management." *Head & Neck Oncology* 1 (2009): 4. doi: 10.1186/1758-3284-1-4.

Mehler, P. S., A. B. Winkelman, D. M. Andersen, and J. L. Gaudiani. "Nutritional Rehabilitation: Practical Guidelines for Refeeding the Anorectic Patient." *Journal of Nutrition and Metabolism* 2010, Article ID 625782 (2010). doi: 10.1155/2010/625782.

Mental Health Daily. "Vyvanse Approved for Binge Eating Disorder: How It Works, Benefits & Risks." http://mentalhealthdaily.com/2015/02/06/vyvanse-approved-for-binge-eating-disorder-how-it-works-benefits-risks/ (assessed August 2, 2015).

Meule, A., V. von Rezori, and J. Blechert. "Food Addiction and Bulimia Nervosa." *European Eating Disorders Review* 22, no. 5 (2014): 331–337.

Mirasol. "Eating Disorder Statistics." http://www.mirasol.net/learning-center/eating-disorder-statistics.php (accessed July 20, 2015).

Mitka, Mike. "Research Suggests Pathological Gambling Is an Addiction Issue." *News@JAMA* (May 18, 2011). http://newsatjama.jama.com/2011/05/18/research-suggests-pathological-gambling-is-an-addiction-issue/.

Mozaffarian, D., T. Hao, E. B. Rimm, W. C. Willett, and F. T. Hu. "Changes in Diet and Lifestyle and Long-Term Weight Gain in Women and Men." *New England Journal of Medicine* 364 (2011): 2392–2404.

Murphy, R., S. Straebler, Z. Cooper, and C. G. Fairburn. "Cognitive Behavioral Therapy for Eating Disorders." *Psychiatric Clinics of North America* 33, no. 3 (2010): 611–627. doi: 10.1016/j.psc.2010.04.004.

Nate, Miyaki. "Four Reasons to Eat More Calories (and Carbs) at Night." Livestrong.com (April 16, 2015). http://www.livestrong.com/article/557830-4-reasons-to-eat-more-calories-and-carbsat-night/.

National Association of Anorexia and Associated Disorders. "Bulimia Nervosa." http://www. anad.org/get-information/about-eating-disorders/bulimia-nervosa/ (accessed June 5, 2015).

National Eating Disorders Association. "Bulimia Nervosa." http://nationaleatingdisorders.org/ bulimia-nervosa (accessed July 30, 2015).

National Eating Disorders Association. "Factors That May Contribute to Eating Disorders." http://www.nationaleatingdisorders.org/factors-may-contribute-eating-disorders (accessed July 3, 2015).

National Institute on Drug Abuse. "Drugs, Brains, and Behavior: The Science of Addiction." http://www.drugabuse.gov/publications/drugs-brains-behavior-science-addiction/drugs-brain (accessed July 14, 2015).

Nestle, Marion. "Why Does the FDA Recommend 2,000 Calories Per Day?" *Atlantic* (August 4, 2011). http://www.theatlantic.com/health/archive/2011/08/why-does-the-fda-recommend-2-000-calories-per-day/243092/.

Nestle, Marion, and Malden Nesheim. *Why Calories Count: From Science to Politics.* Los Angeles: University of California Press, 2012.

New Scientist. "Why We Need a Siesta After Dinner" (June 5, 2006). http://www.newscientist. com/article/dn9272-why-we-need-a-siesta-after-dinner.html#.VXcVMuzbKP8.

Oxford Dictionaries Online. "Adequate," def. 1. http://www.oxford dictionaries.com/us/definition/ american_english/adequate (accessed November 2, 2014).

Paddon-Jones, D., E. Westman, R. D. Mattes, R. R. Wolfe, A. Astrup, and M. Westerterp-Plantenga. "Protein, Weight Management, and Satiety." *American Journal of Clinical Nutrition* 87, no. 5 (2008): 1558S–1561S. http://ajcn.nutrition.org/content/87/5/1558S.long.

Pankevich D. E., S. L. Teegarden, A. D. Hedin, C. L. Jensen, and T. L. Bale. "Caloric Restriction Experience Reprograms Stress and Orexegenic Pathways and Promotes Binge-Eating." *Journal of Neuroscience* 30, no. 48 (2010): 16399–16407. doi: 10.1523/JNEUROSCI.1955-10.2010.

Parker, G., I. Parker, and H. Brotchie. "Mood States Effects of Chocolate." *Journal of Affective Disorders* 92, nos. 2–3 (2006): 149–159.

Pietiläinen, K. H., S. E. Saarni, J. Kaprio, and A. Rissanen. "Does Dieting Make You Fat? A Twin Study." *International Journal of Obesity* 36, no. 3 (2011): 456–464. doi: 10.1038/ijo.2011.160.

Pike, K. M., D. Wilfley, A., Hilbert, C. G. Fairburn, F. A. Dohm, and R. H. Striegel-Moore. "Antecedent Life Events of Binge-Eating Disorder." *Psychiatry Research* 142, no. 1 (2006): 19–29. doi: 10.1016/j.psychres.2005.10.006x.

Pool, E., T. Brosch, S. Delplanque, and D. Sander. "Stress Increases Cue-Triggered 'Wanting' for Sweet Reward in Humans." *Journal of Experimental Psychology: Animal Learning and Cognition* 41, no. 2 (2015): 128–136. doi: 10.1037/xan0000052.

Poulsen, S., S. Lunn, S. I. Daniel, S. Folke, B. B. Mathiesen, H. Katznelson, and C. G. Fairburn. "A Randomized Controlled Trial of Psychoanalytic Psychotherapy or Cognitive-Behavioral Therapy for Bulimia Nervosa." *American Journal of Psychiatry* 171, no. 1 (2014): 109–116. doi: 10.1176/appi.ajp.2013.

PsychGuides.com. "Shopping Addiction Symptoms, Causes, and Effects." http://www.psych guides.com/guides/shopping-addiction-symptoms-causes-and-effects/ (accessed August 5, 2015).

Redman, L. M., L. K. Heilbronn, C. K., Martin, L. de Jonge, D. A. Williamson, J. P. Delany, and E. Ravussin. "Metabolic and Behavioral Compensations in Response to Caloric Restriction: Implications for the Maintenance of Weight Loss." *PLOS ONE* 4, no. 2 (2009): e4377. doi: 10.1371/journal.pone.0004377.

Redman, L. M., and E. Ravussin. "Caloric Restriction in Humans: Impact on Physiological, Psychological, and Behavioral Outcomes." *Antioxidants & Redox Signaling* 14, no. 2 (2011): 275–287. doi: 10.1089/ars.2010.3253.

Renki, Margaret. "Are You Destined to Inherit Your Mother's Body Shape?" *Women's Health* (December 14, 2009). http://www.womenshealthmag.com/style/inherited-traits.

Rikani, A. A., Z. Choudhry, A. M. Choudhry, H. Ikram, M. W. Asghar, D. Kajal, A. Waheed, and N. J. Mobassarah. "A Critique of the Literature on Etiology of Eating Disorders." *Annals of Neurosciences* 20, no. 4 (2013): 157–161. doi: 10.5214/ans.0972.7531.200409.

Riley, Gillian. *Ditching Diets: How to Lose Weight in a Way You Can Maintain.* Full Stop Publications: 2001, 2009, 2013.

Rollins, B. Y., E. Loken, J. S. Savage, and L. L. Birch. "Effects of Restriction on Children's Intake Differ by Child Temperament, Food Reinforcement, and Parent's Chronic Use of Restriction." *Appetite* 73 (2014): 31–39. doi: 10.1016/j.appet.2013.10.005.

Rosenblum, Cookie. *Clearing Your Path to Permanent Weight Loss: The Truth About Why You've Failed in the Past, and What You Must Know to Succeed Now.* Real Weight Loss for Real Women, 2014.

Salamone, J. D., and M. Correa. "The Mysterious Functions of Mesolimbic Dopamine." *Neuron* 76, no. 3 (2012): 470. doi: 10.1016/j.neuron.2012.10.021.

Sanchez, M., C. Darimont, V. Drapeau, S. Emady-Azar, M. Lepage, E. Rezzonico, C. Ngom-Bru, B. Berger, L. Philippe, C. Ammon-Zuffrey, P. Leone, G. Chevrier, E. St-Amand, A. Marette, J. Doré, and A. Tremblay. "Effect of Lactobacillus Rhamnosus CGMCC1.3724 Supplementation on Weight Loss and Maintenance in Obese Men and Women." *British Journal of Nutrition* 111, no. 8 (2014): 1507–1519. doi: 10.1017/S0007114513003875.

Scheer, F. A., C. J. Morris, and S. A. Shea. "The Internal Circadian Clock Increases Hunger and Appetite in the Evening Independent of Food Intake and Other Behaviors." *Obesity* 21, no. 3 (2013): 421–423. doi: 10.1002/oby.20351.

Schmidt, U., and I. C. Campbell. "Treatment of Eating Disorders Can Not Remain 'Brainless': The Case for Brain-Directed Treatments." *European Eating Disorders Review* 21, no. 6 (2013): 425–427. doi: 10.1002/erv.2257.

Schwartz, Jeffrey M., M.D., and Sharon Begley. *The Mind and the Brain: Neuroplasticity and the Power of Mental Force.* New York: HarperCollins, 2002.

Schwartz, Jeffrey M., M.D., and Rebecca Gladding, M.D. *You Are Not Your Brain: The 4-Step Solution for Changing Bad Habits, Ending Unhealthy Thinking, and Taking Control of Your Life.* New York: Penguin, 2011.

Shaw, J. A., D. B. Herzog, V. L. Clark, L. A. Berner, K. T. Eddy, D. L. Franko, and M. R. Lowe. "Elevated Pre-morbid Weights in Bulimic Individuals Are Usually Surpassed Post-morbidly: Implications for Perpetuation of the Disorder." *International Journal of Eating Disorders* 45, no. 4 (2012): 512–523. doi: 10.1002/eat.20985.

Shire. "About Vyvanse for Adults with Moderate to Severe B.E.D." http://www.vyvanse.com/binge-eating-disorder-treatment (accessed July 12, 2015).

Slate, Steven. "Do Drug Addicts Lose Control of Their Drug Use?" Clean Slate Addiction Site. http://www.thecleanslate.org/drug-addicts-lose-control-drug-use/ (accessed August 3, 2015).

Sofer, S., A. Eliraz, S. Kaplan, H. Voet, G. Fink, T. Kima, and Z. Madar. "Greater Weight Loss and Hormonal Changes After 6 Months Diet with Carbohydrates Eaten Mostly at Dinner." *Obesity* 19, no. 10 (2011): 2006–2014. doi: 10.1038/oby.2011.48.

Spinardi, Josie. *How to Have Your Cake and Your Skinny Jeans Too: Stop Binge Eating, Overeating, and Dieting for Good, Get the Naturally Thin Body You Crave from the Inside Out.* Walnut Creek, CA: Twirl Media, 2014.

Standish, Alen. *Before I Eat: A Moment in the Zone Guidebook: Real-Time Tools to Manage Eating Urges and Food Cravings.* Kansas City: Standish Media, 2014.

Stice, E., K. Burger, and S. Yokum. "Caloric Deprivation Increases Responsivity of Attention and Reward Brain Regions to Intake, Anticipated Intake, and Images of Palatable Foods." *NeuroImage* 67 (2013): 322–330. doi: 10.1016/j.neuroimage.2012.11.028.

Suchy, Sara. "Why Protein Makes You Feel Full Faster." *Health Central* (July 12, 2012; updated June 9, 2015). http://www.healthcentral.com/slideshows/why-protein-make-you-feel-full-faster/.

Sumithran, P., L. A. Prendergast, E. Delbridge, K. Purcell, A. Shulkes, A. Kriketos, and J. Proietto. "Long-Term Persistence of Hormonal Adaptations to Weight Loss." *New England Journal of Medicine* 365, no. 17 (2011): 1597–1604. doi: 10.1056/NEJMoa1105816.

358

Swenson, Rand, ed. "Limbic System." *Review of Clinical and Functional Neuroscience*. Dartmouth Medical School, 2006. https://www.dartmouth.edu/~rswenson/NeuroSci/chapter_9.html.

Taylor, MaryGrace. "How to Drink Apple Cider Vinegar for Weight Loss." *Prevention* (September 6, 2013). http://www.prevention.com/weight-loss/how-apple-cider-vinegar-could-slim-you-down.

Teff, K. L, S. S. Elliott, M. Tschöp, T. J. Kieffer, D. Rader, M. Heiman, R. R. Townsend, N. L. Keim, D. D'Alessio, and P. J. Havel. "Dietary Fructose Reduces Circulating Insulin and Leptin, Attenuates Postprandial Suppression of Ghrelin, and Increases Triglycerides in Women." *Journal of Clinical Endocrinology and Metabolism* 89, no. 6 (2004): 2963–2972.

Tribole, E., and E. Resch. *Intuitive Eating: A Revolutionary Program That Works*. New York: St. Martin's Griffin, 1995, 2003, 2012.

Trimpey, Jack. "Orientation to AVRT-Based, Family-Centered, Addiction Recovery" (2010). https://rational.org/index.php?id=90.

Trimpey, Jack. *Rational Recovery: The New Cure for Substance Addiction*. New York: Pocket Books, 1996.

Umberg, E. N., R. I. Shader, L. K. Hsu, and D. J. Greenblatt. "From Disordered Eating to Addiction: The 'Food Drug' in Bulimia Nervosa." *Journal of Clinical Psychopharmacology* 32, no. 3 (2012): 376–389. doi: 10.1097/JCP.0b013e318252464f.

University of Cambridge. "Hormone Regulates Fondness for Food." *ScienceDaily* (August 11, 2007). www.sciencedaily.com/releases/2007/08/070809172258.htm.

U.S. Food & Drug Administration (FDA). "FDA Expands Uses of Vyvanse to Treat Binge-Eating Disorder" (January 30, 2015). http://www.fda.gov/NewsEvents/Newsroom/PressAnnouncements/ucm432543.htm.

Vinken, A. G., G. P. Bathalon, A. L. Sawaya, G. E. Dallal, K. L. Tucker, and S. B. Roberts. "Equations for Predicting the Energy Requirements of Healthy Adults Aged 18–81." *American Journal of Clinical Nutrition* 69, no. 5 (1999): 920–926.

Volkow N. D., L. Chang, G. J. Wang, J. S. Fowler, D. Franceschi, M. Sedler, S. J. Gatley, E. Miller, R. Hitzemann, Y. S. Ding, and J. Logan. "Loss of Dopamine Transporters in Methamphetamine Abusers Recovers with Protracted Abstinence." *Journal of Neuroscience* 21, no. 23 (2001): 9414–9418.

Wang, G., A. Geliebter, N. D. Volkow, F. W. Telang, J. Logan, M. C. Jayne, K. Galanti, P. A. Selig, H. Han, W. Zhu, C. T. Wong, and J. S. Fowler. "Enhanced Striatal Dopamine Release During Food Stimulation in Binge Eating Disorder." *Obesity* 19, no. 8 (2011): 1601–1608. doi: 10.1038/oby.2011.27.

WebMD. "Binge Eating Disorder Health Center." http://www.webmd.com/mental-health/eating-disorders/binge-eating-disorder/ (accessed April 3, 2015).

WebMD. "Who We Are." http://www.webmd.com/about-webmd-policies/about-who-we-are (accessed April 3, 2015).

Werdell, Phil. "Science of Food Addiction." ACORN Food Dependency Recovery Services. http://foodaddiction.com/resources/science-of-food-addiction/ (accessed July 31, 2015).

Wesley, M. J., T. Lohrenz, M. N. Koffarnus, S. M. McClure, R. De La Garza II, R. Salas, D. G. Y. Thompson-Lake, T. F. Newton, W. K. Bickel, and P. R. Montague. "Choosing Money over Drugs: The Neural Underpinnings of Difficult Choice in Chronic Cocaine Users." *Journal of Addiction* 2014, Article ID 189853 (2014). doi: 10.1155/2014/189853.

Wierenga, C. E., A. Ely, A. Bischoff-Grethe, U. F. Bailer, A. N. Simmons, and W. H. Kaye. "Are Extremes of Consumption in Eating Disorders Related to an Altered Balance Between Reward and Inhibition?" *Frontiers in Behavioral Neuroscience* 8 (2014): 41. doi: 10.3389/fnbeh.2014.00410.

Wilson, James. *Adrenal Fatigue: The 21st Century Stress Syndrome.* Petaluma, CA: Smart Publications, 2001.

Wilson G. T., C. M. Grilo, and K. M. Vitousek. "Psychological Treatment of Eating Disorders." *American Psychologist* 62, no. 3 (2007): 199–216. doi: 10.1037/0003-066X.62.3.199.

Withnall, Adam. "Pornography Addiction Leads to Same Brain Activity as Alcoholism or Drug Use, Study Says." *Independent* (September 22, 2013). http://www.independent.co.uk/life-style/health-and-families/health-news/pornography-addiction-leads-to-same-brain-activity-as-alcoholism-or-drug-abuse-study-shows-8832708.html.

Wolf, Rob. *The Paleo Solution: The Original Human Diet.* Las Vegas, NV: Victory Belt Publishing, 2010.

Yoo, Audrey. "Why You Crave Junk Food When You're Sleepy." *Time* (June 11, 2012). http://newsfeed.time.com/2012/06/11/why-you-crave-junk-food-when-youre-sleepy/.

Your Eatopia: Science Based Information on Remission from Restrictive Eating Disorders. "I Need How Many Calories?" (September 14, 2011). http://www.youreatopia.com/blog/2011/9/14/i-need-how-many-calories.html.

Zendequi, E. A., J. A. West, and L. J. Zandberg. "Binge Eating Frequency and Regular Eating Adherence: The Role of Eating Pattern in Cognitive Behavioral Guided Self-Help." *Eating Behaviors* 15, no. 2 (2014): 241–243. doi:10.1016/j.eatbeh.2014.03.002.

Acknowledgments

I want to especially thank all of the men and women—binge eaters and former binge eaters—who have shared their experiences with me, who have told me about their successes as well as the areas where they needed more guidance, who have been open to revealing their challenges in recovery, and who have served as an inspiration to keep working to provide further help.

I am deeply grateful to Amy Johnson for providing a wonderful contribution to the pages of this book, and also for being an amazing colleague to whom I feel confident referring binge eaters for coaching, knowing they will receive the support they need.

I also want to thank the other experts who have shared information and advice in this book—notably, Katherine Thomson for providing so much guidance in the second half of the book, as well as Cookie Rosenblum, Pauline Hanuise, Stacey Cohen, and Richard Kerr.

Additionally, I appreciate the hard work of my editors—Penelope Franklin, who helped in the book's early stages, and Cindy Nixon, whose support, flexibility, and attention to detail made this book a reality—and of my cover designer and friend, Sarah.

And finally, I'd like to thank my family.